Sibling's Haven

Sibling's Haven

SAFE IN WARTIME DEVON

By Angela Stead and Hugh MacBride

ryelands

First published in Great Britain in 2013
Copyright © Angela Stead & Hugh MacBride 2013

Frontispiece: *Hugh with his wife, Roslyn, centre, and sister,*
Angela at a recent exhibition of her paintings.

British Library Cataloguing-in-Publication Data
A CIP record for this title is available from the British Library

ISBN 978 1 906551 36 0

RYELANDS
Halsgrove House,
Ryelands Business Park,
Bagley Road, Wellington, Somerset TA21 9PZ
Tel: 01823 653777   Fax: 01823 216796
email: sales@halsgrove.com

Part of the Halsgrove group of companies
Information on all Halsgrove titles is available at: www.halsgrove.com

Printed in China by Everbest Printing Co Ltd

Contents

Acknowledgements

The authors are profoundly grateful to Roslyn, Kilmeny, Phoebe and Julian MacBride, Hugh's wife, daughters and son, for their help in preparing the text and pictures in this book, without which it could never have appeared.

Preface

In 1935 when I was eight, Penguin booksellers introduced paperback books.

There were ten of them with orange and green covers. One of them was navy blue. It was called *Autobiography* by Margot Asquith. It's got to have been a Sunday when I picked up this book because my father was at home and I asked him "What's autobiography?"

My father explained and he ended up by saying, "Personally, I prefer my fiction labelled fiction."

I did not always understand my father because his conversation was largely not intended for children, but I used to pay attention when he talked to me because he made me feel clever and grown up. I knew what 'fiction' was so I was much amused by his remark which was to me the height of sophistication and wit.

Now I am beginning what may or may not be my autobiography, I remember what my father said. So anyone who also prefers their fiction labelled 'fiction' has been warned.

You may, however, rely implicitly on my brother's account and what his wife Roslyn has unearthed on the internet.

*Ten days before the declaration of war in 1939 their
father, a senior newspaper man, drove Angela,
almost twelve, and Hugh, three and a half, to Devon,
fearing devastating air raids at any time.
Boarding together for much of the time at the same
schools, but separated by their ages, these are
their independent accounts of the war and its aftermath
seen from two very different points of view.*

Angela Stead and Hugh MacBride

PART ONE
Angela's Story
by Angela Stead

I was born Angela Mary MacBride on Sunday 4 December, 1927 in a nursing home in the Queens Road, Richmond, Surrey. It was run by a kind and efficient lady called Miss Skipworth whose insight into children was such that she knew when a very ill little boy asked for a little cabbage on a plate that he meant a Brussels sprout. I was a large baby and my birth was prolonged and at one time despaired of. My paternal grandmother gave a melodramatic account of how my father had been asked whether

he wanted his wife or his baby to survive. However an experienced and elderly physician called Dr McGuire, and the above-mentioned Miss Skipworth, made this question unnecessary as he eventually got both. I had a huge distorted head, which caused my Uncle John to say to my mother, "Good God Kitty! The

Miss Skipworth, a friend of Miss Prendergast (Granny Phyllis' particular friend) and presumably also of Phyllis, some years before my birth. The photo has 'R.M. Skipworth. Matron 1914-1919' written on the front and 'Bedford College, Regents Park' on the back.

child's got water on the brain." Luckily it dispersed, but my head and jaw are asymmetrical to this day and my nose was all over my cheek until about fifty years later when I got around to having it straightened. Shortly after my birth it became apparent that I had started my intra-uterine life as a twin. My mother breastfed me lavishly for nine months. Then one day she tied up her breasts, as was not uncommon then; and went back to work, which was.

My mother and father were both journalists and met in Fleet Street. My father had been in America for the *Daily Express* and he had returned to find that my mother, newly appointed, had annexed his desk filling it with all the rubbish you'd expect from a working girl who cared about her looks. My father tipped all this into the wastepaper basket, with imprecations. That was before he saw my mother: they were engaged three days later. Lionel Murray MacBride was born in 1902. His mother, Phyllis Davy, had run away to join a repertory company. Here she met an Irish charmer whom I know only as Mr Roberts-Carter. They married and a short while later my father was on the way. Roberts-Carter disappeared never to be heard of again. Phyllis was obliged to return to her family whom she recalled bending over her while she was in labour pointing out

Granny Phyllis' miniature photo-frame shows my father as a boy, but underneath his picture we found what we assume to be the only existing one of his father, William Thomas Roberts Carter, her first husband – my grandfather.

that her pains were her punishment. It was a successful deterrent, as she never had any more children. About three years later Phyllis married Tom MacBride, a Civil Servant in Ceylon (as it was then). Phyllis had a glamorous time in Ceylon and didn't return until Tom died about fifteen years later. Meanwhile my father's name was changed by deed poll to MacBride and he was raised in Richmond by his grandmother Mrs Florence Davy, whose husband, Dr Davy, was descended from Sir Humphry Davy's family, and his

Phyllis and Tom MacBride in Ceylon.

*Phyllis' and Tom's home in Ceylon
(from her personal notebook).*

Mrs Davy – my Great Grandmother.

young Aunt Margot. Mrs Davy was a gifted musician and music was taken so seriously in the family that my father vowed it would never play a part in his own children's upbringing. His uncle, Murray Davy, was a temperamental, but well known operatic baritone, and my father was a good pianist and had a pleasing tenor voice, but it was all made so tedious that it put him off classical music for life. Mrs Davy was eccentric, once giving away my father's bicycle to another boy. (My father had to go and get it back.) She wore huge black hats decorated with half birds and jet beads. My father once put a tooth-brush into her hat and it stayed there undetected for weeks.

When my mother was pregnant and living with Mrs Davy, the latter suddenly rose up from the lunch table, went out and returned with a Staffordshire pottery zebra under each arm. "You're a very nice girl" she said, "And you shall have my zebras!" The zebras are still here: one dread-fully broken, but repaired. Incidentally they are not a pair.

My father loved his Aunt Margot who had taken his mother's place. She fell to her death on the stairs of the Richmond house when my father was about ten, pushed, it is said, by an evil spirit. My father recounted a similar experience on that staircase. My mother when she lived there was told by Mrs Davy not to go downstairs at night and the cat would never go upstairs at all. This house was used later as a probation office and I have wondered how the ghost got on then.

My father went to Colet Court and subsequently became a scholar at St Paul's School and got a senior scholarship. He was good at Classics and English and stayed until he was nearly nineteen. He shot for St Paul's in spite of being short-sighted. He obtained a scholarship to Oxford which he refused, was taken on as a cub reporter on the *Richmond and Twickenham Times* writing imaginative and informed copy, and moved on to Fleet Street in a short while.

Murray Davey's debut at Covent Garden.
He sang in the first two Operas on the poster.

My father had small watery eyes and a small mouth clustering round a huge Roman nose and a receding chin. These unpromising features did nothing to mar his attractiveness to women. He had an intractable stammer, sticking on a word sometimes for minutes on end. This was said to be from not being allowed to write with his left hand. My father never appeared to bother about his stammer at all and he didn't, as I soon learnt, like to be helped out. Years later, in a completely right-handed family I did have a left-handed son.

My mother, Kathleen Mary Hogg, was born in 1904. She was the youngest of four children. Augustus Hogg her much-loved father was a doctor in Shardlow, Derbyshire. He claimed to be descended from James

Above right: *Connie, John, Cyril and my mother at Shardlow in about 1912.*

Opposite: *My father in1930.*

My Mother's family home at Shardlow in Derbyshire.

Hogg, the Ettrick shepherd. Her mother, Amy Hayes, came from Appledore in Devon, the granddaughter of 'Bully' Hayes, who was allegedly a pirate. It was not a happy marriage. My mother was constantly upset by noisy quarrelling. Augustus had a 'shooting accident' early in 1914 leaving the family hard up. Amy ran a boarding house in Derby for a time and my mother went to Derby High School for Girls. Throughout her girlhood she was 'adopted' for longish periods by a kindly and aristocratic family at Haddon Hall and a family called Dove whose daughter Mary was her great friend. Mary died in her twenties of tuberculosis. She was a gentle, even-tempered, girl, quite unlike the opinionated literary uncooperative teenager that was my mother. Miss Darke, her headmistress, saw in her something unusual nevertheless and, thanks to her, by the time my mother left school she was amazingly well read, and interested in Early English. Miss Darke arranged for her to go to Oxford but my mother decided to go to work on the local paper instead.

My mother was good looking with huge green eyes and a lovely complexion, enhanced by two round pink spots on her cheekbones. Her hair was brown, fashionably styled. Her figure was good and she was

Left to right: *Uncle Cyril, Aunt Connie (with bandaged arm), my mother (holding Gyp), me and my grandmother with Poosie.*

rarely seen without full *maquillage* and a smart dress. She needed glasses but never wore them. My mother loved male admiration right up to the day she died and there was always a lovesick young man hanging around, more or less fruitlessly, while I was a little girl. Looks and talent got her into Fleet Street quite soon. She had great originality too in pottery and drawing and this was eventually to make her a lot of money and acclaim. After I was born my parents moved into a rented place in Richmond called

Above: *My mother at her Confirmation.*

Above right: *At eighteen.*

Below: *In her twenties.*

Right: *Mary Dove, my mother's great friend.*

WE HAVE LOVED HER IN LIFE
LET US NOT FORGET HER AFTER DEATH.

OF YOUR CHARITY PRAY FOR THE
REPOSE OF THE SOUL OF
MARY DOVE
(OF MASSON MOUNT. MATLOCK)
WHO DIED ON JULY 21st 1925
AGED 21 YEARS.
MAY SHE REST IN PEACE. AMEN.

Plane House, named after a large tree in the front garden, which was actually a sycamore. Plane House is not an easy name to dictate to someone, but the postman was used to delivering letters to 'House'.

I can't remember a thing about it, but I have been told that I was a large square infant with no hair nor willingness to walk until I was about two. I made up for this by great facility in communication, dismissing the seaside as 'wet and dirty', learning poetry and joining in adult conversation whenever I got the chance. By this time maybe it had dawned on me that, unless I earned attention to myself in some way, I'd get left to my Nanny. My parents were fond of me, but neither was going to pass up a much more interesting life, watching the little bud slowly unfold. I can't remember when I realised this but it certainly influenced my childhood and probably my adult life as well.

The first incident that I can recall was vivid indeed. We'd moved out of Plane House when I was three and a half and rented a dark over-furnished old-fashioned place in Halford Road, Richmond. My parents saw this as a stopgap, but we were there until I was five. I had a jolly, easy-going Irish Nanny called Tipper, which was short for Tipperary. There was a cook. My granny Phyllis had been widowed and was living with Mrs Davy. She was a frequent and amusing companion. She made up long stories about a family of wooden penguins who lived in a little oval box. When they got out they used to eat too much tipsy cake and were realistically sick into an ashtray. She could also be persuaded to buy tiny crackers in a box from time to time. She was, however, tiresomely addicted to the doings of Princesses Elizabeth and Margaret Rose.

My mother was pregnant again and due to be delivered any day. This unwelcoming house had a big, bare attic which everyone thought I should like and it was designated my playroom. What I did like about it was the gas fire, which nobody had noticed. I used to go up into the attic and turn it on and off with the dear little gold tap at the side. One afternoon my mother caught me doing this and she gave me the most brutal smacking. I had probably been smacked before because it wasn't unethical then, but this was an onslaught. I lay on the floor crying while my mother stormed downstairs shouting "I've got to go into hospital at any moment. There are three people in this house and nobody can be bothered to look after Jill," (which was by then my nickname). I can now sympathise with her desperation, but the effect on me was that wild horses wouldn't make me go into that attic again – a bit like the Red Room – or turn on a gas fire for years.

My mother had her baby a few days later. It was a girl, Loveday, and she was stillborn. My father told me about it and I'm afraid I replied that perhaps it wasn't so bad as we didn't really need another little girl. Next day my father took me to see my mother. Somebody took me down a long dark corridor, opened a door and nudged me in. My mother was sitting in bed facing the door and when she saw me she began to cry with her hands up to her face and her hair falling over them. She looked too unlike my mother for me to speak to her or go a step nearer so I went out very quietly shutting the door behind me. Back in the corridor somebody said "How was your mother?" I replied "Mummy looked very well," and burst into tears.

When I was nearly four my mother decided that I should go to school and this was sensible because I was surrounded by grown-ups and their only attempt to find a child of my own age to play with had not been a success. Dear little Isobel "did not want to come and play with Jill" because Jill was nasty to her and would not let her touch any of the toys.

School was an instant success. I went to a wonderful old-fashioned establishment called Sesame in Marchmont Road. It was co-educational and run by two sisters, Miss Lee and Miss K-Lee. This school was still going when I grew up and I wished that my children could have gone there. Girls wore green, box-pleated tunics, a white shirt and a green tie and a fringed girdle. Outside they wore a green beret with a lily badge on it confirming that the Misses Lee must have been devotees of John Ruskin. It was in a large house with ground floor rooms that could be partitioned off as necessary. Upstairs were more classrooms and the sisters' rooms above that. Every day the whole school had registration and prayers. For a while I, as the youngest pupil, sat on a little stool beside Miss Lee's table until somebody younger turned up. I was in the kindergarten. Transition was across the corridor, which had dark red linoleum and led by a rickety iron staircase to a large and shabby garden where we had break. In kindergarten there was a sandpit in the window recess, a piano, bricks and books and paints. There was little emphasis on formal learning, but we were expected to behave properly. In Transition they sat at little tables and did sums and letters, which I greatly envied. I only stayed for half a school day, but on my fourth birthday when asked what I wanted to do I said I would like to have lunch at school. This was duly arranged and in honour of the occasion all the pupils were given one little biscuit with an iced star on it.

I was learning to read at home as well. My mother taught me out of a red book called *Reading Without Tears*, and if I had been tiresome I was not allowed to have my reading lesson, but in spite of this I could soon read quite well. During the following school year I missed quite a lot of school. I had my tonsils out in Miss Skipworth's trusty nursing home, probably removed by Dr McGuire. I remember a sore throat and some promised ice cream that turned out to be blancmange. Not long after that I got whooping cough badly and was reduced to a thin child rather than being square and robust. I went to convalesce at Selsey Bill. I imagine Tipper went too, but all I can recall about it was that it was far too cold to bathe or paddle and that there was a disused railway carriage in the garden as a playroom.

That summer I had a much happier visit to the seaside. Tipper, Granny Phyllis and I went to Manaccan across the Helford River to stay with her sister, my Great Aunt Natalie Joan Engelhart and her family. There were a lot of people there in a house with a veranda looking out on the sea. I suggested to Granny Phyllis that it might be prudent to swim on the sand at first (presumably sand was acceptable by now) and this we both did satisfactorily. It wasn't long before we ventured into the real sea and I still

Self and unknown admirer at Manaccan.

Self at Manaccan.

have a photo of myself hand-in-hand with a middle-aged man among the rock pools. Nobody was ever able to identify him. Our one-piece bathing suits are identical. In these suspicious times that photo looks very naive and might bring a knowing smile to the lips of some. Then people were not so ready to jump to conclusions. Obviously child-abuse went on long before the 1920s, but I am equally sure that, a lucky child, nobody ever did anything frightening to me: maybe because I would have been certain to tell. I was an outspoken child. The first time I went to the pantomime and the principal boy came on I said loudly "How silly! She's a girl!" The gentleman in front of me turned round and said "That's right my dear, it is very silly." My mother told me to shut up.

Aunt Natalie and her teenage sons were to play an important part in my life later on. The elder, Jock, was made a butt of silly jokes. I guess he would have been glad to have strangled this cocky, self-important little girl, but he was to get more than his own back in 1939.

When I was five we moved from Halford Road to Strawberry Hill near Twickenham, but before we got to Strawberry Hill we went to live in the Bingham House Hotel beside the Thames, below Richmond Hill. It was fun. It had a games room with a ping-pong table on which other children played, but I was too shy to try. There was a big gentle Alsatian dog. There was a vast, light dining room with your own table and each one had a great many silver spoons, cruets and sugar sifters on a white tablecloth. Best of all was our waiter. He was dark and foreign and charming due probably to the presence of my mother.

While we were staying there, Granny Phyllis took me to Courlanders in Richmond to pick up my glasses. My mother had noticed I couldn't read the names or numbers of buses which were part of our 'What does that say?' exercises. How my eyes were tested I don't know, but when they put my specs on my nose the whole world sprang into focus. Everything was amazingly smaller than it had been and the first thing I did was to stumble over a paving stone outside the shop and cut my hand quite badly. I walked back home to the hotel bleeding and tearful where my hand was done up in a smart white bandage and my darling waiter made a huge fuss of me and gave me a peppermint cream. I have the scar on my hand to this day.

26 Waldegrave Gardens was another rented house and my parents lived there until my father's death in 1968. I ran round the garden shouting, "I'm Jill! I'm here!" This extrovert outburst didn't bring any answering cheer. I lived there until September 1939. About this time Tipper left, preferring to look after younger children. My father took me out one Saturday morning. When we got back she was gone. I was resentful about not saying goodbye: I loved Tipper dearly. I got another minder very soon. Her name was Lesley, the daughter of a clergyman. I was to get to know plenty about her family later on. What I did not know was that she was having a torrid affair with a married man on Thursdays, her day off, but my mother did, and highly approved. Lesley looked like the archetypal clergyman's daughter. She looked after me loyally for several years, but she was never fun like Tipper.

The next problem was school. Strawberry Hill is about three miles from Richmond and no way could I be taken and fetched from Sesame. My mother made enquiries and found there was a Montessori School known as Miss Walton's, five minutes' walk away from our house so I was enrolled in the Autumn Term. Unlike Sesame, this school and I did not get on right from the beginning. I probably was missing Sesame, but what really got up my nose was that we never did anything sensible. What was the point of learning to tie bows on bits of card? Why couldn't you begin a picture of a house with the roof just because that wasn't the way to build a real house? Lesley alerted my mother that I had stuck my tongue out at the school when she fetched me home. Sure enough, Miss Walton soon requested that my mother should go to see her. I was left in the beautiful garden and they went up to the modern Swedish school building. I have only my mother's account for what happened next. Miss Walton quite kindly asked her if little Angela had ever had any investigations into her development as she appeared to be very backward. My mother replied that she had had lots of problems with little Angela but that had not been one of them.

"What schoolwork was I doing?" asked my mother, assuming it might be too hard.

"We don't do any formal work at this stage, Mrs MacBride."

"What about reading?"

"My dear Mrs MacBride, Angela is not nearly ready to start reading."

My mother said no more but called me in from the garden saying shortly, "Go to that bookshelf, get out any book and read some of it."

"Mrs MacBride, that is out of the question!"

I gabbled off a few lines from some book or other. The upshot was that we left, never to return, but it cost my father a term's fees. So it was back to Sesame, being called Jill, going into Transition and causing my family a good deal of inconvenience. For some while my father, who never got home before midnight, used to drive me to school in his Austin Seven and his pyjamas, returning to bed afterwards. I lived in dread that one day he'd get out of the car in front of everybody and I would be mortified. Lesley fetched me in the afternoon and we went home on the bus. I was still a long way from my school friends, but next door there were two girls both older than me. I made friends with the younger and we played together a lot of the time. I was the one who was tolerated and told I was a baby which was good for me. In one field I was way ahead: the facts of life. Sheila and Edwina had devout Catholic parents, attended a convent school and knew nothing about babies at all. My mother didn't offer information until I asked for it, but when I did she gave me a factual answer I could understand. I did not know that reproduction was not a subject for casual conversation. Quite soon Sheila and Edwina knew all I did. This went down badly with their parents and for a while Sheila and Edwina were not allowed to play with a 'dirty-minded little girl'. My mother stepped in, had a chat with next door and told me bluntly that some people did not like to talk about that sort of thing, odd though it might seem, and to leave the subject alone. Friendly relations were resumed after a while.

My parents had been bright young people. My mother's hair was shingled, her skirts were short, she wore gorgeous shoes and a bust flattener. They had an 'open marriage' which meant real infidelity on my father's side and meaningless flirtations on the part of my mother. My father had a secret life, which he concealed more or less from my mother right up until he became ill in 1964. Being on the editorial side of a national newspaper gave him all the cover he needed. At home my parents seemed very happy.

They were always good-mannered, constantly talking and often my father would say something softly into my mother's ear, which made her giggle and blush. I was curious about this and my father would say it was 'a grown up joke'.

"Tell me a grown up joke," I would beg; and sometimes he did. It must have been hard to dredge up clean ones.

My mother would always change after tea in case my father came in early. They never separated in spite of a good deal of grief later on.

By day neither of them was there and in the evening my mother got taken out by a long line of swains. She made a point of being in on Saturday afternoon and gave me what is now called 'quality time'. She read to me, she took me swimming and rowing at Hampton Court. She trailed with me up to the British Museum over and over again to look at the Egyptian mummies. She knitted a skiing outfit for a teddy bear two inches high. I didn't mind my parents' absence in school time.

In due course I 'went upstairs' at Sesame and had my own desk and exercise books. We learnt French out of the 'French Box', which was a dolls' house that could be assembled if you knew the right words. Otherwise the teaching was quite formal. We did spelling, tables, learnt poetry by heart, sat still and left with what was then regarded as a solid grounding. We had stars for good work. Handwriting was important but we also did physical exercises in the garden – running and high jump – at which I became pretty good and dancing class at which I was uncooperative.

During the holidays I knew for certain that my parents were out there somewhere making things interesting and funny while I was stuck at home with Lesley. We had a dachshund by then called Mitzi and we took her for walks. Mitzi was an incorrigible thief and used to weep real tears when she saw her lead. As might be anticipated she got very fat. I had lots of books, painting stuff, sewing things and animal toys I loved. I never liked dolls. By today's standards I didn't have many toys and next to no pocket money. When I was six I was given a fairy-cycle and I rode it until I was eleven. I was given a bit of garden space too, but I never did much good with it. We had a cat and four sex-mad tortoises. Children were really expected to get on with it in the thirties so I never expressed my longing for my parents or maybe never comprehended it at all. It made me again, quite subconsciously, anxious to excel, to be clever and naturally I overdid this and was a bumptious little show-off in adult company, whose hands must have itched to give me a good smacking.

Exciting things did happen. My mother, Mitzi and I were driven to Brooklands to take part in a motorised beauty competition, an outing which a particularly persistent boyfriend had organised. He was not pleased to find that Mitzi and I would be going too. We won this tasteless event. The boyfriend was delighted. I bounced up and down on the back seat of the car shouting, "We won! We won!" and my mother did not restrain me as it made her feel less of an idiot.

Much worse, my Uncle Cyril, then a car salesman, arrived to take us out for a ride in a brand new Rolls Royce he was delivering to a customer. I was copiously sick on the back seat. We rushed back to our house to clean it up and I still wonder how they managed to get rid of the smell. This was the beginning of my being severely travelsick and I can remember long car journeys feeling dreadful and complaining all the time. My father then changed the Austin Seven for a Chrysler and I was put in the dickey seat, which was better for everybody. Often on Sundays in the summer we drove out of London to a large house called Blue Shutters.

This belonged to a successful couturier called Phoebe. She had been my Uncle John's lover for many years, but he had suddenly married somebody else and gone off to plant coffee in Kenya where he died from the long-term effects of a motorcycle accident. Phoebe had known my mother for years and dressed her for nothing. Phoebe's clothes were never mass-produced and she had made hand-knitted clothing high fashion. She made a lot of money and was generous with it. I owe her because being a plain child in glasses, she would not let my mother dress me up in the puff-sleeved pastel net party dresses and daisy decorated hats which made me look like a young pig. My mother was disappointed with me because I was not pretty and I knew it. Phoebe rescued me from curl papers, let me grow my straight hair long, put me in shorts and told me I was 'une jolie laide'. I asked her if I could have a black velvet party frock. My mother was horrified, but Phoebe said "Indeed you can, black velvet is ideal for a child's complexion." She made it for me quite plain and it must have looked better than pink net.

Blue Shutters had a beautiful sloping garden with fields at the bottom. It had its own wood full of spring flowers and a patio and a rockery full of minute rose bushes, which you must never step on. The best thing of all was the swimming pool where my Aunt Connie taught me to swim. Eight years older than my mother, Aunt Connie had worked for some years in the Belgian Congo as a pharmacist. She had broken her arm badly in a motorcycle accident and was back in England to have it reset. She was

Aunt Connie aged 23.

blonde and beautiful and a terrible tease. "Would you like a strawb, Jill?"

"They're not strawbs, they're strawberries," I would reply, red with indignation. "No they're not, they're strawbs."

"They're STRAWBERRIES !"

I am now beside myself.

"Shall we all drink Jilly-wee's health now? Happy days Jilly-wee!"

I hated that name and thought that having my health drunk was an insult.

My mother would intervene fairly soon and say, "Connie, leave the child alone for heaven's sake!"

Still she taught me to swim in Phoebe's pool, probably by taunting me into taking my feet off the bottom.

We went on holiday every summer to the Seaview Hotel on the Isle of Wight. I loved the sea by now, collecting shells and being allowed to go on the beach by myself. By now I was about eight so had become less of a pain. I could swim a quarter of a mile, paced out by my father, was a success at school and didn't need to draw attention to myself all the time.

One Spring holiday I went to stay with Lesley's family. The Reverend Arnold and his wife lived in some out of the way village in Wiltshire. They were both elderly. Rev. Arnold was more or less blind and Lesley's sister Joan had Down's Syndrome. Joan was about thirty and her only interest was her beautiful dolls' house which occupied her all day and which I was not allowed to touch. Mrs Arnold disliked me, being a real authoritarian. She lent me a farthing once for a 'farthing dip' in the village shop. I repaid the farthing when I got back to the house only to be told it was 'dirty' and had to be shined up with Brasso.

The best thing about this grim household was Lesley's other sister, Mary who was horsey. She summoned up a small grey pony for me, taught me how to rise to the trot and took me out every afternoon for long rides on the leading rein. She was accompanied by a handsome, cheerful man so maybe I was a useful chaperone. I hope she married him if only to get away from home.

Another person with whom I cut little ice was my maternal grandmother, Granny Hogg. She lived in Ockbrook, Derbyshire, opposite a Moravian cemetery where everyone was buried standing up to give them a head start on the Day of Resurrection. My grandmother had a large family of dogs and cats who all sat in their places without moving at feed times as an outward show of her inner determination to make everyone conform to her ideas of behaviour. She was a devout churchgoer, going to 8 o'clock communion on an empty stomach and again at

Above: Granny Hogg with Poosie and Annie's dog at Spondon.

Granny Hogg's house in Spondon, near Derby, with her maid, Annie, holding her own dog – a mongrel which Granny used to take for walks with her dogs but was always careful to explain that it was her maid's dog if she met anyone. She moved to nearby Ockbrook before long.

Matins, taking me. I blotted my copybook straight away because when the church organ began to play I began to cry uncontrollably like a dog howls when someone sings. My mother was blamed for this. One of her dogs, Gyp, was fond of me and when, as happened fairly often, I was banished to my bedroom, Gyp would whine miserably outside the door. My grandmother was an indefatigable walker and gardener and she thought I was a wimp. She had a toad in the cellar.

Her servant, Annie, was kinder to me. She had some funny opinions among which were, "There aren't any vitamins in my lettuces after I've washed them," and "I don't hold with girls who get themselves murdered." Once when I was visiting we went from the station in a taxi. On the way there was an emergency stop and I broke the windscreen with my head. The taxi driver was very cross about this and said that my mother should pay him. She said for him to get lost and Annie put raw steak on the lump on my forehead.

My grandmother nagged my mother into sending me to church and when I was a little older I did indeed go to church all by myself. My grandmother died having her gall-bladder removed during an air raid in the war.

Granny Phyllis by now was living in an extremely respectable private hotel near Guildford. Like my mother she was immaculately dressed with white marcelled hair. She would never, never have had it dyed blue. She was a pretty woman with regular features and had a faithful old flame who lived in the hotel also. She wore rouge and powder very discreetly and smoked cigarettes in her room. Much emphasis was placed on table manners and politeness – subjects that little girls could raise being fairly limited. I stayed for short periods there and enjoyed myself hugely because I loved going through Granny Phyllis' jewel box and telling her what I would like to have when she was dead. In Ceylon

Another old friend, Claude Donaldson-Selby, who also lived in the hotel.

29

she had had a good eye for collecting jewels and getting them well set. Granny Phyllis would also tell me stories about Ceylon. One was about a lady who teased an elephant at a durbar. The elephant seized her and held her upside down with his trunk. Like all the other ladies she was not wearing knickers because of the heat.

In Granny Phyllis' psyche there was a different person from her respectable exterior; she knew a lot about horse racing and had a bookie somewhere in the hotel. I was permitted to be with the gardener who let me plant violets in tiny earthenware flowerpots. These I used to try to sell to the other guests.

I did like my godmother, Francesca. My mother met Francesca when she was on her honeymoon on the Isle of Wight. Francesca was being bullied by some women in the common sitting room. My mother noticed this odd looking, small, frightened young woman, routed the women and rescued her. Francesca was 'educationally challenged'. The daughter of a judge and, with an equally brilliant brother, she was an embarrassment. They sent her to Cheltenham Ladies' College where she was utterly miserable. She was small and plump with straight fair hair, cut in a pudding bowl style, and a small-featured face reminiscent of Down's Syndrome, but not so marked. She wore a beret, a brown tweed coat and skirt, thick Lisle stockings and sensible shoes. My mother once tried to smarten her up and put on a bit of makeup, but Francesca cried so terribly that my mother took pity on her and gave up. By the time I was eight, Francesca lived in a mansion flat near Victoria Station. She had a maid who looked after everything. Francesca spent her days wandering about the Army and Navy Stores and every week she got on a train to Strawberry Hill for the afternoon. This continued up until the outbreak of war. She worshipped my mother. Francesca had lots of money and loved spending it on marbles of which I had a great many, carefully sorted out and kept in little cloth bags. The Army and Navy had a wonderful range, notably great big 'alleys' with colourful spirals inside. They cost half-a-crown, a fortune then. We took ages choosing them. I never actually played marbles. I would spend hours arranging them and haranguing them like little people. When the war broke out Francesca's maid departed. Francesca was left to fend for herself.

I wasn't over-indulged. I had to save for anything I wanted. In an art shop in Twickenham I saw a tiny paint box and I, Lesley and ten hard-saved shillings went to buy it. They let me look at it but it turned out that it was a miniaturists paint box, full of costly watercolours. It cost two pounds ten shillings. I wasn't given it, needless to say. Comic papers were not exactly forbidden, but were open to derision. I had few sweets and was too hard up to buy anything but the cheapest aniseed balls and liquorice bootlaces. That's how it was until I was nine – then things changed.

My mother was pregnant again. By the time I was told, the baby wasn't too far off. My mother had a new young doctor and he told her to diet and to take plenty of exercise which meant that twice a week she walked along the towpath from Strawberry Hill to Richmond Hill which is a good way by any standards. We had some tedious trips to baby shops where my taste was always consulted as being 'nearer to the baby'. This regime paid off as on 16 February 1936 one Sunday morning my mother was delivered of a boy, John Anthony Hugh, after a four-hour labour and just as the doctor came into her bedroom. Hugh was slightly premature but he weighed six pounds, which was an improvement on me. He was quite healthy at his birth. My father wasn't there because he was hastily taking me to stay temporarily with Granny Phyllis' best friends in Richmond. These people had a large number of cocker spaniels and a gay son called Boy. Granny Phyllis abandoned her air of fastidious gentility on one occasion and told him he would get 'cancer of the back passage' if he went on like that.

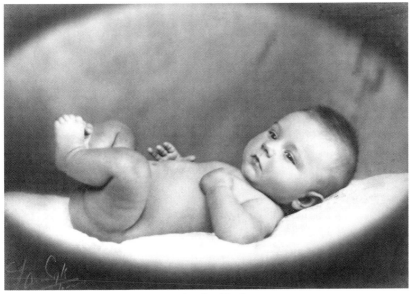

My brother Hugh.

The next few weeks were not typical of my parents. I couldn't express this, but it made me very unhappy and was a poor start to moving over for a baby brother when you have been an only child for nine years.

After the birth my mother lay in bed for four solid weeks doing absolutely nothing but feed her baby. She had a monthly nurse who waited on her hand and foot. Lesley had departed a little while before. Why I don't know, but the arrangements for me to stay with the families of good school friends (both boys incidentally) had come unstuck so I ended up with a family I didn't know in Richmond who had a child of four. They were nice to me, but I longed to go home to see my new brother. Somehow it got overlooked. After about a fortnight the nurse came out to fetch me in her car but took me back to Richmond at bedtime. I guess in retrospect that my being at home would have been difficult.

When I was eventually allowed home, things were going badly. Hugh's permanent Nanny had arrived but he had developed gastro-enteritis due allegedly to the negligence of the monthly nurse. Hugh wailed constantly and the doctor said he must not be allowed to cry. My mother, my father, his Nanny and the cook carried him about, singing and rocking him day and night. I never to this day hear 'Teddy Bears' Picnic' without remembering the foreboding and tension in the household. It was touch and go. This time I certainly didn't want Hugh to die. He gradually recovered. My mother kept her milk. Anxiety abated, but it left her in permanent dread that Hugh was getting ill. Having a new baby meant that

My father and mother with Boy Richards (left) at the Wedding of his sister, Gwenda, in 1930. He died of leukaemia after the war; his ship was off Japan, downwind of Hiroshima, when the atomic bomb exploded.

my mother was at home most of the time. By then she was a feature writer for the *Sunday Express* and every week her secretary came to take orders and carry off the latest instalment of the adventures of the heroic Sarah Snail for the children's page. Mother was Uncle Mac of the Choc-Toc Club as well. Sarah Snail was drawn out on Bristol Board with special pens and woe betide any child who might even think of touching either. The pictures were accompanied by a storyline in verse. My mother had been raised on the *Ingoldsby Legends* so she was a good versifier. Sarah Snail would be thought of now as pathetic, but she survived for several years and was certainly original.

Maybe my mother's reduction in income caused some difficulty in maintaining the lavish style in which we lived. Hugh had a Nanny. There was a resident cook general called Emma who was Cornish. She was also a dedicated Salvationist and she had had an enormous gallstone removed which she showed me sometimes. Like the Provincial Lady, my mother never did a hand's turn. I can picture her in the kitchen only once when she iced some notes of a hymn tune onto a cake made by Emma for some Salvationist festivity. Money matters were never discussed in front of me, but my father became less cheerful and talkative and was even more frequently away from home.

Hugh became the centre of my mother's universe. She did sincerely love me, but I had never given her such agony of mind. Hugh was always her favourite. He was a loving placid child and grew up to be a loving, kind adult so I in retrospect cannot complain, having been neither.

By the end of the year I would have outgrown Sesame and took the entrance exam to the Old Vicarage School for Girls on Richmond Hill. This school had once been select and old-fashioned, but when it moved and expanded it became a respectable all round girls' school with games, gym and swimming, art and music. The teaching was formal, but not uninteresting and they worked us quite hard with homework every night. Miss Lee and my new headmistress, Miss Cross, were friends as many girls went from Sesame to the Old Vicarage. Miss Lee tipped me as a high-flier but I ruined my reputation during my entrance exam. I could answer all the questions but my fountain pen wouldn't write so I was terribly slow. Did I have the sense to ask the person invigilating for something else to write with? It never occurred to me. At the Old Vicarage School we wore a grey tunic without a girdle, a pink-striped shirt, grey socks, black shoes and a hat with 'OVS' on the ribbon. In the summer we wore pink dresses, which could be any design your mother decreed. You also had to have a white aertex shirt and a grey skirt for games and you got into trouble if your kit was not all marked with Cash's nametapes. New girls were put in a House. They were boringly called after the points of the compass. There was no Sorting Hat! I was in East, a despised house **full** of under-achievers and wore a little round yellow brooch.

There was an important rewards and punishment system which was based on loyalty.

A 'quarter star' was awarded for good work and a point off for minor misdemeanours.

A 'quarter stripe' was bad not least because you had to tell the whole school how you got it at a special assembly where you revealed your achievements for the past week. I got one once for rushing into a music lesson and bouncing a bit against the piano. The night before I had to own up I didn't sleep at all. The direful moment arrived. "What was the quarter stripe for?"

"Jumping up against the piano."

When the whole school stopped laughing Miss Cross said very severely, "You'd better come and see me at break."

When I got to her study, more dead than alive she merely said, "Behave more sensibly in class in future," and let me go.

Miss Cross was not approachable. She taught Scripture and she was often accompanied by a huge Great Dane which would do rude things on your leg if given the chance.

I was very happy here nevertheless. We had gym with a vaulting horse, made a felt rabbit with a carrot in its paws in 'craft'. I won the Pilgrim's Progress for Scripture. I was lucky enough to find school easy and was always well placed in class. I might have been a fair game for teasing because of my plain face and glasses, but I was in the netball team and also knew how to give as good as I got; I had a couple of fights, fortunately not found out.

In my second year I was nearly eleven. I was allowed to travel to school by myself in the bus. A supercilious older girl called Avril got on at my stop, but we didn't speak because she hated the sight of me. When I left for school no one was up except Emma who allowed me to have tinned peas and black treacle on toast for breakfast. We started Latin in a ladylike way using a book all about girls and doves and not much syntax (a year later I was to eat massive crow about this, but I am anticipating). I got my netball colours. I had two good friends, Sheila and June, an enemy Sylvia, and a fat shy girl who was hopeless at everything except for her talent at drawing. Most memorable was Heather who was being groomed to be an ice skating star. One time we all had a letter to take home announcing a visit to the British Museum. Heather's mother replied that she didn't see any point in Heather's joining in because she was going to be an ice skater. My mother fell off her chair laughing. Years later I stayed in a house with a top professional ice skater. Thinking that this must be a fairly closed shop I asked her if she knew Heather. She didn't, so maybe Heather should have come to the British Museum.

At home, Hugh was less fragile but still raised with great emphasis on hygiene. When he began to crawl I was scared of being responsible for him in case he put anything dirty into his mouth. He didn't eat well after he was weaned and many subterfuges were employed to feed him. Thursday was Nanny's day off. Francesca came over for the afternoon. Due to a lack of practice my mother made heavy weather of bathing, feeding and changing Hugh and was always in a bad mood by the time I got home from school. About five o'clock my mother sent me upstairs to turn on the dreaded gas fire in the nursery.

Out of school Sheila and I spent much time clashing about in the road outside our house on roller skates. They were clamped onto one's shoes with a little key. I wore my key on a string round my neck because if it got lost you would never be able to take off your roller skates. We went to a roadhouse some Sundays called 'The Ace of Spades'. I scared the pants off everyone in the swimming pool by climbing up to the highest diving board and jumping in. Everyone clapped, but I didn't realise. In the late Autumn of 1937 I was got out of bed to hear King Edward VIII's abdication speech and we all sang, 'Hark the herald angels sing, Mrs. Simpson's pinched our King!' at Christmas.

That year my mother organised a stunt where she and I went Christmas shopping with a pound note donated by her newspaper. I bought an inflatable rubber dachshund, a bowling hoop far bigger than I was, toys for Hugh and presents for everyone else. Getting that hoop home on the tube was newsworthy in itself. A photo of me appeared next Sunday surrounded by my purchases. My mother painted that hoop all different colours and I played with it a lot.

I listened to Children's Hour and it was fashionable to baa like Larry the Lamb in 'Toy Town'. I went to the cinema, but not on Saturday mornings which my mother thought common. Instead we went shopping ending up in a French Patisserie in Richmond. I always had a Madeleine, but it sadly didn't have the same effect on me as it did on Proust. I went to a film one evening with my parents. It was called *San Francisco*. It began quite frivolously with a catchy tune and ended up with horrific scenes of the earthquake. I kept my parents up all night.

My mother had read many books to me by now. I loved the Lowood School chapters of *Jane Eyre*: *Holiday House*, *Seven Little Australians* and *The Family at Misrule* by Ethel Turner and many others. I was not supposed to read *A Century of Creepy Stories* because I got too scared and around about this time I did get insomnia. My parents would leave a light on outside my open door, but when they went to bed they turned it out thinking I was asleep. I lay stiff with terror for what seemed like hours and became so pale and wan I was taken to the doctor. He prescribed patent groats which were disgusting. Sooner or later I started sleeping properly again. Surprisingly, I was allowed to keep pet mice. I got two – Albert, brown and Victoria, white. Albert had many children. Luckily the babies came out a silvery beige so they could be disposed of for two pence each at the local pet shop. My mother loved Victoria and Albert and they may have laid the foundations of the Kitty MacBride Happy Mice. This again was far into the future.

By 1938 everyone was beginning to be aware that there was going to be trouble with Hitler's Germany. My father who was on the staff of the *Daily Herald* was certain there would be a war. My mother began to learn German and to go to First Aid classes, coming back with alarming instructions about how to cope with poison gas. The Munich Crisis came and passed. We were sent to stay on a mink farm in Kent for a few days, but came home when Chamberlain returned announcing 'Peace with honour'. People became even more anxious as they were fitted with gas masks and an Air Raid Precautions booklet was sent to every family.

For a schoolgirl the summer passed easily enough. I took grade 1 of the Royal Drawing Society examinations and my picture was reproduced in the yearbook. I was becoming interested in drawing and painting, but had never shown much aptitude so everyone was surprised except my mother who of course had seen it coming all along. I got a special recommendation for swimming. Hugh had a new Nanny. She was small and lame and wore a built-up boot. She was gentle and kindly and far nicer to me than I was to her. I was expected to take the entrance examination for St Paul's School for Girls in the Autumn of 1939.

In August 1939 we went, Nanny, Emma and all to a rented house at Angmering-on-Sea. My father stayed on in London. It was a quiet holiday for me. The weather was not good and I spent time mooning about, writing poetry, reading and drawing. In the last days of August my father suddenly appeared. He made us spend one hectic day packing up everything Hugh and I and Nanny had with us. The next day we were all bundled into the car and driven for hours westward until we got to Okehampton and looked around for somewhere to stay. We found a guest house called Pixy Nook at Sticklepath. Nanny, Hugh and I were installed and my parents departed. My father thought that England would be bombed and occupied within days so he and my mother did not expect to see us again. Some mothers did go into the country with their children for the duration of the war, but my mother was far too keen on being part of the action even to consider it. Her grief on leaving us must have been overwhelming, but she told me later that both of them felt mainly relief that they had done their best to keep us safe.

I wasn't particularly upset because I was sure they'd be back. I flew my kite in a nearby field, heard the local quarry exploding at midday and painted some pictures. It never occurred to me to think about Nanny. Hugh was happy with her so he was fine. The weather was lovely. At eleven o'clock on Sunday 3rd September we all gathered round the radio to hear Mr Chamberlain announce that we were at war with Germany. Somebody began to cry.

In the afternoon a taxi arrived to take us to where we were going to stay permanently. This was Lifton Park near Launceston. The place had been taken over by a boys' preparatory school called Moffatts. Jock Englehart was the headmaster. Term had not yet begun properly, but there were some few boys already there.

Lifton Park was a long two-storey house with a sweeping drive in front and an imposing hall and stairway. Above and behind this there were master bedrooms and large reception rooms. Further from the front the rooms became smaller and ended up with sculleries and kitchens. There was a dairy and some outhouses. Horses had been stabled on the home farm about two hundred yards below. The house was handsomely set with woods behind and large lawns in front. There were many exotic trees and plants and some noisy peacocks. Inside there were left behind glass cupboards filled with objects d'art that must have been valuable. Over time they gradually disappeared. The previous owners had gone, never to return. In 1969 I went back to Lifton Park and most of it was a ruin. Someone was living in the front of the house, but the lead from the roof behind had disappeared and giant Bay-Willow-Herb plants were growing out of the eaves. Hens scratched on the sweep. I'm only a hundred miles from Lifton Park, but somehow I never went back again. This fortnight before term began saw in me a complete change of personality. I became a hoyden. I didn't wear my glasses, cast aside my uncomfortable orthodontic device, tore my clothes and ran yelled and fought as well as the boys. We were entirely unsupervised as I suppose the staff were working flat out to get the place organised. Gradually more and more people arrived. In the end there were twelve girls most quite young. Some had mothers with them, presumably helpers. Hugh and Nanny got a little poky room at the back of the house. I virtually forgot them. I even forgot Albert and Victoria who had come all this way with me. I think Nanny let them go. I don't suppose they lasted long and I feel ashamed about this even now. The girls' dormitory was a spacious front bedroom with three tall windows. We had camp beds; mine didn't have a mattress, but I slept like a log anyway. We girls were frankly not welcome in the school. We ate apart, we were not included in games and we older ones were severely treated for minor misdemeanours. We once had a pillow fight and our punishment was to sweep up leaves on the wooded church path during the games period every day for a month. One of us was whacked and another was made to write out a long sentence one thousand times for saying 'bloody'. I was a cousin, but I was not guilty of using this to my advantage. I never owned up to any relationship, especially to my Great Aunt Natalie whom I never addressed as anything but Mrs Englehart. The masters were addressed as 'Sir'. Masters, matrons and other people's mothers all became my enemies for a long time. We five elder girls made it our business never to be conspicuous and disappeared into the landscape most of the time.

Mavis Locke, Maureen Sharp and self bathing in the Tamar.

The other four girls became an important part of my life. There was Mavis who was heartily disliked. She was an infuriating, foxy-faced, rather spiteful girl. She once hid my glasses and I nearly killed her by strangling her with her tie. Luckily Maureen who was older and much stronger than me broke it up. Mavis' mother lived in the Arundel Arms in Lifton. Mavis was academic – more than just bright – ending up in the scholarship class and learning Greek. Diana, who had a big brother Tony, was about ten, but kept up well. Her mother worked in the school and they had a little brother the same age as Hugh. Her family were nice to me later in the war, having me to stay and giving me a good time.

Maureen was the daughter of the maths master, Captain Sharpe. Her mother worked in the school as well. She was my best friend and I fortunately met her again later on. Her parents, in holiday time, were kind to me including me in outings probably because Maureen refused to go anywhere without me. She was dark with a face that would be handsome and striking when she grew up. At this time she had huge features, a lot of wiry hair and was strong and mature for her age. I admired and envied her. She was thoroughly unacademic and in a form below mine, but being a strong rider she was often let out of class to help with the ponies which came every week for the school's riding lessons. Maureen had to eat an egg every morning in her parents' room because the food at Lifton Park was extremely scanty. She made a fuss about this as she deemed it disloyal. She didn't get on with her father who was disappointed by her lack of progress especially in maths and he rubbed it in. It didn't help that I was bright. Maureen never held this against me at all.

Pat was an amazing girl. She was a little older than me. She had pale hair, a pale complexion and rather protruding pale blue eyes. She had no need of prettiness because she was strong, full of energy and did everything outstandingly well. She rode brilliantly, winning an adult hunter trial on one of the teacher's horses. She could gallop and jump like a horse, holding a flowerpot in each hand. She was a good artist, played the accordion and was clever in class. Best of all she was equable and kind, taught me to ride on a carthorse, and never made me feel like the ignorant weedy person I was by comparison. Pat became a well known West Country vet, eventually married the man who had given us riding lessons at Lifton and came to an end not inconsistent with the life she had lived so intensely.

School came upon us one dreadful day. The classrooms were upstairs in the middle of the house and in winter freezingly cold. It took the masters no time at all to find out that I was miles behind in Latin and maths, the only subjects that mattered. I could get by in all the others. Every school day was identical – maths, Latin, break, French, English, then dinner, Saturdays included. From two till four the boys had games, then afternoon school Monday to Friday. Supper came next then bed. On Sundays we went to church, wrote supervised and allegedly censored letters home and the rest of the day was free. I realised that if I did not make heroic efforts in

Latin I was destined to endless detentions or worse. Captain Sharp took trouble with me in maths and I don't remember its being unduly difficult. By Christmas I caught up. No teaching method ever devised could be worse than French taken by Mr Engelhart Senior. He was strange and frightening wandering about the house muttering and sometimes half-clad. His room was rather too near our dormitory for comfort but he never actually came in. In the classroom he used to dictate what seemed to me to be an incomprehensible stream of language; nor did he tell us what the passage was about. You then went up in turn – he underlined nearly every word – and sent you back to 'put it right'. You could go up ten times in a lesson and get nowhere. When you got the French right (this could take you literally weeks) you had to translate it. I remember some of these passages to this day and I also remember bursting into tears. This method of teaching turns you into a good guesser but it's short on grammar as I was to learn when I went to my next school.

Mrs Engelhart took English. She had been a sentimental novelist writing as Natalie Joan. I have never seen a copy of any of her books anywhere since. The trouble with the Engleharts was that they were all frighteningly unpredictable. Mrs Engelhart in a good mood would read to us John Buchan in class and sometimes in the evening. In a bad mood she was vitriolic and gave out draconian punishments. She was the one who caught us pillow-fighting. Once somebody in the dormitory had a terrible cough. Mrs Englehart who slept in a little room nearby described this cough 'like some disgusting old man'. She was also nasty about people who wet their beds. Her second son David took our form for Latin and we learnt gender rhymes every day, four lines at a time. He laid into me at the beginning, but when I'd caught up he let me alone. He was to be called up soon. Mr Ingrams took his place.

There was also a geography master, Mr Jackman. He lived with a large family in the south lodge of the estate in great confusion. I was a bit sorry for him if anything.

I feel sad writing about Jock Englehart. Much later on I got to know him well and loved him dearly. He died in 2000. At Lifton he was a figure of terror. He had a study where he whacked naughty boys. He was sarcastic and made one feel small. I had a Damascus road moment outside his study plucking up courage to go in to be told off. Both the Englehart brothers were expert musicians, especially Jock who became a famous pianist. In his study was a grand piano and Jock was playing what I now know was Mozart's Study in C. I could hear it through the door and went in. Jock said,

"Do you want to listen?"
"Yes please Sir."
He played for quite a long time. If life were idyllic I would never have been afraid of him again. This didn't happen but soon after this I was found to have a true and pretty voice and I had more rapport with him when there was music going on.

One day he dictated a poem to us. It went like this:-

Away, haunt thou not me,
Thou vain philosophy!
Little hast thou bestead
Save to perplex the head
And leave the spirit dead.
Unto thy broken cisterns wherefore go,
While from the secret treasure-depths below,
Fed by the skyey shower,
And clouds that sink and rest on hill-tops high.
Wisdom at once, and Power,
Are welling, bubbling forth, unseen, incessantly?
Why labour at the dull mechanic oar,
When the fresh breeze is blowing,
And the strong current flowing,
Right onward to the Eternal Shore?

This poem is by Arthur Hugh Clough. I learned this 70 years later! It is called 'In a Lecture Room'. This seems quite hard for people of twelve?

Jock would have to have a biography all to himself. He was a unique and talented man. When he was eighty we had a wonderful evening in the Acorn Theatre in Penzance where he played grand piano, my daughter sang and her boyfriend played guitar. They begged Jock to come back to do a gig, and if he'd lived, he certainly would have done so.

We girls had our meals in a little scullery at the back of the house. Some of us had jars of honey or jam, which could still be obtained if you had some money, and scraped them out obsessively. When you are a child you don't really recognise privation. Was I hungry? Probably. Was I cold? I remember huge itching chilblains and knitting some mittens, but all these things had become so much a part of one's life I took them on board unthinkingly. We were all underweight, but I only remember being ill once and then only for a day or two. I must have felt dreadful because the matron I went to see was far from sympathetic and, besides, she had a dubious bull terrier.

I was always covered in cuts and bruises and once got a bad cut on my thigh, but I didn't say anything about any of them. Once I caught my finger in a chaff cutter. Another time I was bitten by a rat. I did tell Nanny about this. She was still at Lifton then. She put bread poultices on my hand which came off black.

These injuries occurred on our idea of heaven – the farm. Lifton Park Home Farm was below the house and invisible as if some Henry Crawford had 'done away with the offices'. When we first ventured down there were two huge horses and a carter, but not for long. The farm was run by a Mr and Mrs Vanstone, their son Bernard, known as Bossky, and a small strong man called Little Egg. We managed to win the heart of the irascible Mr Vanstone. Mrs Vanstone kept us from starving because every day we went to milk the cows she made us drink a pint of milk and gave us a huge piece of homemade bread or saffron cake with cream and jam. I didn't like cream and said so. Mr Vanstone got hold of my plaits and force fed me some cream! He'd never heard such nonsense.

Little Egg at Lifton Park Home Farm.

I think we began by standing about timidly. Then Little Egg suggested we put out the cows' feed and we soon felt important because we knew each one's rations. We then went to fetch them in and marvelled how every cow knew her place in the shippen. Soon we were quite happy pushing in and fastening the chains round their necks. There was a huge good-tempered Devon bull who stood outside the farmyard until his harem came out. He had about thirty wives, mostly large Devon cross cows, some black and some spotted. There were a few Guernseys and one Jersey cow. Cows had horns then. One time we went to fetch the cows for milking. The bull was far away from the herd at the end of the field. We reasoned that he could stay there as he was not going to be milked. When the bull realised his cows had gone he galloped after them damaging every gate he came to. We got into trouble, but luckily nobody said that we couldn't come again. When Egg went to fetch the cows he rode on Jim who had been the last bus horse in Launceston. Egg didn't use a bridle. He just steered Jim with a little twig vaulting on and galloping all over the field like a Red Indian. Pat could do this and one of us would be on behind hanging on. We adored Jim and used to take him for rides when he should have been having a well-deserved rest, as he did all the carting for the farm and for a carthorse he wasn't very big. For sheer good nature and gentleness I have never met a horse to rival dear long-suffering Jim.

While the cows were feeding, their udders had to be washed in warm water with a cloth. Then the milking began. Our favourite was Sparky, a huge spotted cow on whom Mrs Vanstone taught us to milk. We got the knack quickly thanks to Sparky's forbearance. When you'd milked out every last drop, (and sometimes Mr Vanstone came over and checked), the milk had to be tipped into the cooler in the bottling room. This was high and a big bucket of milk was hard to lift. I spilt some once and there was trouble because spilling milk was the unforgivable sin. We became able to milk three or four cows before we had to hasten back to school. An unwelcome job for any of us children was to milk a cow with mastitis because we milked more gently. The cow would have her hind legs tied together and sometimes struggled so hard she fell over.

Mavis didn't like milking so she was Mrs Vanstone's favourite and helped her with bottling the milk and in the dairy. Mr Vanstone had a shop in Launceston and a milk round so there were many bottles to wash. The water for this was pumped up from somewhere by one hundred quite stiff strokes. Bottle washing was enlivened by a vigorous part singing of such topical gems as 'South of the Border', 'The Isle of Capri', 'Run Rabbit' and 'There'll be Bluebirds Over'.

Maureen and I stayed at school in holiday time which allowed us to be on the farm as much as possible. The following summer we saved hay and learnt how to bind a sheaf in the corn harvest. The reaper and binder made nearly all the sheaves but those near the hedges had to be done by hand. We made stooks and were shown how to build the corn stack with their sheaves inside. Once when we were harvesting we saw a German plane coming over pretty low. Egg picked me up and flung me into a ditch. When the reaper and binder had nearly finished rabbits ran out from the decreasing circle of cover to meet a terrified fate from dogs and men with sticks. I was past being compassionate, but I never killed a rabbit myself. We went to fetch illicit cream in Mr Vanstone's van and became adept at keeping a bucket of milk from spilling en route. There was a harness pony, Mary, so borrowing poor Jim we went for long rides. There was an orchard on the farm. In the autumn we were sent to pick apples. There were enormous soft bluish ones for cider which were pressed on the farm and some varieties, like 'Pigs' Noses', I have never seen again. The EU Regulations would doubtless have forbidden them all to be grown by now.

The time I revisited Lifton Park I also went down to the farm and there was Bossky unscathed from his service as a rear gunner in the RAF He was not displeased to see me. He told me that his father, who had always been brutal to him as a boy, loved us girls, and would look at his watch saying, "They'll be down here soon." He went on to tell me what a nuisance we had been on the farm. This was a blow because we assumed that we had always been helpful and hard working. When I told Maureen this, she too was most indignant. Mr Vanstone had long ago died of a stroke, but Mrs Vanstone was still living in Launceston. Bossky asked me to go to see her, but we were en route for Cornwall and I knew to delay would cause a big family fuss, so I said I couldn't. I wish I'd gone.

The day I lived for, apart from farm, was riding day. Every week in term time Mr Bert Piper from Chillaton would trek over to Lifton Park with eight or nine ponies. We were divided into ability groups and had an hour's lesson in a large sloping field near the house. Because of riding in Wiltshire I was found not to be a complete beginner and was promoted to the next class up. Best of all was helping Bert bring the horses over and take them home if you were competent enough. Taking the horses home also meant going to the Chillaton Arms where we drank real cider regardless of the fact that we were all under age.

We once had a gymkhana with a Novice Riding Class. I got a green rosette, but Mavis won the class outright which was gall and wormwood.

Closely connected with horses was Mrs Lasson. She was a tall slim elegant woman with a 'tally-ho' accent and she resembled a horse as well. Her husband was in the army. She taught the younger children and she owned the chestnut thoroughbred that Pat rode to victory in the Hunter Trials. I loved Mrs Lasson because at Christmas she gave me a white Swiss-style knife with two blades, a hoof pick and a needle embedded in the side. I named my knife 'Sixth Finger'. Years later I was struck to read that Ivan Denisovich named his knife 'Ten Days' which was the length of time a man spent in the cells if his knife was discovered by the Siberian labour camp warders. I kept Sixth Finger safely until I was nearly sixteen when I gave it away as a love token.

Hugh and Nanny stayed at Lifton Park for a few months; then they moved into the household of a Doctor and Mrs Lea for Nanny to take care of their two little boys. This was better for everybody. Hugh loved Janet Lea who treated him like a son. Before Nanny left Lifton she made me a blue dressing gown which reached to my ankles at first, then ended up above my knees. This was magnanimous of Nanny because I was never cooperative with her. I fear that Hugh is getting short shrift in this story. We did not see much of each other until later on in the war.

We met one day a week when we girls went down to Lifton Village to do Guides taken by Mrs Lea. I thought Guides was a complete waste of time and was eventually thrown out.

It was a long time before I saw my parents again. I only twice saw them together throughout the whole war. My father went into the Ministry of Information which was in the tall London University Building. It was no sinecure. He worked week in week out and did fire-watching all through the Blitz. He got an OBE for his contribution when the war ended. My mother became an ARP warden while she was waiting to be called up to be a Publicity Officer in the ATS. She was drafted to central London to help in the Blitz, and once stayed alone with an unexploded land mine keeping people away until the Bomb Disposal Squad arrived. She also had to learn about housekeeping as Emma had gone back to Cornwall. The phoney war did not weaken our parents' resolve to keep us children out of London. When I saw my mother again after the war began, she never stayed more than two or three days so maybe I've telescoped a few visits into one, which is after Hugh and Nanny had gone to live with the Leas. My mother made cigarettes for herself in a little rolling machine and Hugh had spent weeks picking up fag ends for her to resurrect. There was a fuss because my long hair was entangled, too difficult for me to comb out. Mrs Sharp washed Maureen's and my hair from time to time, but nobody was there to plait anyone's hair in the mornings. My mother got my hair untangled with scissors. She was quite rough because she was angry and remorseful, but not with me. It soon tangled up again. Nobody thought to cut my hair so I could look after it myself. It didn't worry me at all. My mother stayed at the Arundel Arms in Lifton. It was an excellent hotel in the war and it still is. At this time the Arundel Arms did a marvellous pre-rationing breakfast with bacon and egg and mushrooms, tomatoes and fried bread followed by toast and limitless butter and marmalade. One time my mother was leaving after breakfast and I had walked down from the school to say goodbye. I couldn't eat a thing because I was so choked with tears. Poor mother. It was a sad parting for her. It was to become more cruel for her later when she got leave because I would have little or nothing to do with her.

Being a boy's school there was great interest in the war. Pins were stuck in maps, strategies discussed. We knew all about Dunkirk. In our own real lives, events seemed far away. There must have been a certain amount of petrol. To eke it out we had a pony trap drawn by Mary. We girls used to harness her up and drive the trap unsupervised. Surprisingly there were no accidents.

The boys themselves impinged little upon us. They were merely people we did lessons with. Sometimes they jeered at us if we met them outside. Some stand out. Tony Vivian, Diana's brother, I remember because I went to stay with them at Woking later on. I met him again once when he had an attachment to my sister-in-law. There was a very senior boy who looked like Balloo, three brothers called D'Arcy all bidding to rival that fictional god. There was a clever boy in my class called Dodwell, who knew all the words to the Gilbert and Sullivan operettas by heart. I met his sister, Philippa, half a century later at a concert at Lusaka Cathedral. She was a missionary she said, but that was about all she told me because I was obviously outside the pale. A boy called Julian, red headed and Scottish, kept us laughing. That household name, Dudley Sutton, was several years younger than me, but even then he had the sort of personality that presages fame. That summer at Moffats we did a performance of Humperdinck's *Hansel and Gretel*.

I was Gretel. My father visited us round about this time and Jock told him that I might consider singing as a career.

Common Entrance was looming for the boys in my class so I had to leave. Pat had already gone. Mavis was going to a top academic boarding school. The Sharp family were planning to retire to Somerset where Maureen went to some prim girls' school which she hated. She was allowed to leave altogether quite soon and she went to work on a farm. Diana still had another year to go at Moffats.

In the spring holiday before I left I went to stay for a week at Ardock Lodge at Lewdown four miles away to see how I liked it. Ardock was a small school started by a Mrs Hilsden. It had been joined by Commonweal Lodge, a school from Purley, much to its academic advantage. The London part of the school was still on holiday. I loved everything about Ardock. There were ponies, and delicious porridge for breakfast. Mrs Hilsden was a remarkable person and the few other children were friendly. I was longing to come here to school. I had the happiest time for about four days.

One morning we had a little gymkhana. I fell off my pony and hurt my knee. My kneecap was actually broken, but I did not know this until years later when I hurt the same knee falling over a railing watching two camels mating at the zoo. This time my knee was properly X-rayed and the evidence was found.

I was carried into the sickroom. My already too-small jodhpurs had to be cut off, to my great distress, and my leg was splinted onto a padded bit of wood. Dr Lea was summoned. For about three days I was in agony, not much alleviated by aspirin. Everyone at Ardock was incredibly kind. They let me stay an extra week to make up for my accident. I couldn't stand on my left leg and had a broom for a crutch for some weeks.

Sometimes the doctor would examine my still swollen knee.

"Please, can I go riding?"

"Not yet I'm afraid."

I would go away fighting back tears.

At the end of my last term at Moffats I won prizes for Latin and English. One doesn't often really read school prize books, but the latter was the Everyman edition of Modern Humour. Eighty percent of it was above my head, but I loved that book and have it still. I also won a cup for getting most badges in the year. A badge was a bit of red ribbon on a safety pin you pinned onto your jersey. Because I was a girl my name couldn't be engraved on that cup, but they gave me ten shillings which was far more satisfactory.

That summer Maureen and I got a ferret. He cost five shillings and came equipped with a barrel for his cage. We called him Diogenes or 'Ogi' for short. Ogi was a big ferret, yellowish in parts with redcurrant jelly eyes. He was very gentle and never bit.

We used to let him out on the rough parts of the garden (by now the whole place was pretty dilapidated). Ogi would disappear down a hole and we would have to wait there until he came up again which might well be a long time. He was fed on rabbit or little bits of meat from the kitchen. When I moved permanently to Ardock I was allowed to take Ogi with me as Captain Sharp wasn't taking any ferrets anywhere. The first night he spent at Ardock Ogi disappeared. There was a handyman called Trumper who I think stole him as he was a perfectly good working ferret. I was upset but was distracted from my grief by the arrival of Commonweal Lodge en masse.

This put a whole new complexion on things. Most of the girls were tidy town dwellers and when they saw me shabby, far from clean and heathenish they withdrew the hems of their garments in no uncertain fashion.

This antipathy towards me was not helped because when we were all sorted out into classes, I was put into Lower Fifth where one began to prepare for School Certificate over the heads of big, mature girls a year older than me. I was tall by then but thin and under developed. Everybody but me had their periods both in my class and in the class below and this was to be so until I was over sixteen.

My unpopularity did not end with the girls.

"How am I expected to read the handwriting of a scrubby schoolboy?"

Miss Clarke taught us English, was obsessed with deportment and extremely sarcastic.

"Do you really not know what a reflexive verb is?"

Thus Miss Bray the Headmistress,

"You must learn all these tenses as soon as possible."

"Leave assembly at once and go and wash the mud off your knees."

"You are all covered in hay like a stable boy."

"Where is your compass/ rough book/ protractor/ painting rag?"

These are just a few of the slings and arrows I remember from those first days. All that Latin I'd learnt got forgotten until I was about sixty-five.

As before at Lifton, I adjusted. I became rather better-washed, learnt to write legibly and took more care of my belongings I began to be better regarded because I could ride and handle horses, sing well and I was good at art. I became accepted as a mildly amusing eccentric.

When the two schools were joined up there were about fifty pupils. Ardock was an old house on the A30 which had belonged to the Baring-Goulds and like Spring Terrace in Richmond, there was a ghost.

The Ghost's Tale

A woman's ghost haunted the main staircase at night. Only young children could see her. My brother aged about 5 said she wore a long grey dress with white accessories. Older people knew she was there however.

Some years later Ardock was burned to the ground. It was never rebuilt. The first time I drew in on the A30 the yard and fields had been made into a Service Station, I had some coffee and began chatting to two women who were on duty. I spoke of the ghost and they looked concerned but had more to say about the teachers at the school: "Funny bunch of wimmen they was!" They were too.

My next encounter with the ghost was roughly thirty years later with my son and his wife. We were given an unenthusiastic welcome by a man in the yard but when I mentioned the ghost, the atmosphere changed and he sent us indoors to meet his wife. Inside there was a huge new building containing a banqueting hall for corporate functions. One wall from the original Ardock Lodge had been used in its construction. The rest of the land had become a stud farm and it was good to think of horses there again after all this time.

The wife was a little reticent to talk about the ghost. Then she opened up a bit and told us that when her daughter, then aged four, went across the huge room full of tables, someone unseen always held her hand. She also said that when a photogravure of the lady had been taken down from the wall for some reason, they had found some broken chairs in the morning. I called out:

"Oh Ghost are you happier now there is so much activity around you?" Suddenly the air around me grew bitterly cold and my spine was frozen. I was certain she was there. My son and his wife did not notice but I think the proprietress did.

My back felt cold for quite a while when we got back into the car. I fervently hoped that the ghost had not hopped in after me!

***

Less imposing than Lifton Park, Ardock was a large country house. There were about eight bedrooms and three large rooms downstairs and a good big kitchen with an Aga. Madamoiselle felt the cold and was always running into the kitchen "To sit on ze Aga Khan". A dark passage leading to the back door was used all the time. It led out to the yard where there were stables, a two storey barn and a wooden building which served as two classrooms.

Ardock had two large sloping fields for the ponies and looking away from the A30 there was a handsome view of rolling fields and woods with Dartmoor in the distance. I was to paint that landscape many times, I did this once by moonlight and was very surprised to find in the morning that I had got all the colours wrong. As I was fifteen at the time you'd wonder that I didn't have more sense.

The Lower Fifth were taught in a conservatory on the south side of the house, hot in summer, but freezing in winter. At first there were five of us but two soon left. The academic standard was high and of the remaining three, two of us got Matriculation Exemption from our grades in the School Certificate Exam and the third certainly passed all right.

For the next two years they worked us hard. We had lessons all morning; the early afternoon was games, riding (if it was your turn), running a 2 mile course, picking hips for the war effort or just going for a walk, then afternoon school, then prep. The school met twice a day for prayers. Commonweal Lodge had a strong C of E tradition and while the two schools were together religion was orthodox. When Commonweal returned to Purley two years later Mrs Hilsden made our assemblies wildly non-denominational.

Mrs Hilsden took us for maths. She was a charismatic person and I have much more to say about her later. She was a clever teacher though sometimes I suspect that she was only two pages of the textbook ahead of us. We admired her enormously and worked to please her. She also taught botany which I loved. Miss Bray taught French with Mam'selle begging us to "Liez, liez bind it togezzer". Miss Clark, Miss Bray's partner taught English. I was to go home to Purley one holiday together with Miss Bray and Miss Clark and I came to like Miss Clark somewhat better. History was taught by Miss Belt, a thin colourless spinster with a thin colourless mind. She made her subject direfully dull. Our period was 1789 to 1914, a sensa-

1943, Joan Hilsden with her horse Carry On *at Ardock*
West elevation of the building in the background.

50

tional time. It was a world record how little history we absorbed in two years. Our art teacher was called Milly Millar and she rode over from Okehampton every week on her pony, Willow. Her hair was in black curls above which sat a brightly coloured bandeau. She wore plenty of make up and an artistic manner. She was an expert wood engraver and draughtswoman. She told me I should go to the Slade School and make painting my career. I ignored her advice stupidly because by then I was going to save suffering humanity.

We did a lot of singing and every Sunday evening we had 'musical appreciation'. This music came from huge 78rpm records of which there was a vast collection. I loved some of them, but flagged somewhat during long Beethoven symphonies. Nobody fidgeted, so as well as enlarging our musical vocabularies, it was good practice for the Ring Cycle at Covent Garden later on. Margaret Thistlethwaite taught singing and piano. She was a slight, blonde, pretty girl who looked about sixteen. She had just graduated summa cum laude in piano from the Royal College of Music and was soon to get married. Six years later I went to her house in Kensington. She was very happy and the place was solid with music and children.

Ardock was full of clever people and the atmosphere was never static. This was because they were all cooped up together so that emotions ran high among the staff; love affairs waxed and waned with exultation and tears. This all went right over my head.

Margaret Chiverton known as Chivvy was Mrs Hilsden's partner. She was a tall exophthalmic woman but she had nothing of the shakiness one connects with thyrotoxicosis. Her energy and common sense kept the whole place from falling apart. She was a P.E. teacher and she arranged riding, country dancing, games, the timetable and all the mundane things which can make a school a shambles unless someone organises them properly. She was always fair and always kind. About twenty years later, I met her by chance with her sister at Dozmary Pool near Jamaica Inn. There she told me something which shed a great light on how I was treated in my later schooldays and which I never suspected for a moment.

Mrs Joan Hilsden was the brightest star in the Ardock firmament. She was a shortish, stocky person with fair hair and a dark complexion. Her husband was in the army and I only remember seeing him once. She looked rather like 'Napoleon aboard the *Bellerophon*', heavy jawed with arms akimbo. Like Napoleon, she was an autocrat and a great big ham.

We all adored her and some of us got to sleep with her, but not I. I was not nearly personable enough and anyway was soon to have heterosexual fish to fry. So far I have not painted a flattering portrait of her. Sexually her behaviour was irresponsible to say the least. She managed to wreck the medical career of one girl who was begged to 'come back to look after the horses' and did so only to be emotionally embroiled all over again. Other teachers were also involved. This was all done more or less discreetly. I knew nothing whatever about any of this. Having condemned her I must hasten to describe a generous, lively asexual side to her nature and I benefited. One holiday a visiting parent allowed me to have a go with her oil paints. I did quite a good job and Mrs Hilsden bought a set of oil paints for me. She once lent me a pretty taffeta dress to go to a dance given by the American army stationed nearby.

She was bookish and guided me into reading Tolstoy and many rather lesser works concerning reincarnation in ancient Egypt and visitors from other planets. She taught us all to think on our feet, to make up our minds and to speak fluently. About this time I began to stammer, though nowhere near as badly as my father. I wasn't unduly sensitive about it. It disappeared when I sang. The hurly-burly of the two schools under one roof diluted Mrs Hilsden's personality somewhat. Later when Common-weal went back to Purley, leaving her as headmistress with about twenty-five pupils, she went right over the top. She was at her best during the holidays. She organised picnics to the Fairy Pool on Dartmoor taking all the ponies and bikes available. We would ride across an open space called Galford Down taking turns to ride or to cycle. Mrs Hilsden would ride on her handsome black mare Carry On. When we got to the Fairy Pool we would swim in the freezing water. She also took us to swim in a disused quarry full of bright blue water. That was the first time I ever saw a naked man. She was unrivalled at getting petrol and food from unknown sources.

Mrs Hilsden's mother, father and sister lived at Ardock. Her father had been a major serving in the Somme in the First World War. He had had both his hands blown off and had survived by holding his arms above his head until help came. At mealtimes he wore false hands but mostly he pottered around outside performing miracles with his two stumps. He was a stickler for things being done properly and got me into trouble because I emptied a dustpan onto his head out of the top storey of the stable block. Mrs Hilsden's brother John was to be killed at Salerno. I can remember her screams when she got the news.

There was not room in the main house for everyone so girls slept in places nearby. I slept in the house because every morning I got up and milked two cows. Trumper milked them at night. After about a year the cows were sold so I slept out at the farm like the others. It was a mile walk uphill on an empty stomach and, as it was Devon, often raining. All the senior girls slept at Lewtrenchard, the late Reverend Baring-Gould's vicarage, and where we went to church. One time a woman visitor leapt to the piano in the middle of supper and began to play 'Onward Christian Soldiers' to our embarrassment. I have left Mrs Nixon Eckersall till last because indirectly she had the most emotional impact on me. She came to the school the term before I was due to take my exams. She became the School Secretary. Mrs Eckersall was a handsome horse-faced woman. She had a withered leg from polio as a child, but got around briskly all the same. She was well educated and aristocratic. Her husband was in the army and by him she had had a little boy and girl. By a previous marriage she had a fourteen year old son Robin. Robin was a tall, skinny handsome boy a little younger than me. He was academic and knowledgeable which he did not try to disguise. The first time I saw Robin he was making a figure out of clay, rather well. He informed me it was a position from the dance repertoire of Margaret Morris of whom I had never heard. Our conversation was an acid affair of one-upmanship. Where Robin had been at school before I have no idea nor why it was decreed that he should join our form for the following term when he would be taking scholarship examinations for various public schools. He was not the only boy in the school. He was joined in our class by Reggie who was presumably at the same stage. Reggie fell hopelessly in love with Stephanie as Robin was with me. Nobody did any work or revision for weeks until someone realised why. Robin and Reggie were moved to the class below.

I loved Robin. We longed to do we knew not what but we never did. For a few nights in Spring we slept in the same room and would go out in the moonlight to hold hands and kiss. When term time began we both thought touching was unsuitable except when really out of the way, but this did not stem our passion in the least. It gave my amour propre a wonderful boost to be the beloved of one of only two boys in a whole girls' school. Robin loved my energy, skinniness, bare feet and untidy hair and Robin was to me my east and west. *Et ego in Arcadia vixi* but not for long. The School Certificate Examination soon came upon us. This exam was approximately the standard of 'O' level which was to be introduced some years later. For School Certificate you had to pass in English Language, Maths and a modern language, plus three more subjects all at the same time and, if you failed one of these three you had to sit the whole thing again.

The Examining Board sent your school a detailed breakdown of your exam results so your teachers knew exactly how you'd done. Having got the basics one year you could add other subjects the next year. This was called 'patching'. I got my matric exemption by the skin of my teeth which was better than might have been expected.

At this time Robin was sitting all by himself upstairs doing scholarship examinations for a number of public schools. He passed the lot, but Mrs Hilsden and his mother chose Shebbear College in North Devon because it was nearest to Lewdown.

Commonweal Lodge went back to London for good at the end of the Summer Term 1943. I saw the bus pull out of the gates with, for the first time, a sense of loss and foreboding.

The summer passed in a green and yellow melancholy. Firstly Robin wasn't at Ardock for the greater part of it. We wandered out into the horses' field not knowing what to say, too sad to hold hands. Somebody called for him to get into the car. Secondly the exam results hung over my head. Thirdly we were all very busy rearranging the house which could just about contain the reduced school. We always had to turn to and help with washing up and keeping the school reasonably clean and so forth because, apart from Maud our heroic cook, and Trumper, there were no domestic staff that I can remember. Maud was a small dark lady no longer young. She was wonderfully good tempered and did miracles with the food and would make a little picnic for you if you were going to be out all day. I think she made the bread for the school. There were no foreign bodies like fleas in it as there had been at Lifton. When you cut a slice off a loaf for someone else at table you asked 'Bessie or Badger?' Bessie was the top of the loaf and Badger the square bit at the bottom. I have never heard anyone ask this again. Being fifteen by now I worked very hard that summer redecorating, putting up bunk beds and helping to carry furniture from one place to another following Mrs Hilsden's hectic instructions. One evening Chivvy asked me to go out for a walk with her. She seemed distracted and I thought maybe she'd had a fuss with Mrs Hilsden. With hindsight I think she was plucking up courage to tell me I would have to leave Ardock because my father had not paid my school fees for two years. Why my father did not pay them remains a mystery to this day. He sent no money for my clothes. He did not pay the Lees any money towards Hugh's upbringing. Presumably he did not pay Moffats. My mother was by then a Junior Commander in the ATS Her pay only just covered officer's expenses she could not avoid and she was always short of money.

I never knew anything about this at all as Chivvy could not bring herself to tell me. It showed how kind and generous the Ardock people were at heart. In reality I did get given a great many more chores than other people and, as time went on, was treated badly. I suppose charitable feeling was overlaid by the school's increasingly rocky financial situation. I never suspected any of this and thought it was I who deserved extra work or to be left out. It slowly ate into me and destroyed my self confidence. That chance meeting at Dozmary Pool made me understand exactly why I wore cast off clothes, that my shoes were too small, that I was eventually to be treated as a second class citizen. By then it was too late to be angry with my father for bilking out of his responsibilities. I did ask him about it once and he said, "At the end of the war your school did sue me for your school fees but, luckily, it went into liquidation before I had to pay them," and that was that. The exam results arrived. I was one mark short for a credit in maths, but I got Matric exemption after Miss Bray had written to the Board of Examiners. Until I heard it was alright I felt I had failed miserably. I was drained after that exhausting Summer Term. It was very hot. Next term I was to be ill. I already had styes and boils which I did not report. A strange man was staying at Ardock, father of twin pupils. He had large dark eyes with their white showing above and below the iris. He read my palm telling me I would never get to be a doctor, which I had decided to do when I left school. He said he foresaw something else he would not tell me. There was no time to ride. Robin came back a few days before the new term. We were overjoyed to see one another, but it was different. Robin was preoccupied with his impending departure for Shebbear. I was downcast and dreading his going away again.

Ardock under Mrs Hilsden's rule was changed. There were few rules, but more criticism and it was easier to offend. She made me Head Girl which I hated and feared because though I was the most senior pupil academically, I was expected to organise girls older than me. Two of them, Patience and Barbara known as Paddy and Bandy, rose into prominence and were the bane of my life. I successfully begged Chivvy to let somebody else be Head Girl. Mrs Hilsden told me I lacked character.

It was decided that I should take Maths again. Also I did two further subjects called Physics-with-Chemistry and Biology. I was left to get on with it most of the time and I did dissections doggedly on my own. Someone's father posted me a lobster to dissect. It was still alive when I unpacked it. I tried to anaesthetise it and it wouldn't die.

Physics-with-Chemistry did not call for practical work but I enjoyed messing about in our so-called laboratory. At the end of the school year I obtained a distinction in Biology, a credit for Physics-with-Chemistry and I bumped up my result in Maths. At the beginning of that last school year at Ardock I started fainting for no reason and I was running a temperature. Nobody ever got to the bottom of it but Dr Lea told me I had to give up games. Luckily they let me ride. Mrs Hilsden let me paint horses all over the dining room walls. I wrote regularly to Robin. I sent him all my sweet coupons. I gave him Sixth Finger. He wrote back but it was difficult. Shebbear was a rough-and-ready place and writing to a girl would have exposed him to ridicule. He was fairly happy at Shebbear as he was good at running and not victim material. Mrs Hilsden and his mother occasionally went to visit him. Once they took me. We went across country through lanes with many gates which I had to open. Unlike ordinary mortals, Mrs Hilsden had an uncanny gift of finding her way about.

It was a bitterly cold January day. The visit was not a success. Robin was displeased to be seen with a girlfriend and after a short while he went back to the other boys.

Balm for my sad soul that autumn was Toast. She was a large rangy black mare who had been loaned to me by a handsome young army officer. I looked after Toast as well as I could and she raised my failing spirits. That Boxing Day we all rode to the local meet. I was looking forward to cutting a bit of a dash on Toast. However it transpired that Mrs Hilsden was going to ride Toast. I was relegated to some smallish pony.

By spring army lorries thundered up the A30 in a continuous convoy day and night. Chivvy's setter bitch was run over. Toast did not care for lorries so we spent time cowering in the ditch beside the A30, not able to get back to the stables.

In spite of our internecine upheavals the war did not forget us. Night after night Plymouth lit up the sky like a giant firework display. We listened to the news all the time. A girl called Joan's brother was burned in his bomber and became one of Dr McIndoe's guinea pigs. We knitted balaclavas and prayed for victory in church every Sunday.

I do not exactly remember when Judith Weare came to teach at Ardock.

She had fair straight hair tied back in a ponytail and an odd but interesting convex face. She wore crimson corduroy skirts and brightly coloured knee socks. She was not bowled over by Mrs Hilsden. She shuddered to the depths of her intellectual being at the mere mention of horses. She had a First in English from an Oxbridge college and was an energetic and stimulating teacher.

I had Art lessons by myself with Mr. Lazenby. He taught me the history of art, about the Golden Section and he analysed pictures to help me to understand their composition.

I met Mr Lazenby again about twenty years later in a hospital outpatients. He was working at Colet Court in London and put in a good word for my son when he took that school's entrance examination. Nicholas was not grateful to Mr Lazenby because he was always being told how poor at art he was by comparison with his mother.

We had a production of *Hansel and Gretel*, cadged from Jock Engelhart. I was the witch this time, and my performance unhinged some little person from High Trees who was removed howling.

I had some one-to-one singing lessons later that year. Miss Thistlethwaite had gone, much to our regret. This new teacher was the shape women assume when they sing a lot of Wagner. Her mashed potato contralto voice grated on my ear. As I was no longer a treble she decided I was to be a contralto also and made me sing lots of soppy songs. I rebelled eventually over the Recitative leading into 'Ombra Mai Fu' which I could not sing to her satisfaction.

The examination class below me had about eight pupils. Diana Vivian had arrived from Moffats. She was able to carry on with Latin because Miss Weare was there to teach her. The ruling spirits were the aforementioned Paddy and Bandy. Paddy was small, blonde and baby-faced. She came from a horsey family in Bovey Tracey. She was an elegant rider and had experience in the show-ring. However she made a great fuss about riding beforehand because she had lost her nerve. I went once to stay with her when relations were amicable. Paddy's mother told Paddy she could not understand why she had brought home someone who was such an unsuitable friend. Bandy was a Jewish girl, tall, dark and well-developed. She too rode well and was allowed on Carry On, Mrs Hilsden's mare. Both were in Mrs. Hilsden's inner circle which made them conceited and scornful though neither was unduly clever in class or talented in any other way. By the time I left school I was delighted to think I should never have to see either Paddy or Bandy again. My good friend was Pat Molloy. I met her once after the war then she went to live in Australia. She was older than me and as far as I remember had no examinations to take. Pat was a remote intellectual girl, well read and articulate.

During the lull in the air raids that year, I went to stay with her family. Mr and Mrs Molloy lived in a large block of flats off Hampstead Heath. They were the kindliest people. Mr Molloy was in publishing and we used to discuss with him in detail the botany textbook we never got round to writing.

In the Summer Term I suddenly acquired a relation. The connection was tenuous, but Peggy and I insisted that we were cousins. Peggy and her sister Yvon came from Moffats. Peggy was sensible and good company. Yvon was musical and intelligent but shy and sensitive to the point of instability. That summer there was some enemy action in Devonshire. German planes randomly unloaded bombs but as far as I know there was no loss of life. An ARP centre was set up about half a mile from school and we elder girls took turns to be messengers. One Sunday morning Peggy and I got on our bicycles to do our stint. The phone rang. A bomb had exploded in a field about two miles away. Some Captain Mainwaring was to be informed at once by messenger. I was quick off the mark. I took the message, ran to my bicycle and climbed on to pedal resolutely uphill. The pedal fell off and my bottom came painfully in contact with the saddle. I ran back seized Peggy's bike and set off again. When I arrived Captain Mainwaring looked down, "Little girl, you are bleeding."

To my surprise I was, all over his carpet. The spike which held the pedal on had made a deep three inch cut in my calf. I wasn't all that far from school so I rode back there and made my bloody, stealthy, guilty way to the bathroom to get a plaster or something when I passed out. Someone came in, the blood was staunched and I was made to lie down. About three hours later Doctor Lea came by and put some stitches in my calf without any anaesthetic. I got some moderately deserved kudos from this incident including a letter from the Home Guard saying I had shown 'True British pluck'. I sometimes wonder how I would have reacted if I had known I had cut myself. My mother was very pleased with me indeed.

All my schooldays at Lifton and Lewdown I was treated with generosity by other girls' parents. That spring I went to stay with Diana's family near Woking. We went riding twice. There was an enormous flowering cherry tree in the garden. It was in full bloom so I painted a picture of it to give to Mrs Vivian. While I was working away I heard a woman singing in

Italian somewhere nearby in a heavenly disembodied voice.

I went to stay with Peggy's family in the summer at Blue Anchor near Minehead. Though the European war was to continue till next summer, the overall concern about it was becoming relatively less poignant in contrast to the anxiety caused by the Normandy Landings. For one thing you could go on the beach at Blue Anchor and in Minehead the hotels were busy.

One day we cycled out to Luccombe, to visit a beautiful house on the edge of Exmoor. Peggy's family had some involvement in this house, but exactly what it was I have forgotten. More memorably, they had a goat which galloped off with its rope under my knee joint giving me a deep and painful burn. Peggy and her sisters wore bright blue socks which I coveted. Their mother kindly sent me a pair when I went back to Ardock.

About this time I also went into Somerset to stay in Bishops Lydeard with the Sharps and to Hinton St George to stay with Mrs Eckersall. Both were rather disappointing because Maureen was working as flat out on her farm as Robin was on his. I felt somewhat like my mother who in her infrequent visits to Ardock was all but ignored. The most emotional moment I had with Robin was when he told me ruefully that he had lost Sixth Finger.

The school used to give me train money for these trips and Chivvy would sometimes take me to the station in the car; otherwise I had to walk like everybody else. Devon was full of little country stations before Doctor Beeching swept them away and the train was how people got about if they thought their journey was really necessary. What happened at the other end was my business and I hitched all over the place on my own. None of the drivers ever alarmed me in any way and sometimes I would share some dinner or was taken out of their route to be nearer my destination. At that point I was shapeless and thin so maybe none of them was that desperate. When you get breasts however plain you may be it is always open season for impertinent remarks as I was later to discover. Sometime that summer Audrey came to Ardock. She turned out to be a living portent of what my last school year would be like. She was nineteen years old and had worked in an office after she had left school. Why she had elected to go back to school I could never understand though I was to spend much time with her. Audrey had a younger musical sister already at Ardock who was funny and attractive. Audrey was neither. She was tall and dark with sloping shoulders and big legs. She moved and spoke with great deliberation. I am at a loss to describe her nullity and feel I am being unfair to her because she faithfully followed me through many vicissitudes. She was an ardent Christian Scientist and tried vainly to make me read *Science and Health*. I guess her mother didn't pay Ardock any fees for her and it wasn't long before we were lumped together as charity children who could be put to do any number of disagreeable things. We were about as far away from the Hilsden clique as it was possible to get.

That summer term was to be the last at Ardock. The school had decided to move to Fairford, Gloucestershire. When I came back from my visits away the place was in turmoil. Some horses were sold, furniture was being packed up. Audrey and I worked so hard that we never got to know the overall plan. Early in September furniture vans arrived, the remaining horses were boxed. Everyone else was to go by road to Fairford. Audrey and I were to cycle to our local station, get on the train to Swindon then cycle to Fairford. We were the last to leave. I cannot say I, like Marion Dashwood, was deeply moved about going away from a place I had loved: but I was regretful. We also were a bit late for the train, a complication not envisaged by Jane Austen.

The new school was to be renamed 'Wings'. The badge was a rearing Pegasus surmounted by the words 'They shall mount up as eagles'. Millie Miller designed this logo. She came with us to Fairford and married the school bursar who decided later to become a woman.

The building from which we were all supposed to mount up as eagles was a rambling forbidding place which had been recently used as a mental hospital. Indeed at the beginning there were still strange ladies urinating in the garden of the women's block. All the doors of the place were self-locking so unless you had a key you could easily be imprisoned. There were many eerie mirrors about the place when we arrived. When there was no more furniture to lug about Mrs Hilsden set me to painting poets' names on the upstairs doors. Audrey's and my room was Dryden: 'very apt' said someone.

Audrey was going to take School Certificate. I was set to do the London University Intermediate Examination in Science in one year by correspondence. This involved practical work for which there were no facilities. The standard of this exam was far beyond School Certificate and was meant to take two years. I did my best but there was no one to help me, it was dull and often I could not understand it at all. Sometimes I slacked off in Dryden, reading and writing poetry or long letters to Robin, but I knew there would be trouble if I did not keep up, so I copied large chunks out of my course book and passed muster. As at Ardock, Audrey and I had a good deal to do as well. I got up and lit the fires downstairs. In Devon there had been wood, but here we had bad quality coal and the fires were hard to light. One of these fires was in Paddy's and Bandy's study where they would sit smirking while I grovelled in the grate. Pride prevented me from saying anything. Some horses had come with us from Ardock and they were put in the stables. The ex-medical student looked after them mostly, but I fed them in the evenings. Audrey was scared of horses, but she and Mary Baker-Eddy loyally came to help me. The horses had also to be exercised which I did by myself most afternoons. One time a huge rope fell from the sky from a glider attached to a plane about a hundred yards from me and Carry On. Fairford was at this time given over to the air forces of all the Allies. In the holidays overseas Air Force men would come on leave to Wings. There were one or two girls there who were worth chatting up. I was not one of them. These guys played cards all day and went out in the evening

At Christmas I went home to London to stay a few days with my father. My mother was based in Bristol, working flat out, exhorting the population to give blood. We hadn't seen her for months. She designed posters, wrote copy for papers, organised and spoke at meetings. Her boss was Sir Lionel Whitby the famous haematologist, a difficult man. My mother got on all right with him. After VE Day mother applied for and got a compassionate discharge from the ATS. She was totally worn out, emaciated and near to the nervous breakdown she was to have later on. If she had not left the ATS early she would undoubtedly have had recognition for her work.

Up in London I visited the Ministry of Information and I met C. Day Lewis a little of whose poetry I had read. My father took me to a Greek restaurant and ordered me Turkish coffee so that as he said "you'll know not to have it next time."

By the Spring Term I was sick of horses, fed up with Audrey and everything else. I wrote to my mother begging her to let me leave school and go into the ATS. I was seventeen by now, but boarding school does not engender maturity. She was also worried that if she connived at saying I was eighteen she might get into trouble so she wrote back telling me to stick it out till I had done my exams. I was changing as well. I'd filled out, I was becoming rebellious in thought if not in deed, far from the eager cheerful little girl I had been. Robin came to visit and took a fancy to a jolly girl called June, so I suffered the pangs of love unrequited as well.

For the past year or so Mrs Hilsden had been prone to feeling faint (I once caught her outside Ardock's front door late at night), being unwell at certain times and showing dramatic signs of exhaustion. To be fair her brother's death may have had something to do with this. When she emerged after one of these incidents she was the usual centre of attention and full of things for Audrey and me to do.

At Wings these malaises became more frequent. Once I was summoned to cut her fingernails. Trays were taken upstairs by the faithful.

Some interesting people came to stay at Wings. One was the Maharajah of Patiala who had a daughter in the school. He was a jovial portly man and I was disappointed that he showed no evidence whatever of limitless wealth. Ida Haendel the famous violinist came for a while. We thought she was wonderful because she was so young to be able to play the violin like that. Mrs Hilsden recked naught of V rockets which were causing alarm and damage in London by then. The older girls were taken up to hear Ida Haendel play Beethoven's Violin Concerto in, I think, the Wigmore Hall. After a pause in announcing this I was included. I felt disloyal because I had enjoyed the Mozart part of the programme more. My father was angry that I had been allowed anywhere near London at this time.

Once the headmistress of a finishing school in London came out to spy out the land with a view to joining forces with Wings. Her school was called 'Cygnets' and I have no idea of what the curriculum consisted except that girls were taught to get out of a car with decency. That evening we elder girls were sent in to meet her. She gazed with undisguised horror at our clothes, speech and general deportment, but she went a bit far when she said scornfully,

"I suppose none of you girls would know what French composer wrote a Spanish Opera?"

I said, "Bizet," and saved Mrs Hilsden's bacon, but in spite of that the merger never took place.

Miss Weare produced *Twelfth Night* at the end of the spring term. I wanted to be Feste, but by then I was quite busty so a thin girl called Pat got Feste and I got Sir Toby Belch. When I got over the chagrin I enjoyed acting drunk.

In the Summer Term I went to London to take the Intermediate Examination in Chemistry, Physics, Botany and Zoology. All the papers and the practical examinations were completely beyond me, but only later that summer when I got the humiliating failure notice did it really hit home. Sir Lionel Whitby had told my mother that I hadn't got a chance in hell of passing and that I should be prevented from taking the exam, but nobody took his advice.

On the way back to school from my examinations I got to Waterloo too early for my train and wandered out into the surrounding streets. A hairdressers announced 'Hair Purchased Here' so I went in and asked them, "Would they buy my hair?"

My waist length hair had been a burden to me since Mrs Hilsden had decreed that I was too old to wear it down my back in a plait. I used to put it in a bun and in various Swiss-style braids, but it was always falling down. The hairdresser said my hair was an unfashionable colour being light brown with a greenish tinge (Robin used to sing, "I sigh for Jilly with the light green hair"). The hairdresser gave me three pounds however and he trimmed what was left neatly about my ear lobes. Unlike Jo March I did not put the money to unselfish use. I bought a tennis racquet.

The storm when I got back to school was force ten on the Beaufort Scale. My mother was informed; my father, who was by then in Australia, was wired express. He sent back an laconic telegram reading "What comma your caps Crowning Glory question mark screamer. Love father".

Someone showed me how to wrap my hair round an elastic on my head as many service girls did.

While I was away taking my exams Mrs Hilsden had another visitor. This was her husband John discharged from the army. I heard he gave Mrs Hilsden an ultimatum to choose immediately between her Wings way of life and going away with him. She chose Wings and John Hilsden left, presumably for ever.

I left Wings just after VE Day. I went to say goodbye to Mrs Hilsden. She was in her bedroom. I knocked on the door and she called me to come in. She was in her vest and droopy knickers and any scales that might have remained before my eyes fell off. I said goodbye and I went downstairs vowing never to have anything more to do with horses, never to eat porridge again or to live in any institution. I kept none of these resolutions.

A few days after I got home the telephone rang and it was Mrs Hilsden asking if I would come back to teach the younger children. My mother answered the phone and gave her a short impolite answer. I never heard of her again.

***

I was delighted to have left school, but life at Waldegrave Gardens was not to be easy. My mother and I were strangers. She was close to a nervous breakdown and I was wary of her. After a while she began to pour out all her troubles. She felt guilty about this and said so, but she couldn't help it and I was the only person around.

This was because my father had gone to Australia. He had been gone about six months taking up a job as a Publicity Officer at the British High Commission in Canberra. He flew there in a flying boat which took several days. Once this plane threatened to come down on land which, as my father said, " Was too serious to be alarming."

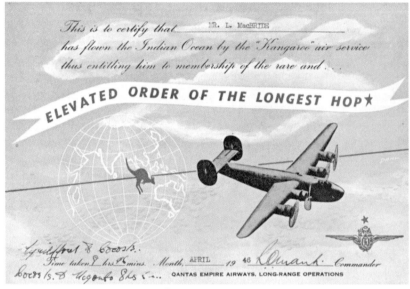

Memento of a somewhat alarming flight!

True to form he was sending home little money which did not help my mother's state of mind.

Hugh came home about this time. I feel remorseful that there has been so little about him for all this time, but the only excuse I can offer is that we did not see much of each other. Nanny left the Leas around 1943. I hope the Fates treated her with kindness. Hugh had moved to High Trees and I saw him sometimes, but Ardock kept me so busy there were few opportunities to meet. Being away from his mother had left its mark upon Hugh causing him to be an overly quiet, self-contained, late developing little boy. He made no outward attempt to read until at about seven he discovered the natural world and someone heard him reading "Pearl-Bordered Fritillary" aloud to himself. When the school left Devonshire, High Trees moved into the women's block at Fairford, when the patients had gone. I saw a little more of him then, taking him out sometimes to a café in Fairford and treating him to beans on toast, out of the money remaining from selling my hair.

When Hugh got home he was in poor health. He had a knee infection which would not clear up. Things looked up when he met Bradley, who was about eighteen; most days he and Hugh would go fishing. Bradley would come round in the morning, we would make sandwiches for the pair of them and off they went with their rods and stuff, returning late in the afternoon. I am certain there were no unsavoury overtones in this relationship. Bradley had the same interests as Hugh aged nine, but could be trusted to cross roads and take care by the river. Sometimes coming home with fish which was ceremoniously cooked and eaten, less appetising ones were given to the cats, Buttercup and Ugly. The only disadvantage about Bradley was that he wouldn't go home and had to be led tactfully to the door and put outside.

Because the house had not been lived in for some time there was clearing up and cleaning to do. Houses were all shabby then. After we had done that I was at a loose end. I had been so accustomed to being organised by other people that I didn't know what to do with my time. A fair amount of it was spent listening to my mother getting her troubles off her chest.

In 1942 my mother had been called up into the ATS and spent three months in Basic Training. She liked the military life, enjoyed the physical exercise and found it interesting to be with such a diversity of females. On her first twenty-four hours leave she rushed back to Phoebe to make her uniform fit properly. After Basic Training she took some incomprehensible IQ tests and was sent to OCTU from which she emerged as a Second Lieutenant. She spent a while as a Catering Officer and went on to work for Sir Lionel Whitby with the rank of Junior Commander.

Mother met dozens of people, mainly male, because she was an excellent chess player. I knew the moves from about five years old, but I was never any good. At one OCTU interview my mother was asked what interests she had. She replied that she played chess.

"You don't look in the least like a chess player to me," said some disdainful army officer. My mother was looking smart and handsome in her well fitting uniform. "May I take that as a compliment, Sir?" she replied.

Playing chess she had met an officer in the Kings Royal Rifles and they fell in love. I knew very little about Carl, but the affair went on for some time and mother did mention him longingly when she came to visit me on leave. He gave her a costly copy of *The Oxford Book of English Verse* with a cryptic dedication on the flyleaf in the smallest handwriting I have ever seen. Owing to their being much apart, my mother had romanticised their relationship. A short time before my mother's discharge they got together for the weekend and it was a disaster. My mother started walking round Bristol at night when she should have been in bed. She got a compassionate discharge from the ATS.

One day, soon after we had all got home, my mother cheered up, we put on such finery as we possessed and went up to London to look at the shops, have a drink in a pub and go to the pictures. When we got to Leicester Square we saw that the photos taken by the Allies, when they went into the concentration camp at Belsen, were to be seen in a cinema nearby. We went in. We have become hardened to images of suffering and cruelty nowadays. It was different then. My mother and I came out weeping and shaking. "What do you want to do now?" asked my mother. "Let's just go home," said I.

We started to have visitors. The first was Robin. His relationship with me was a little awkward at first, but we soon resumed where we had left off. Robin was used to being in a household where there was no money and he turned out to be good at cooking. When he was due to go home he rang his mother and asked if I might come too.

Captain Nixon Eckersall had been demobbed and the family were living at St Leonards-on-Sea, the Ardock days forgotten. By then we could get out onto the beach to swim. Once I made a pig's ear out of getting my bathing suit on and my newly acquired bra off without baring my breasts. Robin and George, Robin's younger half-brother, were eyeing my dilemma with interest. George's father said "Do you need any help?"

This made it all the more mortifying. By this time Robin and I were keen to go to bed. The only time we nearly did make it our activities were interrupted because George was discovered watching us through a crack in the bedroom door.

An unwelcome visitor was a woman who had worked with my father in the MOI and had had an affair with him. She was a fattish doughy-featured individual. As soon as she could get my mother alone she would tell her exactly what she and my father had done in bed. This had a morbid fascination for my mother. I hated this person, but it was hard to confront a woman of forty when you are seventeen and your mother appears to be welcoming. The end came abruptly when Uncle Cyril arrived at our house. He told her to get out.

Next on the scene was Donald. He was a large, comfortable, good tempered man. He came from Northumberland where he had been a baker before the war. He was in the Engineers and his aim in life was to invent a speaker that did not distort the human voice at all. He did do this later and my mother helped him to organise a publicity stunt where a soprano sang behind a screen; then Donald's device was turned on and we all had to guess which was which. Unfortunately we could.

At this time Donald was devoted to my mother. He slept, for decency's sake, on the sofa downstairs, but he didn't stay there all night. He wanted her to leave my father when he was demobbed and go up north with him. My mother was soothed by his protectiveness, but even though she was fond of him, she didn't want to do a lifetime's baking in Northumberland.

One afternoon the doorbell rang and standing on the step was a good looking young RAF Officer. On his uniform he wore a DFC ribbon which mother instantly recognised. This guy had been a messenger at mother's ARP station and she had taken him under her wing, lending him many of my books which I never got back. My mother and Alan were delighted to see one another. Their service experience gave them much to talk about. I was completely ignored. Mother persuaded Alan to take me out to the theatre for which she paid. He made no bones about his indifference to me. I responded with a mixture of dislike and humiliation.

We went to see Phoebe. She had spent the earlier part of the war struggling to keep her business going. One dark rainy night she was driving home to Blue Shutters when a man thumbed her down. Phoebe stopped the car, the man got in, produced a revolver and told her to drive to Brighton. He told her that he was a Nazi agent and that he would kill her outright if she tried any nonsense. When Phoebe got him to Brighton he smashed her head in and left her for dead. She had a brain haemorrhage and could not speak for some time. She gradually got back her speech, but the attack left her feeble and disabled. When we saw her again she was very frail, but not so lacking in spirit that she couldn't tell me that she wondered where the confident, chatty little pre-war girl had gone? She found some emerald green silk and made me a dress with red appliqued flowers on it. I was touched, but I rarely wore it because it was so unlike other people's dresses. She died soon after.

Phoebe had a nephew called Bill. We had met as children once and had behaved badly at an Easter Egg Hunt at Blue Shutters. Phoebe had often told my mother how pleased she would be if we were to marry. Bill turned up at Waldegrave Gardens. He was stocky, strong and not bad looking. He took me to the theatre to see *Perchance to Dream* by Ivor Novello. This romantic start was a boost to my morale and it wasn't long before Bill became a permanent fixture at home where he stayed for some weeks before he started a course in horticulture. He begged me to become engaged to him so I did, mainly because we were doing some heavy petting. I soon regretted it because Bill was boring. He got on well with my mother. He was splendid in the house, lit our uncooperative boiler and reestablished the now tortoiseless garden. We went up to London for the VJ celebrations and got stuck in a huge crowd in Piccadilly Tube Station. Bill managed to jam us into some cranny as the crowd surged by. Some people were crushed to death that evening.

My exam results arrived. I knew they would be poor, but I didn't expect to fail the lot. I felt my whole school career was a failure and that I was wearing a notice round my neck for all to read that I was a dunce. Vainly did my mother tell me crossly that it was not my fault. About this time I met my ex-classmates Medusa and Stephanie in London. Stephanie has passed her Higher School Certificate in Sciences, in spite of having spent much lesson time in the Air-Raid Shelter. Commonweal Lodge had stubbornly kept to the syllabus. She was going to Medical School in September and she deserved it. Sadly I thought I had thrown all my chances away. We were seriously in want of money. Either I or my mother would have to go out to work and we decided it should be me because somebody had to be at home for Hugh and my mother was not mentally or physically fit for work. A friend of my mother's worked as a secretary at the Paint Research Station in Teddington. She told us they were in need of a junior technician so I was taken on at two pounds a week.

My failed exam results were still hanging over my head when I arrived in the Analab, the chemistry side of the Paint Research Station. However Mrs L. the brisk cheerful woman who was in charge treated me as if I knew absolutely nothing so I was able to relax and sometimes to come up with a relevant remark. I got on with the other girls. Pam was a chief technician. She was petite and precise, in her late twenties, and had nearly finished the degree she had worked for at night school. She had a sick mother and not much fun. Winifred was an intelligent outspoken girl in her early twenties. She did research instead of routine work.

She was not at all pretty and took little trouble with her appearance; in spite of this several of the young men at the PRS were mad about her. She went out with one or another for a while then cheerfully dropped him for someone else. Tina was junior like me. She had a good voice and we used to sing together when Mrs L. was out of the way in spite of Pam's disapproval. We were overheard and asked to sing at the PRS Christmas party.

All undergraduates were made to go to Night School whether they wanted to or not. Most nights in the week we walked to Teddington Station and went to Battersea Polytechnic to study Science, getting home at about nine p.m. Battersea Station at eight p.m. on a cold winter's night after a whole day's work and not much to eat is a cheerless place, but I was not alone. Many of these people stuck it out for years and eventually got degrees in Science at the PRS' expense. Night School served me well because when I went to Sydney University the following year, I was let off practical Chemistry.

In the New Year I was moved to the Physics Department. The head, Miss Tilleard was a gentle put-upon lady no longer young. Because I had got a distinction in Art at School Certificate I was set to draw pictures of factory floors complete with people working machines. The wall, floors, machines and the workers' clothes were coloured by me in what I considered to be restful or stressful or stimulating combinations of colours. After

*1946. Physics Department at the Paint Research Station, Teddington.
Miss Tilleard (centre) was the Head. (Mike Birbeck indicated).*

a month or two the powers that be thought I could be more usefully employed so I was sent to the National Physical Laboratory nearby to be taught to use a Hollerith machine. My memories of this incredibly tedious device do not need to be recorded.

By then Bill had left and I was glad to see him go. He wrote me a letter every week and I hope I replied as the engagement had not been officially cancelled. At the PRS there were young men who were not as inaccessible as I had imagined. I began to hope I was not as plain as all that. There were flirtations and banter at work which included me. There were societies you could join when it wasn't Night School. The department went out to lunch together at the British Restaurant in Teddington (price one shilling) or the Greasy Spoon where the food was rather better. I stopped grieving about having lost my chance of going to Medical School and the exam disaster faded into the past. About this time I met Mike Birbeck. It was at a bus stop in Twickenham at lunchtime. We were both going back to the PRS for the afternoon's work so we got on to the bus together which seemed a trifle indecorous. Mike was slender with a hatchet face and good features. He had just come down from Clare College, Cambridge where he had been a scholar. He had been directed to work at the PRS where he was helping to

Self with Mike.

make one of the first electron microscopes in England. Mike came from a famous Potteries family. He was unpopular at the PRS because he was aloof and did not join in the badinage around him. This made him more intriguing to me. Eventually I persuaded him to come to our house to see our cats. He had a meal with us and we had silverside which he hated but ate politely. Food was to be rationed until the fifties so it was always a headache. Off ration you could get whale meat and something dark red and fishy called snoek but not much else. People carried a bag around with them just in case they passed a shop which happened to be selling something off the ration that day. The Black Market was going strong, but we wouldn't have used it: anyway we were too hard up. Mike did not flirt with my mother and she never forgave him. He didn't flirt with me either, but we eventually got round to holding hands and kissing goodnight. We were accepted as an un-enterprising item, went to lunch together with another physicist called Peter and walked to Teddington Lock. The lunch break at the PRS was fairly flexible. Mike was agile and could jump over the rowing boat lock with his hands in his pockets. He had got a Half-Blue for Hockey at Cambridge and was in the PRS hockey team, but he played down being athletic because he thought it made him look un-intellectual. At the weekends we went up to town. London was geographically in ruins, but the Arts were surfacing again. Theatres and concerts were plentiful and cheap. We went as often as we could and sat in the gods.

In the early summer my mother got a letter from the Diplomatic Service informing us that, as my father was going to do a second tour of duty in Australia, we would be eligible to travel to Canberra at the Government's expense. It took a while to sink in and we were not as ecstatic as one might imagine. Mother's heart failed as she anticipated all the hassle. I felt settled and unadventurous. The only person who was keen to go was Hugh who had started at a prep school in Sheen. He disliked it and invented many unusual illnesses to get off going. There was a lot to do. We sub-let the house through an estate agent and very lax they were. Bill took over the cats. Robin wrote and asked me to come to stay and I wrote back telling him I was going to Australia. I didn't see Robin again for many years and when I did I was glad I was not his multiparous, kind, industrious wife.

On the last evening I said goodbye to Mike. We were regretful but we both felt that we'd meet again. We were to marry some years later. The carriers collected our luggage and we were sent off to Tilbury to get our first glimpse of SS *Themistocles* of the Shaw-Savill Line. She had been a troop ship in the war and when I discovered that she was on her last

SS Themistocles. (State Library of Victoria).

voyage before she was broken up I was upset as I thought she was a handsome vessel. She carried about forty passengers. We had a smallish, upper deck, four berth cabin. This was hard on my mother because she still wasn't sleeping, was easily upset and needed more privacy. We couldn't believe it when we had our first meal on board. It was served in style by the stewards and Hugh and I were dumbfounded. The Barber's Shop sold limitless chocolate. In the Bay of Biscay it was rough but only Hugh was so seriously ill that the ship's doctor had to be called. He discovered that Hugh had bought and eaten ten Mars Bars all at once.

We were to be on the *Themistocles* for ten weeks because we were not going through the Suez Canal but round the Cape to Durban then across the Indian Ocean to Freemantle, Adelaide, Melbourne and Sydney.

It is said that travel by sea makes people lustful, but though I did not behave myself at all well I got off that ship *virgo intacta* more or less. I attracted a married man. It was certainly not due to my irresistibility but because Jim's wife Kathleen refused to have sex with him or so he said. Jim was fifteen years older than I. He was tall and serious and Scottish. He was taking up a post at the University of Sydney. Kathleen had been a psychiatric social worker and had the unstable temperament not uncommon among those who work with the mentally ill. Being in a strop with her husband on board a ship was ill advised. Doubtless due to sexual frustration Jim gave me credit for being more academic and more attractive than I was. We read poetry together. I knew a lot of poetry having been used to learning it both as child and adolescent. Kathleen said poetry was silly and stumped off to their cabin. Jim, though sorely tempted, had a Calvinist's conscience so he never technically committed adultery. Just as well because Kathleen relented in Adelaide and she got pregnant immediately. Jim and I said a private goodbye in Melbourne and he bought me a book of T. S. Eliot's poetry. Another time a man who was travelling alone and had paid me little attention heretofore took me up to his cabin and we lay down on his bunk. 1 realised I'd been stupid, told him I had my period and escaped.

My mother knew nothing about my activities. She had become more depressed and irritable since we had left home, sometimes leaving the table abruptly at mealtimes and wandering about the deck at night. She was in turmoil about seeing my father again and wondering what he had been doing behind her back. (This proved to be no idle premonition). My efforts to keep an eye on my mother made her cross. Luckily she found a companion in Mr Nelkin. Mr Nelkin was in his sixties. He was Jewish and gave off an aura of money. He was always to be seen in the costly immaculate suit, the waistcoat and the impeccable linen of the nineteen-thirties. He spoke perfect English with a hint of one who has Yiddish as their first language and had a detached melancholy air like J. Alfred Prufrock. We were not at the Captain's table, but the First Officer's which caused some passengers to look sourly upon us. Mr Nelkin was also at our table and he unbent towards my mother, called her Kitty and made her feel better. He and mother would sit on deck safely in the shade, a parasol over my mother's head. Mr Nelkin used to chide her because she allowed me to play deck tennis and expose my skin to the sun. His usually calm voice would rise and his accent become more pronounced as he scolded:

"That perfect peaches and cream complexion will become tanned by the sun and her bloom will be gone forever."

His words fell on deaf ears. I did indeed play a lot of deck tennis, became good at it and won a Deck Tennis Knockout Competition outright. There was a pool on board and when we sailed over the Equator I was covered in shaving soap and thrown in as is customary. There were other children for Hugh to play with. There was another girl my age on board. We did not get on. My mother must have upset her mother as well because they gave a party somewhere in the Indian Ocean with the sole purpose of

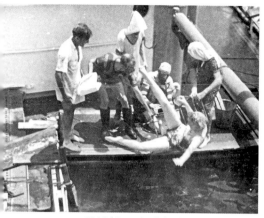

*1946 'Crossing' the line ceremony
aboard* Themistocles – *Me airborne!*

not inviting us.

It was agreeable on board. We made bets on the distance the ship had travelled the previous day, were waited on by obliging friendly stewards, played Housey-Housey and hung over the ship's rail watching the sea for hours and hours. The ship's repertoire of music was limited and the Ink Spots were with us from morning to night. Whales and flying fish caused everybody great excitement. Sometimes you'd be allowed to go on the bridge and take the wheel which made the *Themistocles* veer suddenly and cause passengers to look up in alarm.

When we docked at Durban, Aunt Connie was there to meet us. She told us what a long, dusty journey it had been by train but I was too ignorant to take in the distance from Salisbury (the capital of Southern Rhodesia, as it was called then) to Durban. We went to her hotel to have dinner and I saw active apartheid for the first time. My aunt treated black people as if they were not there. She told us the "Blecks" had to ride on special buses, were herded into townships and were forbidden to use the same lavatories as white people as if it had been ordained since the beginning of time. The black waiters in the hotel stood behind our chairs with lowered eyes while we ate. She told us about her farm outside Salisbury and her staff of servants. We said,

"What did they eat?"

and she replied

"Oh kaffir meat and mealies."

My mother and I were disgusted and ashamed and said so. Aunt Connie replied in her clipped South African accent,

"Kitty, just shut up about things you don't understand."

My mother said hotly she didn't have to understand, she just had to look around.

This rift between my mother and Aunt Connie was never healed. When Aunt Connie revisited London in the sixties and saw the black people in buses and dress shops and holding hands with white people in the street she said it made her feel sick.

In the eighties Aunt Connie died and left me and other members of the family a lot of money. We unanimously agreed that her staff should be sent back to their villages with what seemed to us parsimonious annuities, but her executor said that would be plenty. We never saw a penny of our money because of Mr. Mugabe's financial policies. Soon after I was to live in and out of Southern Africa for nearly ten years. I could never condone apartheid, but I became better informed about the associated problems.

Durban has a great curved, sandy beach extending to the horizon. When I saw it I asked if I could go swimming. There were no nets then so Aunt Connie said, "Not unless you fancy being eaten by a shark."

We went to a snake park. My mother liked snakes and allowed their keeper to hang several around her neck. Hugh and I felt that though we weren't exactly afraid of snakes we did not want to be festooned with them as well so we vanished quietly into the crowd.

By the time the *Themistocles* docked in Adelaide we were delighted to be in Australia at last. After ten minutes of being on Australian soil I got into trouble with the police for jay-walking. We went to a café for breakfast and were each served a huge plate of eggs and steak which would have been one person's meat ration in Britain for a month. It was raining in Melbourne and at that time the city was not architecturally inspiring. It was a gloomy and appropriate background to Jim's and my farewell.

Sydney was magic. Early in the morning we sailed through the Heads into Sydney Harbour and there all at once was the bridge. 'Earth hath not anything to show more fair' wrote the Old Sheep of Grassmere though he was describing somewhere else. The harbour was busy with ferries and little boats and the sun shone over everything. The Opera House had not been built then. We docked at Circular Quay and there was my father come to meet us. There was little emotion because we were too involved with luggage and passports. We didn't have to go through Customs though because we were Diplomatic. We went by plane to Canberra. It was a bumpy ride and gave Hugh and my mother earache but the plane flew low enough to see the Outback stretching for miles and miles and the poor ring-barked trees. Since I left Ardock I had done very little painting. Everything at Fairford had been ugly and Waldegrave Gardens wasn't much better. Seascapes were beyond me and it was many years before I had the confidence to draw or paint in front of people. If there is something you ought to be doing and you are not it is bad for you. Canberra was to wake me up

Ring-barked tree near Canberra. Watercolour, Angela MacBride 1947.

visually and I began to paint again.

Canberra in 1946 seen on the map looked like a dumbbell. At one end there was a big area designed round a series of concentric circles. It was joined by a long road to a small township grandly called the Civic Centre. The road between ran through bush in which was stuck Government House, upon whose steps a wallaby had been seen, the British Legation and the Canberra Hotel. Out on the edges of each end of the dumbbell were sprouting small townships and scattered around the perimeter were various specialised buildings like the Canberra Observatory where I was groped by a man who was to be the Astronomer Royal. He had asked me if I would like to come and look at the stars through his telescope. Luckily somebody drove out to fetch me because this man was known to embarrass girls. The Embassies and the Legations were in the circular area.

My father had rented a house in Mugga Way, a desirable address. In front of our house the Outback sloped steeply upwards then all around for ever. Life was given over to diplomacy and protocol. Nearly every evening we went to a cocktail party. Embassies gave three parties consecutively. We were "second night" guests and the canapes were slightly fresher than they must have been for the "third night" contingent. At Legation cocktail parties we were promoted to "first night" entertainment. Everybody was sensitive about rank and not being invited at all was an insult. Once when my father was away my mother and I dressed up for a party at the Canadian Legation. We walked down one of the circular roads from Mugga Way. When we got nearer to our destination we heard the sound of clippers and when we got nearer we saw it was Mrs Canadian High Commissioner cutting down her hedge to the five foot maximum height demanded by Australian law. We had obviously got the day wrong, said "Good evening," politely, walked all the way round Dominion Circuit and back home.

Having read the invitation properly this time we went down the road exactly the same the next day. One or two people at the cocktail party were looking at us strangely.

"Was the party you went to last night nice?"

"Yes, very nice, thank you."

What they meant was,

"Where did you go and why wasn't I invited?"

Formality gave this part of Canberra an atmosphere of false friendliness that became oppressive. At first I couldn't make out why somebody I had met quite often wasn't more forthcoming. Any pair who became more than friendly were morbidly secretive about it. One young man took me out to play golf. Next day he wouldn't look at me and I don't think it was entirely because I was a useless golfer. My father broke this rule and someone soon made it their business to tell my mother that he had been sleeping with someone else's wife. I cut this woman dead when I met her and my father was furious with me and perhaps afraid. My mother, who had been getting better, was visibly upset. This overt reaction by his family did pull my father up short as far as we knew.

Hugh went to Canberra Grammar School. Soon after, we went to an open evening and propping up a door in the school hall was an Australian ex-serviceman who had been one of the airmen staying at Wings. He was surprisingly pleased to see me, came to our house and chatted up my mother. Garnett did not get much change out of me because he had not taken the slightest notice of me at Fairford.

I lived in Canberra until February 1947. It was hot, dusty and dry and in the daytime nothing happened. I went out painting in the bush and also did a piece called 'The Cocktail Party' which was to win first prize in the Sydney University Art Competition. I had a weighty Australian bicycle and went shopping on it sometimes going across the Great Divide to Civic Centre as if it were another country. My father also used to send me off to Queanbean, a small town about five miles outside Australian Capital Territory to buy gin. You couldn't buy alcohol at all in ACT except drinks in the hotel. One boiling day I cycled forth and duly obtained the gin. I was terribly thirsty by then so I went innocently into a bar nearby to get a drink. The bar at midday was full of men. I reduced the whole lot of them to silence because women were not allowed in public houses. They did sell me some lemonade which I drank surrounded by a deathly hush. When I went out I wondered if they had had to reconsecrate that bar like a church. We had a small garden with eucalyptus trees, kookaburras and a cherry tree which produced a great crop of cherries. Before we could pick them a flock of little green birds like parrots flew down and ate them all. We had a shed in which we found a funnel-web spider. I once shut Hugh in that shed during a quarrel, but the spider to be fair had gone by then.

My mother got a new admirer. Charles was about forty and remarkable looking because he had snow white hair and bushy black eyebrows. He was not a member of the Diplomatic Four Hundred and he appeared to have no occupation. Because he was so popular he went to most of the Diplomatic cocktail parties, but he didn't comport himself as if he had a steel ruler down his spine. He drove a Ford V8 convertible and was the person who rescued me from the Astronomer Royal to be. He lived in the Hotel Canberra and would take my mother and me there for drinks. I was used to playing second fiddle to my mother where men were concerned so I was surprised when he once drove up Mugga Way to take me out to dinner at the Canberra Hotel by myself. There were some disapproving glances from the other tables. He drove me home and kissed me chastely goodnight, but by Canberra standards it was hot stuff.

I went to play tennis at the Dutch Embassy. Someone lent me a pony once and he ran away with me for miles into the Outback. After Christmas my father wrote to the University of Sydney asking if I was eligible to be admitted. He enclosed all my School Certificate Examinations and said nothing at all about failing the Intermediate exam. A board sitting in judgement on overseas applications decided I could enter the first year medical course. I was to live in Newtown at the Women's College known as The Dyke. In February I flew down to Sydney 'Uni' for Orientation Week. At the college I was given a ground floor room with a glass door to the outside world and a homily about being trustworthy and not exploiting this convenient orifice. By the end of the academic year I spent half the night letting students in.

The Women's College was strict. The Principal was Miss Elizabeth Archdale, a famous English cricket player. She was approachable and jolly, but quite unmoved by excuses or prevarications. Everyone was supposed to be in by 10pm You could stay out until midnight if you had a pass. A senior student was on duty to let you in or if she was nasty, report you for being late. Passes till 2 am were granted sparingly and refused if you asked more often than Miss Archdale considered reasonable. Alongside the university curriculum, first year girls doing Science had to stay in twice a week for Physics and Chemistry coaching and we were set written work. We all moaned like anything about this and said crossly that it made us look like schoolgirls. These rules impeded our social lives and men from the other colleges would sneer at our restrictions.

A few girls went to dozens of parties and made it back to college just in time for breakfast. They said that the danger made it more fun. The majority of us were less adventurous and confined our indiscretions to the hours of daylight.

At the Uni there was democratically no selection. If you held the necessary academic qualifications you could enrol for any subject you wanted regardless of however many students had applied. The authorities relied on a large dropout and failure rate. The eight hundred first year medical students were called together and told that fifty percent of us would fail. This was an understatement, as it turned out, because of that eight hundred candidates only two hundred and fifty passed into the second year. In spite of the huge numbers the practical work was well organised. The lectures on Physics and Chemistry were inadequate and Miss Archdale knew this. That was why the science girls were given extra coaching for which nobody was grateful.

After this direful warning Orientation Week was fun. All the University Societies were touting for members. The Freshers at The Dyke got to like or hate one another almost at once. We got lost on the university campus, found out how to get to King's Cross in downtown Sydney on the tram. The tram was noisy and you could hear it coming for miles. You asked for 'two sections please' or whatever. On my first trip the conductor said in an upper class English accent, "Do you want Bucknum Pellis?" and everybody laughed.

In 1947 Pommies were not unduly popular, but not hated. Nobody in Australia ever held my being British against me. They were without

exception friendly and hospitable. Later on girls would ask me,
"Do I sound very Australian?" I used to reply
"What did it matter if you happened to be Australian?"
But it wasn't the answer they wanted. Pronunciation had pitfalls. My
father had a colleague who had been skiing at Mount Kosiusko, but was
losing his holiday tan fast. He met my father going in to work, my father
said,
"You're getting lighter every day."
The man retorted angrily,
"What's it got to do with you what time I get into the office?"
My mother thought a chicken was called a 'chook'. She went to a shop
to buy one and the shopkeeper thought she
was mad.

I decided I would do choral singing and
joined the Sydney University Dramatic
Society. When I signed up, because of my
stammer, I said that I didn't want to act but I
could paint scenery. This was rash. Next
Sunday a man called Jack rang me up and
asked me to help him paint a backdrop for a
play by Carlo Goldoni. When I saw what he
had done I knew with a sinking heart he was
a far more experienced painter than I. He was
scornful, but I managed to paint a passable
trompe-l'oeil bowl of fruit on the table. Next
time I went to SUDS I met John and fell in
love.

John was gay. Inexplicably he fell in love
with me. SUDS was a two layered society;
the inner stratum being homosexual, the
outer straight, but far less creative. John was
part of the inner circle, but I didn't know
because he was so affectionate. Sometimes
he would apologise and say he couldn't go
out because there was a session at someone
called Sam's flat and there would be trouble
if he wasn't there. I never gave it a thought.
Sam was an exceptional producer and made
SUDS famous all over eastern Australia, not

John Mawson.

that there was much competition at that time.

John was pretty, looking like a female version of Cary Grant. He was tall and slender with narrow shoulders and a tendency to mince, but when he forgot about it he was strong, energetic and a good swimmer. He yearned for anything to do with England and longed to leave Australia. This was what at first made him pay attention to me, but he was later to take me home to his family, give me as many poetry books as could be afforded from the sparse Sydney bookshops, ring me up constantly and spend all his spare time with me.

John was reading English and was in his second year. He was writing a thesis on Gertrude Stein. John was witty and iconoclastic. He sang snatches of grand opera to words of his own invention and knew more poetry than I did. He was also unexpectedly practical and good at finding his way about which was useful when he eventually came to England three years later. When he arrived he brought me a gold bracelet as a sort of marriage offering. The woman who wore it through Customs loved John. She never forgave me for not marrying him. Years later I met her at a private viewing at the Royal Academy. We had tea together downstairs and she berated me because she said my perfidy had turned John into a full blown homosexual. John was to die young in Greenwich Village from something that sounded like AIDS.

When I joined SUDS it was just starting a lavish and professional production of *Hassan* by James Elroy Fletcher. John was Ishak. The huge intricate backdrop was painted by Loudon Sainthill. There were many mundane jobs which Sam and Jack snappishly gave me to do. They hated me and I never knew why. In the first term at The Dyke it was customary for the Freshers to put on a play. Miss Archdale thought I'd got some rudimentary literary background, so I was told to produce it. We did the Mechanicals play from *A Midsummer Night's Dream*: it was hard work because nobody wanted to look silly. Thisbe didn't want to wear a padded bra, nor the lion to roar. A stately remote English girl who had also joined SUDS played Theseus and unexpectedly helped me to whip up enthusiasm. I was the wall. It went down well and I was given some kudos. Pride goeth... however. Miss Archdale then bade me produce a play for the University Drama Festival. I asked John to do it and he chose a deservedly long forgotten play by Alfred Lord Tennyson, to be played completely seriously. Diana and John obtained much high flown satisfaction from their performances. This rubbish came bottom at the Festival and Miss Archdale told me I was out for a duck.

John liked coming to The Dyke to have dinner because he said it was like a nunnery and rehearsing this dismal play gave him the entrée. In April John came home to Canberra with me. He was a *succès fou* with my mother, but before we went back to Sydney she told me bluntly that he was homosexual and I must never consider any long term relationship with him as it would certainly lead to untold misery. She said it was an awful pity because he was adorable. I took no notice of this at all.

The middle term saw the opening of the super-colossal production of *Hassan*. When he wasn't involved with the play John and I would go swimming in Sydney Harbour which was foolhardy and to Bondi Beach which was terrifying. I could never decide which I feared most- sharks or big waves. We went skating and rode on the roller-coaster at Luna Park. We went to Paramatta on the ferry to see the koalas. I had spare afternoons because I was let off practical Chemistry and John could plan Gertrude Stein and type her up at night. John had a room at that time in Woolloomooloo and we had plenty of opportunity to make love, but we didn't. I was more than willing, but John planned urgent things for us to do and there was always another day. We did eventually make love, but it was several years later and not part of this story. We went to the cinema often. I never hear 'You Belong to My Heart' from Walt Disney's 'Song of the South' to this day without remembering John and how it felt to be nineteen.

My father was reliably paying my university fees and gave me a small allowance as well. Students had many concessions and when they failed I would resort to my diplomatic ID card. A little money went a long way. I bought an emerald green coat and some agonising red sandals.

The next holiday I spent only a little time in Canberra. I said goodbye to my family who were going home. My father had been offered a high-flying job in the Air Ministry in London and had already gone back to England to take it up. My mother had had a reasonably happy time in Canberra, had played plenty of chess and was more like herself. As usual Hugh had not liked school. We gave a farewell party at Mugga Way and every single thing we cooked went wrong. My mother had been worried that my 'cocktail party' picture which was at that time part of a university travelling art exhibition would arrive in Canberra before she'd gone because all the people drinking in it were recognisable. I never caught up with that picture again, but I've still got some other paintings I did in Canberra. The rest of the holiday we travelled to Brisbane with *Hassan*. I was in charge of the costumes. Apart from being busy and anxious all I remember about Brisbane was drinking Pimms outside some hotel. The train journey from Sydney took three days. At night we lay down on the floor like sardines. When we got to Brisbane which was hot, we all got out of the train unbelievably dirty and tired. Brisbane University put us up and we gave five successful performances. Then we had to travel all the way back to Sydney to face up to the grim reality of exams in the none too distant future.

Sydney was tropically hot and humid. Mosquitoes were everywhere and whenever I wanted to look my best I would have a big swelling eyelid or huge fat cheek. It never occurred to me to buy a mosquito net.

We all began to revise like lunatics. Only those at The Dyke who knew they were going to fail anyway or those who were too clever to have to work went out and came in late. Cosy bedroom chats lasting into the small hours were discontinued.

The students' phone which lately had never stopped ringing, fell silent. John, being one of those who did not need to work, was impatient with me. "Revising is silly," he said "It's too late now so why not forget about it?"

Tempted though I was I remembered what it was like to fail exams.

It was stifling hot in examination week. In the Zoology Practical Exam we had to dissect a stingray and tie little bits of coloured thread around various organs. By the end of the exam two hundred stingrays reeking of formaldehyde in an airless laboratory made everybody feel sick. All we science people at The Dyke were made to sit the Physics Distinction Paper. I wrote some waffly half-baked answers and hoped for the best. Provided you passed the curriculum paper it didn't matter.

Then it was the end of the university year. The Dyke would be closing until February so I was getting concerned about where to live. I was also going to have to keep myself, as my father wrote enclosing a smallish amount of money and told me that it was all I was getting until next year. Several students, including John, were obliged to work through the summer break so I didn't feel unduly hardly done by. Janice an older lesbian fellow student who lived in Sydney with her partner took a misguided fancy to me. This time I knew what she was about and I told her she was wasting her time. She tried to help though and found me a job in a laundry in Strawberry Hills, then a run down Sydney slum. The poor woman who ran this from her small home and yard couldn't really afford to pay me anything but I had to insist that she kept her word as I was broke. Not only was she poor, she was ill and often bent double with pain from what might have been gallstones. She worked from early in the morning until late at night and lived in dread of something being spoiled or lost.

This laundry was run entirely by hand. The clothes were washed in coppers, mangled and then pegged carefully onto wash lines. They were then hand-ironed. The laundry was sorted, the lists were checked and the clean clothes were beautifully packed up in brown paper. The whole place stank of dirty clothes. The heat was equatorial. I went to work here on my twentieth birthday and it was the most horrible day of my life. I was a raw prawn and I dropped a woollen shirt into the boiling wash by mistake and nearly left right away in tears, but the woman was feeling awful and there was nobody else. In a day or two I became more useful and was shown how to iron coloured shirts. I never graduated to white ones. The iron was massive and my wrists swelled up. Luckily I wasn't to do this for very long because John invited me to go home with him for Christmas to Maryborough in Victoria. John was reluctant to go home and hadn't seen his parents for over a year, so they had no option but to accept that he was going to bring a girl home. They were not best pleased about this, but his father thought it was a step in the right direction. John's mother and sister, Pauline, had never heard of homosexuality. We all got on quite well.

During my time in the laundry my face had erupted with acne spots. I had always had a good trouble-free complexion and had taken it for granted. My self-esteem plummeted. It wasn't hormonal acne because it later yielded in two days to sulpha drugs, but I was to put up with it for six months. It influenced me into making a cowardly decision and marred what was left of my time in Australia. John mentioned my skin just once and I burst into tears. He told me it didn't make any difference to us and never spoke of it again.

John's family lived in Maryborough, north of Melbourne in a corrugated iron-roofed house with a wood floor. Rugs were scattered about. There was a piano and photographs of relatives in frames. The windows and door space were covered in mosquito netting so it was dim indoors, but stuffy and hot. There was electric light in the house but no power. There was a shower you used by igniting a few sticks in a tin above one's head and water came down out of a bucket. You had to be quick because the hot water in the shower ran out in no time. There was an outhouse for a lavatory. Very early in the morning this was emptied into a lorry which came by every day. The member of the family who struck me first was a large turkey pecking about happily in the garden. It wanted a few days before Christmas and I fed this bird up until Christmas Eve, when John's father chopped off its head, his mother plucked it and we had it for Christmas dinner! They had had to prepare it so near the day for fear it would "go off". I couldn't eat any of that turkey and the family looked pityingly upon me. John ate his with gusto and I began to see the down-to-earth rural boy beneath the aesthetic literary skin he had assumed when he went to the University. John's father was the editor of the local newspaper which came out once a week. He ran it single-handed, collecting the content, setting up the paper and printing it on site. He was pleased to see John because he could set type and read proofs and had done so since he was a teenager. I went to work there as well. I was good for only menial tasks but I was pleased to go because the printing press was about all that moved in Maryborough. John's father was a large capable man. He looked upon John as one who had inexplicably changed, and not for the better. He was not bewildered or grieved by what John had become, unlike his mother. He quite liked me and asked me about what England was like during the war.

John resembled his mother. She was pretty and neatly made with dark hair and a worried expression. She was musical and in the evenings John or his mother played the piano and we sang songs like "The Last Rose of Summer" or "The Rose of Tralee", and a whole repertoire of comic songs from Music Halls long ago. The family also did what we would now call Line Dancing. I was clumsy at this. John's mother spent her days in a vain battle against dust and hoping that John might eventually come home to Maryborough and do something sensible.

John's older sister, Pauline, put me in mind of Audrey. She was large and plain and she went out to work every day. She didn't have a boyfriend as far as I knew. She was pleasant to me considering she had been made to share her bedroom.

Soon after Christmas I got a telegram from Diana. It read "Chemistry Pass, rest Credits; how perfectly disgusting." John, quoting Emerson, said something about "a bee, ignorant of scientific truths, had made an awful lot of honey."

After about three weeks I was glad to go back to Sydney though I had nowhere to live. As it was I got a room with a finals medical student called "Flower" Firebrace, so called because she was incredibly beautiful. I had never dared to raise my eyes to her in College but she turned out to be a charming person as well as being beautiful.

She was forlorn because she was having an affair with a married doctor and hoped with all her heart that he would eventually live with her: in reality, she was not optimistic.

We both had to get jobs right away but before I started looking around there was a letter waiting for me at the women's College. It was from the British High Commissioner in Canberra and it said that the British Government would not be responsible for my fare back to England unless I left within two months. If I agreed they would arrange a passage home for me. It took a while for me to let this sink in. When I found that a passage cost £250 I despaired of having that sort of money. Deciding to stay would mean I would not see my family for many years, nor did I trust my father to help me financially. I knew in my heart that I was getting nowhere with John, though I loved him no less. I also wondered whether my skin condition was due to the Australian climate and that I ought to see a doctor. I could have been treated through the Medical Faculty but it didn't cross my mind.

I took all this to Miss Archdale who reacted positively as she always did. She told me if I went home I would find it impossible to get a place in a London Medical School, which turned out to be entirely correct. She said she would find me a scholarship to pay for my course and college expenses. She told me I had come thirtieth out of the two hundred and fifty successful examinees. Reluctantly I refused her offer. I asked how to go about consulting a doctor but I couldn't bring myself to tell her why. I imagine that Miss Archdale suspected I was pregnant, so she said "Well perhaps it would be better to go home."

Thus it was that I threw away my second chance of becoming a doctor. There was a huge jam factory in Newtown that could be relied on to provide short term work, but in the summer you could smell it for miles, so we guessed that actually being inside would be intolerable. For three days Flower and I put lids on cardboard boxes. On the fourth day we couldn't face it again, preferring to starve. We ended up in a glass factory which made scientific glassware and cheap glass crockery. We were set to calibrate litre flasks. You sat on a high stool at the flask's eyeline, filled it up with a litre of water (I don't know who had measured that) and marked just below the meniscus with a glass cutter. You did this all day. Something so monotonous empties the mind, leaving it open perhaps for glimpses of the future.

My vision came in the guise of a nondescript girl in a paint-stained green overall. I never actually spoke to her while she went in and out of a room near the factory floor. She was the factory artist and responsible for the ghastly designs on the glass plates. It occurred vividly to me that sometime I too would be a unique person employed by, but working alone in, a large enterprise. That premonition came true ten years later.

Meantime it was miserable to see my fellow students all setting out on their second year while I was working in a factory waiting to go home to no medical school.

Flower went back into college to take her finals. John had started his third year – "Gertrude Stein" had been well received. I saw him in the evenings. I knew we were going to part very soon and I was eaten up with grief.

It was not long before I got a letter enclosing a Quantas ticket to fly to Hobart at a week's notice. There I was to join SS *Drina*, sailing to England. I got an enormous wooden tea chest, packed all my books and things I wouldn't need on the voyage and it was carted away.

The night before I flew off they gave a party for me at SUDS. To my surprise Jack gave me a scarf hand-printed by himself. Diana gave me a book of Villon poems and John gave me a book on Picasso. John and I ended up in bed together somewhere. We didn't make love because we were too drunk and overwrought.

In the morning John went with me to the airport terminal. I got in the coach and put my hand out of the seat window to touch him one more time. He kissed my fingers.

Then the coach drove away.

More than fifty years later with blood long cooled it seems more of a pity that I can't remember a thing about such a remote and beautiful place as Tasmania. I never got the chance to go again.

I boarded the *Drina*, hardly noticing that she was much smaller than the *Themistocles*. She was due to sail to Glasgow with a cargo of apples and twelve passengers. She was not going through the Suez Canal, but from Freemantle to Cape Town and Tenerife, so it was going to be a long voyage.

I got on that boat dirty, tear-stained and unwell. My cabin mate must have been dismayed at having to be cooped up with such a disaster for the next ten weeks. She was a beautician about fifteen years older than me. She told me my spots would be cured by scrubbing my face with a nailbrush every day, so all my time on the *Drina* I was red and sore as well as being relentlessly spotty.

Another passenger was a Roman Catholic priest with whom I used to play chess. I never beat him. He told me I was a born worshipper and would end up as a practising Catholic. This seemed unlikely at the time though thirty odd years later I became a churchgoer.

There was a man of about thirty. He was pale, exhausted and smelled

1948. Coming home on MS Drina.

of blood. He spent much of his time in the doctor's cabin, and was going to England to seek last-ditch treatment. Although the doctor never breached medical etiquette, he looked soberly upon this man. He made it to Glasgow however.

A very short, stocky little man was going to London to make his fortune as a cabaret artist which was optimistic to say the least. He was boastful and macho and I slapped his face when he made a business-like pass at me.

A mousey young girl was going to England to get married. By day two until the end of the journey she slept with the Third Officer. Her fiance was waiting for her on the quay at Glasgow. They embraced as if she had been yearning for him throughout the whole trip.

The crew were a randy lot and it was difficult in such a small ship to stay out of trouble. Once I stupidly went into the Purser's cabin. Nothing much happened and I was making my tactful way out before it did. At the door I bumped into the Chief Engineer, a Scotsman with girls my age, who had been kind and fatherly up till then.

He never spoke to me again.

I was still good at deck tennis and was often to play with the younger officers, which was perhaps the jolliest thing that happened aboard the *Drina*.

At Cape Town my steward asked me to go out with him and I refused. I was nervous of this man because I much disliked the enormous black-heads which adorned his nose.

He had pulled me out of the bath when it was rough in the Great Australian Bight and I had nearly fainted. After that there seemed to be something even more repulsive about him and I knew that slapping his face would be a waste of time. I went up Table Mountain in the cable car with a kindly middle-aged lady instead.

At Tenerife, Eric a somewhat negative young man lent me £1 to buy my family some presents. I had to save enough money to get from Glasgow to London and I was broke as usual. He never expected to see his money again. However, I saw him at a bus stop in Regent Street about three months later. I had £1 on me and I ran up and shoved it into his hand just as he was getting on a bus. It was worth it to see his complete astonishment.

We docked at Glasgow in the late afternoon and the passengers departed. I was stuck because the tea chest full of my belongings was in the bottom of the hold and couldn't be unloaded until the next day.

By evening it was raining and I and the rest of the remaining crew went to a gloomy hotel to have dinner. We had expected a more exciting and memorable evening. The crew drank my health and we went back to the *Drina* to spend the night.

When I and my luggage got eventually to the railway station, the guard told me I couldn't put the tea chest into the guard's van unless it was labelled. Resourcefully, I labelled it with a lipstick because that was all I had.

On the journey to London I got talking to a very young man who took a fancy to me and told me that his parents, who were meeting him at Euston, would drive me and my tea chest to Strawberry Hill. When we reached Euston his parents were far from enthusiastic, and worse was to follow when this boy got lipstick all over his trousers.

They drove me in total silence to my house except for repeated suggestions that I should pay to have his trousers dry-cleaned. I had no money at all so I couldn't offer to do this. They dumped me and the tea chest on the pavement outside 26 Waldegrave Gardens and drove angrily off. I was sorry for that boy; he had only tried to be kind.

I knocked on the front door. Both my parents were there. My mother said, "Where on earth have you been? We were expecting you last night."

My father said "Good God Jill you've grown."

I went in and shut the door on my first twenty years.

***

PART TWO

Hugh's Story

by Hugh MacBride

STRAWBERRY HILL, BRIGHTON AND ANGMERING-ON-SEA

I have it on good authority – that of my mother – who should know, though I don't remember being present myself, that I was born at 10 o'clock in the morning of Sunday 16 February 1936. She phoned the doctor herself when she felt my arrival was imminent, but he, inferring from her demeanour that the situation was not urgent, missed the action and arrived with the midwife only in time to dot the I's and cross the T's.

My mother's account of the circumstances leading up to my birth are worth recording, though we should perhaps note her journalist's flare for making a good story. In the 1920s she had been a star crime reporter for the *Daily Express* but by 1935 she was doing more feature work, drawing a strip cartoon "Sarah Snail" and running the "Choc-Toc" children's club in the *Sunday Express*. Evidently she was still doing some reporting, however, because the proprietor Lord Beaverbrook sent for her and required her to change her account of some meeting or event which had political connotations in which he had an interest. She refused to change her account of what had actually happened and she recounted the ensuing dialogue:

Beaverbrook: "You're fired!"

Kitty MacBride: "All right, you owe me a year's salary".

Beaverbrook: "You'll be very lucky to get it".

Kitty MacBride: "You'll be very unlucky if I don't; I have a contract".

She got the money.

Considering that a few years later Churchill chose Beaverbrook for the crucial post of Minister of Aircraft Production, on the basis presumably that he was a good organiser on the one hand and a five-star bastard on the other, she evidently kept her end up pretty well.

Returning to her colleagues in the newsroom and announcing that she had been fired, one asked:

"What are you going to do now, Kitty?"

"I'm going to go home and have a son," she answered.

And here I am!

It seems that I am rather lucky to be here, however, since at a few months old I got gastroenteritis, still bad news for babies and a killer in 1936. The doctor had the idea that kaolin would help. He explained to my mother that it would form a lining on the walls of the intestines, which seems rather improbable now, but for one reason or another it worked and I survived. At the worst point he told my parents that I must not be allowed to weaken myself further by crying and they spent a whole night dancing in turns round the room to the strains of "Teddy Bears' Picnic" on the gramophone; the only way they could find to stop me crying. I have disliked this tune since I can remember; perhaps it brings back unconscious memories of near terminal tummy-ache.

My mother blamed my nurse for causing my condition by poor standards of hygiene, and replaced her with a much younger woman. She seems to have entered into the struggle to save me with enthusiasm. The first time she saw that my green stained nappy, characteristic of the disease, had been replaced by a more natural condition my parents happened to be entertaining some guests for drinks. Anxious to share the good news, she stuck her head round the drawing-room door, attracted my mother's attention, and held up the dirty nappy!

When I had recovered my mother was desperately anxious in case my illness returned. She bought an Electrolux gas fridge and everything that went in my mouth was sterilised with boiling water – except the end of her dachshund Mitizi's tail which I was found chewing when briefly left unattended on the floor!

At this time we were living in a rather smart four-bedroom semi-detached house in Strawberry Hill near Twickenham, with my sister, who had been born in December 1927. My mother had a still-born child between us, in November 1931, and hearing her speak of it in her old age I felt that she never really came to terms with this sadness.

I should explain at this point that my sister's name is Angela but, before

Above: *26 Waldegrave Gardens, Strawberry Hill, before the war. The gates and railings went for war effort and were never replaced in my time.*

Left: *Me in the back garden.*

Above and right:
Me at Strawberry Hill.

I was born, she insisted on being addressed as Jill. Although she reverted to Angela when I was quite small, I had got used to calling her Jill, and I still do.

I have a rather hazy memory of the house at this time, in particular sitting in a high chair in front of the window of the room used as a nursery, and of the taste of tinned mandarin oranges. My first clear memory is of a trip to the seaside with my mother. I remember being on the beach with her and finding a piece of sea-washed brick – I still feel the pleasure I got from the texture of this material. I searched for all the pieces I could find, and my mother let me put them all into a rather narrow wicker basket she had brought.

I also remember, from the same time, walking on wooden boards, laid not quite touching, to a slot machine which consisted of a large mechanical hen in a glass case. A penny in the slot made it cluck with ever-increasing vigour until at the climax it flapped its wings and laid an egg. I was greatly entertained! Talking to my sister and my mother years later it appeared that she had taken me, alone, to Brighton for a few days around the early summer of 1939, and the hen was on Brighton Pier.

My last memory of Strawberry Hill is looking at my father's car in front of the garage – a small family saloon smartly finished in maroon with black mudguards. From the image of the car in my mind, and the fact that my father (as I now know), who was totally unmechanical, relied on my uncle

Cyril, my mother's brother, for everything to do with cars, and that Cyril sold Singer cars from his showroom at 171 Great Portland St, I infer that it was a Singer Eight. In a matter of days, I think, this car was to play a major role in changing my life, and that of my sister, forever.

In August 1939, I am told, we went on holiday to a rented bungalow at Angmering-on-Sea in Sussex. My mother and sister were there as well as my nanny, a Miss Walsh, but because of the threaten-

Me with Nanny Walsh at Angmering 1939.

94

ing international situation my father, who was News Services Editor of the *Daily Herald*, stayed in London. I remember a low rather dark single storey house with a well worn brick path. Beside the house, with the same sort of path around it, was a vegetable bed in which onions had been left to go to seed. I liked the round seed-heads, especially as they were set off by the worn brick!

I can remember being in a rather ill-lit room with bookshelves on either side of the chimney breast. It was here that a sort of family joke started, involving various places to put a piece of cheese. "Cheese on the books" amused me particularly, but although I have an image of the room in my mind I am not at all sure that "cheese on the books" is a firsthand memory. I mention this because I am very anxious that everything I recount as remembered is a real memory and not something I have since been told about. When I first thought about writing this account I was worried that it might be difficult to distinguish between these two, but having thought about the material I have to put down, I realise that my sister and my mother, let alone my father, were present at almost none of the events I have to describe.

We never finished our holiday!

STICKLEPATH AND MOFFATS

Before recounting my recollections of the last few days before the declaration of war in September 1939, I need to explain, with hindsight, what was happening. When news of the signing of the German-Russian Nonaggression Pact came through to my father on 23 August he feared that this might cause Hitler to order massive air raids, and possibly invasion. He came down to Angmering the same day and said that we must leave for Devon in the morning. In the event, of course, raids did not start for almost a year.

Presumably the Russians were playing for time, as, wisely or otherwise, had Mr Chamberlain at Munich on 30 September 1938. In later years I found that my father was bitterly scornful of Chamberlain for not standing up to Hitler. My boss in the RAF, Flt Lt Bert Tingle, who had worked his way up through the ranks as an armourer, told me that at the time of Munich he had worked for twenty-four hours with bleeding fingers assembling machine gun belts from single rounds 'so that we could put an aircraft in the air which could fire its guns'. The eleven months between Chamberlain signing at Munich [agreement to Hitler's annexation of part of Czechoslovakia] and his declaration of war were not wasted.

My father's aunt Natalie Engleheart and her sons Jock and David ran a school called Moffats at Lifton Park in Devon, near Launceston. Although, so far as I know, he had had no contact with them for some years, and my mother disliked Natalie intensely, he arranged for us to board at Moffats, if the now almost inevitable war broke out. My parents first plan had been to send us to Oslo to stay with a family they knew, but my father realised that Hitler might not respect the neutrality of the Scandinavian Countries and changed his mind, wisely in the event.

Despite his complete lack of interest in things mechanical, my father was a good driver – but hampered by poor eyesight. Years later he told me that the one thing that made him feel guilty was having, throughout his life, lied about it on his driving licence application forms (no test was required when he first took out a licence). I fear that St Peter may well have had other points to raise! Nevertheless he (my mother never had a licence) drove us children and Nanny, to Sticklepath near Okehampton in Devon, and dropped us at the first house offering board and lodging that he saw within reasonable distance of Lifton. It was called, and I remember this, Pixie Nook.

I don't remember anything about this journey. I presume that my mother came to give my father support on the way back, because he turned around and drove straight back to London! On 1930s roads, with 1930s lights, this must have been a truly marathon effort! I was to see him, I think, only once more (at Christmas 1939?) before we went out to join him in Australia in 1946, where he had taken a job in the Commonwealth Relations Office as Public Relations Officer to the British High Commissioner towards the end of the war in Europe, in February 1945.

Sticklepath was a place of terror for me. I was too young, three years and seven months, to be frightened by what might lie ahead if war came, and separation from my mother would not have been a shock as Nanny was there and she looked after me most of the time anyway. My fear came from the quarry a short distance along the road to Launceston, where blasting charges were set off each day at exactly 12 o'clock. I was not frightened of being blown to pieces or hit by flying rocks, the quarry was too far from Pixie Nook for that. It was irrational fear of the sudden, overwhelming loudness of the explosion. It was lucky I was never in an air raid!

After a couple of days or so, Nanny, with excellent psychology no doubt, took me along the road to the quarry, after the day's blast. I held back as we approached the place but Nanny insisted and we went up the steps to a little office raised on legs. There she bought me a small set of building blocks, said to be cut from the stone they were quarrying. I liked these a lot and I am sure the exercise made me feel better about the blasting, though I still hated the bang! I don't remember having the little stone blocks after we left Pixie Nook so I suppose they must have been left there.

After what I remember as a few days, but must have actually been ten, on the second of September when Mr Chamberlain made his fateful announcement that we were at war, we moved on to Moffats at Lifton. I don't remember this much shorter journey, either.

The house at Lifton Park, which now housed Moffats School, was a grand one with just two storeys, and broad paved terraces with stone balustrades around the front and side. It still stands but is very dilapidated

Above: *Lifton Park in 1832*
by J. Thomas after T. Allom.

Right: *A recent photo of Lifton Park.*

Me with unidentified children at Lifton Park.

now. The school owned the large park in which it is set, which was thickly wooded with mature trees, mostly beech, with luxuriant growths of rhodo-dendrons in a remarkable variety of colours. Near the house there were lawns and flowerbeds planted mostly with azaleas. The sulphury smell of azaleas still reminds me of this place, and the memory is not an unpleasant one. A family of peacocks lived in the grounds and the sound of a peacock's call has the same effect on me.

My father's Aunt Natalie I remember only as a malevolent presence in the background.

I shared a rather small room with Nanny and am sure she looked after me very well, though I don't remember very much about it, except the time I had a sudden and very vigorous nosebleed as I was getting out of bed. Nanny stopped it very quickly and I am sorry now that I don't remember how!

My most vivid memory of that room was a stack of fairly small cardboard boxes which arrived sometime before Christmas, presumably in a larger box which was too big to keep in the room, which Nanny put in the corner covered roughly by some piece of cloth. I knew they were for me and was very excited by them. They proved, when Christmas came at last, to contain a clockwork train set with a single small circle of track. I think the spring of the green engine broke very quickly but it gave me a lot of pleasure while it lasted.

Moffats was really a boy's preparatory school but they took a few girls including Jill and Maureen Sharp, the daughter of Captain Sharp, the Maths master. Jill and Maureen became good friends. She lives in Devon and we went to see her quite recently. I suppose the school only accepted the girls because of the war.

There were no other children of my age and obviously no one to teach me, although I remember being parked at the back of a class of boys and chanting "amo, amas, amat, amamus, amatis, amant" with them. It was quite a few years before I discovered what this strange incantation meant!

I spent my time roaming the large grounds of Lifton Park. I think there must have been rhododendrons in flower pretty well all my time at Moffats and I got much pleasure from them. The brown blotches and speckles in the throats of the white and yellow varieties fascinated me particularly. The other activity which I remember was building little houses out of small sticks, of which there were plenty in the beech woods. These I made by sticking four forked sticks into the ground, one for each corner, placing two sticks between the forks and two more resting on these at the corners. I then had a frame which could be filled in by leaning sticks against the sides and resting them on top. I used to spend quite a lot of time and trouble making these.

Since sticks were my principal playthings I was, at first, dismayed when the whole School was assembled on the wide gravelled area outside the front door and the headmaster, holding up one of those abbreviated cricket bats that I was later to see on sale for beach games, threatened to beat anyone with it if they were seen to pick up a stick! I don't think I could hear everything he said but I gathered that someone had been hurt in some game with a stick. After a bit I decided that this could hardly apply to the harmless twigs I used and that there was never anyone to see me in the woods in any case.

The ground rose quite steeply at the back of the house and a driveway had been dug out along the building with the bank held back by a stone wall. At the high point the bank had been excavated to make an underground wine cellar or dairy or whatever. It was quite big and served as an air-raid shelter for the whole School. I can remember Nanny waking me up in the middle of the night and carrying me, wrapped in blankets, to this shelter where we sat on wooden benches. I don't know whether this was a practice or an actual alert, though I think we had to wait quite a long time before going back to bed so perhaps it was an alert, but nothing happened.

The ground above the door of this shelter had heather and yellow flowers I now know to be hypericum, Rose of Sharon, growing on it. On sunny afternoons, and most of them were sunny in 1940, I would go to this place and creep cautiously towards the edge of the bank where a large adder was nearly always coiled up in the sun. I was well aware that the snake was dangerous and kept my distance, but it had a fascination for me.

One of the things I remember about the house was the fine broad staircase, leading down to the large hall, opposite the front door. I always came down this one step at a time, leading with my right foot each time. I knew this was childish and I tried to make myself put my left foot down before the right in the normal way, but I never quite had the nerve while I was there. More recently, when my knee and hip joints are feeling unreliable, I tend to revert to my early technique!

Towards the end of my time at Moffats the may came into flower and I picked a sprig to decorate our room, but Nanny forbade me to bring it into the house because it might bring bad luck! More disappointingly she wouldn't let me keep a splendid peacock's tail-feather for the same reason. I now suppose that with the very real threat of air raids and invasion hanging over everyone it might well have seemed a bad time to push one's luck; then I put it down as a rather sad example of the oddness of grown-ups! My mother told me years later that Nanny was a Catholic and, as war loomed, she had asked with intense feeling if she could hang a Saint's medallion round my neck to keep me safe. Naturally permission was given; evidently it worked!

Jill has told me since that she and the other girls spent quite a lot of time at the farm which adjoins Lifton Park, and I remember going there with her once or twice. I was particularly impressed by the oxeye daisies which grew about the farmyard.

Not very long after the may flower incident, and therefore about the early summer of 1940, I was taken away from Moffats and went, with Nanny, to live with the family of Dr Maurice Lea in Lifton Village.

LIFTON

Dr Lea was the local GP and he lived with his family in a rather long thin old house on the opposite edge of the village from Lifton Park. With some converted outbuildings it now houses three families. Dr Lea was about forty and his wife Janet, whom I thought very beautiful, was a few years younger. They had two sons, Patrick a bit under four years older than me, and John whom I regarded as my own age but I now know to have been distinctly younger. There was another boy Roger, the same age as Patrick, although of smaller build, who was also an evacuee, though I don't think I knew that at the time. No doubt they were glad of a similar companion for John.

Nanny and I shared a small room at the far end of the house, towards Tinhay, with beams and a rather complicated sloping ceiling. To reach it one had to go up the stairs in the middle of the house, rising from the hall with the front door. On a shelf on the left as one started up the stairs was a tank with small goldfish. One was bigger than the others, less highly coloured with rather large ungainly fins. Dr Lea said it was a *shubunkin* and he was clearly proud of it. My long-suffering wife Roslyn has looked it up on the internet and found that this species was not bred until the 1930s and must indeed have been of some note to ichthyologists in 1940, but I liked the little goldfish better!

Further up the stairs one reached the level of a frieze with a pattern of cherries, on the probably rather old parchment coloured wallpaper, which greatly appealed to me.

I don't know why, I don't think the initial reticence was on my side, but I didn't see much of John at the Lea's to start with. Nanny amused me in our room by making a scrap-book, making pictures with stencils and water colour paints, and 'transfers' (nearly always a disaster) bought from a shop in the village. I can also remember playing with one of those wooden frames with holes through which wooden pegs can be driven with a small mallet and making patterns with coloured wooden tiles. After a while I started playing with John and sometimes the elder boys. After spending so much time by myself at Moffats this was a welcome change and there-after there was usually something interesting or exciting going on. John and I became quite good friends although we never really hit the same wavelength. The other three boys' great enthusiasm was collecting butter-flies, inspired by Dr Lea, who had a splendid collection of butterflies and moths in a tall cabinet with thin drawers. He would open it to show it to

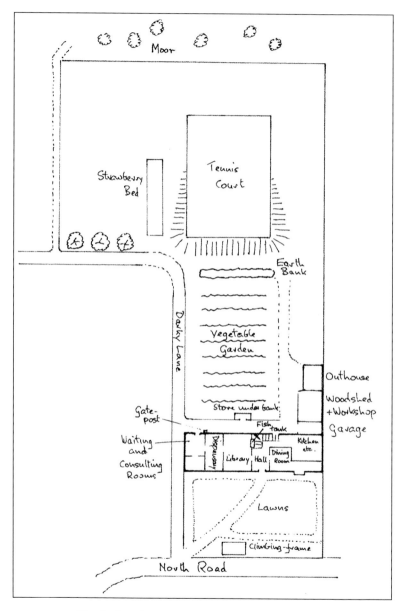

*Sketch plan of Dr Lea's house, The Cottage, & garden
at Lifton in 1940, drawn from memory.*

us from time to time, as he did with his collection of mineral samples, which also fascinated me. Butterflies were more plentiful then than they are now and no one thought anything of killing the odd one for their collection. Most people prefer to use a camera these days, including me, for I am still excited by them.

I had better explain how butterfly collecting is actually done. The insect is caught in a rather long tapering net mounted on a circular frame with a fairly short handle. Once inside, the net is folded over to keep it in and the killing bottle, consisting of a screwtop jar with a cotton wool pad on top of some chemical to kill the insect quickly without discolouring it, is manoeuvred inside the net until it can be closed with the insect inside. Before the dead specimen stiffens it is set for display with the wings further forward than their rest position on a cork-covered board with a groove down the middle and sides sloping slightly away from it. A single pin through the thorax holds it in the groove and narrow strips of cellophane held over the wings with pins keep them in place until the specimen becomes stiff.

I was keen to join in this activity and Nanny make me a butterfly net from some curtain netting. I don't know who made the frame for it. Dr Lea provided the chemicals for the killing bottles; Patrick's and Roger's had a couple of handfuls of potassium cyanide crystals under the cotton wool. I remember seeing Dr Lea take down the sweetshop-style bottle from the top shelf in his dispensary and scoop the crystals out with a table fork. John and I were not allowed cyanide and had to use a wad of cotton wool soaked in strong ammonia solution under the dry layer. This worked well enough but had to be renewed fairly often.

The boys lent me a setting board and taught me to use it, and Nanny sent away for a proper butterfly box for my collection. There weren't very many in it but they survived, remarkably, up to the 1950s when, my mother told me, the cleaning woman who came in a few days a week found the box and cleared out "some old moths". My mother found the box very useful. Some of my specimens were distinctly bedraggled but one or two, notably an orange clouded yellow, not so common in Lifton, was immaculate and perfectly competently set.

Nanny and I were accepted smoothly enough into the Lea household and I heard later that she helped out as receptionist in the surgery, but there was one contretemps not long after we went there. We usually all had lunch together at the dining-room table in time to hear the one o'clock news on the wireless. It was usually read by Stuart Hibbert or Alvar Liddell. Everyone knew the newsreaders names, which they gave at the start of every bulletin. I didn't understand the significance of the news reports, often disastrous at that time, but I remember the grown-ups exchanging sombre glances.

On one such occasion I took against some item of food on my plate and tried to assert my rights by refusing to eat it. I'm not sure what it was but I think it may have been the top part of a boiled egg containing only the white, which I disliked. Eggs – known as "shell-eggs" outside rural areas to distinguish them from the dried egg powder supplied in small brown waxed cardboard boxes by the Ministry of Food – were rationed and in short supply. I now suspect that a doctor visiting in a rural practice would have done rather better than most citizens, so eggs may have carried some psychological loading of guilt. When I continued to refuse and had what I am sure the grown-ups would have called a tantrum, Dr Lea quickly lost patience. He jumped up and dumped me on all fours on the floor, and with my waist clamped between his legs, gave me a hard spanking. I was howling blue murder by now, more from mortification than pain I think, and Nanny took me up to our room. There were no further such incidents.

At this time I was afflicted several times by attacks of ear-ache in the night. I can remember the hopeless feeling that the pain would never stop, Nanny pouring warm oil into my ear, which helped to some extent, and the awful taste of crushed aspirin, even taken with jam on the spoon. As a result of this, as I now realise, Dr Lea arranged for me to have my tonsils and adenoids taken out at Tavistock Hospital. The surgeon was a Mr Mollison.

I was taken to hospital fairly late in the day and I was pretty scared when Nanny and Mrs Lea left me there. I was put on a trolley and given a rather large pill that looked like a miniature reel of yellow cotton. I have a hazy recollection of strange dreams as I lost consciousness, but woke up next day in bed in a ward. I had a sore throat and was given ice cream. I don't remember being there very long; I think I was taken back to the Lea's house the following day.

The Leas were able to get enough petrol to run their two cars. Dr Lea had a smart black Morris 10 which he used for his work. It was kept in a garage which formed part of the outbuildings at the back of the house. He took the boys in it occasionally and I remember, as we drove along an unusually long stretch of straight road, Patrick and Roger discussing whether the car's steering could be locked in such circumstances. Dr Lea told them from the driving seat that continual minor corrections were needed to stay on even the straightest road, which seemed fairly obvious to me. We went about mostly in Mrs Lea's Morris Eight four-seat tourer, though seldom for any great distance. This car, which had wire wheels and must therefore have been the 1933 model, was supposed to be maroon and black, like my father's, but the paintwork had faded from neglect and being kept out of doors. I don't think the engine can have got very much attention either, as I remember we all had to get out and walk while Mrs Lea backed the car up a rather steep hill.

At the Lea's I started going to school with John, as a day-boy, in the kindergarten of a school called Ardock, after the old house it occupied at Lewdown, a few miles along the main road towards Okehampton. It was really a girls' school with a strong accent on riding, though I was later to find that there were a couple of boys of my sister's age whose parents were, I presume, abroad or involved in other war work. Mrs Lea took us, with our gas masks in their cardboard boxes with strings to put over one's shoulders, each day in her Morris Eight.

Most of the other day-children in the kindergarten came from local farms and they often boasted to one another about the types of tractor their fathers had, which were mostly Fordson models. I didn't have very much to do with them, perhaps because I had come with John, but I remember a pair of sisters with long startlingly fair hair. A few of these children were rather spiteful. My attitude was I think, essentially straightforward and trusting and I fell for that the silly riddle "Adam and Eve and Pinch me went down to the river to bathe. Adam and Eve were drowned. Who do you think was saved?" The obvious answer was taken as the mandate for a vicious pinch.

I don't remember very much about the lessons except that they were rather dull. From time to time we practised putting on our gas masks. We seemed to spend a long time looking at books with pictures, which we could not read. One showed fairies with a ladder reaching to the moon. It irritated me. Memorably, one of the books was *Struwwelpeter* with a series of pictures starting with a little boy sucking his thumb, a lanky fellow cutting his thumbs off with a large pair of scissors, and finally the boy standing with his arms by his side, blood dripping from his four-fingered hands and his thumbs lying on the floor beside him. I found this deeply disturbing, not because I was afraid that my thumbs would be cut off if I sucked them – I was dubious about cutting through bones with scissors anyway – but because it seemed so unnecessarily unpleasant. Why would anyone want to put such horrid stuff in a book?

John evidently didn't like the kindergarten either, because one morning at breakfast, but before Mrs Lea was ready to take us to school, he said "I don't want to go to school, let's run away." I tried to point out that this really wouldn't help and no good would come of it, but he insisted and I reluctantly went along with him. We went up the lane beside the house and up onto the moorland, dotted with gorse bushes, on the hill behind the house. Mrs Lea found us an hour or so after we should have left. I was expecting to be punished for this exploit but we weren't even scolded. Mrs Lea seemed relieved rather than angry when she found us.

On the left of the hall as one came in at the front door of the Lea's house was the library. The wall facing the window was filled by shelves holding bound copies of *Punch* which John and I enjoyed looking at even though we could not read the captions to the jokes. Our favourite, needing no caption, must have been published at the time motor lawnmowers became available; it showed a distraught gardener sprinting after his mower as it cut a swathe through an elaborate flowerbed and headed into the road through the open gate. Another book which interested me particularly was *Marvels of the Universe*, a collection of articles on astronomy, geology, natural history and so on with many illustrations, including a colour plate of the canals on Mars, now known to be quite fictitious. I don't know what drew it to my attention in the first place; perhaps the older boys showed it to me. I'm surprised now that I was so fascinated by it when I couldn't read the captions to the pictures. I don't remember doing it, but I think I must have asked Nanny to read them for me. She certainly knew I was very interested by it because, quite out of the blue, she sent away for a copy of my own! I think it cost two pounds, but whether she paid for it with money my parents had given her to get things for me or out of her own, presumably meagre, resources I don't know. I have the book, now rather dilapidated, in front of me as I write.

Another item of particular interest in the library stood on a fairly high shelf in front of the books on the wall beside the door. It was a Hornby '0-gauge' 4-6-2 locomotive, clockwork, in the dull red livery of the LMS (London Midland and Scottish) Railway. It was a beautifully made toy, well worthy of display on the shelf. Rolling stock and one or two smaller engines to match were put away somewhere, and carefully stored in one of the outbuildings were many yards of track mounted on long wooden boards. Dr Lea and the boys set it out in the front garden once while I was there. It covered quite a lot of the garden! The engine ran for a surprisingly long time before it needed to be rewound; compared with my little green 0-4-0 engine and the two-foot circle of track at Moffats, this was the ultimate train set!

I had a few possessions of my own at this time; a large brown teddy bear called Hug-me Major and a smaller one, Hug-me Minor, as well as a zip up pyjama case, black and white in the shape of a panda. I had a very nicely made clockwork Schuko car with steering and gear change which worked. It had come from Germany before the war and its styling was rather progressive: a *deja vu* of the Jaguar 2.4 litre saloon of the 1970s. I also had a small collection of Dinky toy aeroplanes: a Spitfire, a Hurricane, a Blenheim twin engine bomber of the RAF with its asymmetric cockpit, a Junkers Ju 88 – the standard German bomber, with the Heinkel He 111 – and the experimental seaplane (I've forgotten its name) which carried a small plane on its back. These were all very accurate die-cast models and one was encouraged to have them; aircraft recognition was rather more than an interesting hobby at that time!

The Leas had another toy which I liked a lot: a truly enormous Meccano set, quite old. Dr Lea helped Patrick and Roger to build a gantry crane with two towers supporting a track for a trolley with the lifting gear; it spanned almost the whole of the dining-room window bay. John and I helped with the small parts but I don't think we were allowed to play with the Meccano by ourselves, but I was more interested in it than John in any case.

I was much impressed by an indoor activity of the big boys which they called "making a flare". Dr Lea had provided them with potassium chlorate, sulphur and copper sulphate. These were finely ground, separately, in a pestle and mortar and the powders thoroughly mixed together. I presume Dr Lea had warned of the danger of grinding chlorate and sulphur together: the mixture can easily inflame violently at any moment! The mixed powders were put onto a tin tray in the middle of the room, on the floorboards with any rugs rolled well back, and lighted at arm's length with a match. It burnt furiously with a splendid blue flame — and filled the room with the pungent smell of sulphur dioxide! I liked all this a lot, not least the blue crystals of copper sulphate.

Another slightly surprising activity in the bedroom was making marmalade. It happened that all four of us boys caught measles at the same time, and we were all moved into one bedroom, Patrick and Roger one above the other in a bunk-bed. The blinds were kept partly drawn in the day as strong light was thought to be harmful in measles at that time. Mrs Lea entertained us in various ways, the most memorable being cutting up a large bag of bitter oranges she had obtained – such things were rare indeed – and boiling them for marmalade on a Primus stove (an early version of the camping stove which burned paraffin) in the middle of the bedroom floor!

Dr Lea may have seemed casual, by modern standards, in giving the elder boys dangerous chemicals, but the Leas were not casual about teaching us children air raid precautions. We were taught to use a stirrup pump and to fight fire by directing a jet of water at what was burning rather than at the flames. If we had to deal with an incendiary bomb the nozzle on the end of the pump hose had to be turned to give fine spray, as a jet of water would make it explode. We were encouraged to familiarise ourselves with the stirrup pump by having water fights in the garden on sunny days in our bathing trunks. We were also taught how to get out of a smoke-filled room on all fours, breathing the clear air just above the floor, and how we, as small children, could rescue a much bigger unconscious person by rolling them onto their back, tying their wrists together with a tie, or shirt-sleeves, or something and crawling forward with our hands and knees straddling their body and our heads between their arms. Dr Lea was 6 ft. tall and of fairly solid build but I could move him across the floor quite easily if not very fast, in this way. They taught Patrick and Roger to do a fireman's lift as well.

At this time, the late summer of 1940, we went on many expeditions collecting blackberries, and a bit later rose hips, in the surrounding countryside. Collecting rose hips was a national campaign organised by the W.I. who arranged for them to be sent for processing into rose-hip syrup, a good source of vitamin C. They also arranged the collection of wastepaper, always called salvage, aluminium foil ('silver paper') and anything else which could be re-used to help the war effort.

At harvest time of this year the four of us boys went to a farm near Tinhay to watch the crop of grain being threshed. In the farmyard a steam traction engine was driving a threshing machine by means of an incredibly long belt from the engine's flywheel to a smaller pulley on the machine. The belt lashed about and I was amazed that it didn't come off the pulleys. The threshing machine, in the shape of a large rather irregular box on wheels, emitted the chuketa-chuketa rhythm of the barn-dance while the men pitch-forked sheaves into the back, took away the straw discarded at the side and changed the sacks as they filled with grain from the small but steady stream down the chute.

One of the walks we used to take, though it was not the best for collecting berries, was along the railway out of Lifton. It was dismantled long ago now but there were trains, if not very frequently, on it then and I was always nervous walking along the track in case a train came, though we would have had plenty of time to get out of the way! Leaving the line and crossing a meadow took us to what I thought a magical place, where the river Lyd joined the Tamar. I'm not sure why this place made such a deep impression on me, though it certainly was lovely. Catching a glimpse of the flashing colours of a kingfisher there must have added to the magical effect.

Another place we used to go quite often, either by car or on foot, fairly near the confluence of the rivers, was the old water-filled limestone quarry where the other boys and Dr and Mrs Lea used to swim. There was a small beach, although it quickly shelved into deep-water, and all around the rest of the quarry the sides rose sheer from the water. I couldn't swim, and I don't think John could either, but Dr and Mrs Lea used to take us on their backs and swim round the edge of the pool, which was roughly in the shape a broad L, so that part of the trip took as out of sight of the little beach. Here the bushes growing on the sheer walls dipped into the grey-green water making it look impossible to get ashore if anything went wrong. This was quite exciting, but I was always rather relieved to get back on dry land!

One day when Dr Lea came with us to the quarry he led us to the entrance of a tunnel into a stone ridge, and we all went in. He had a torch, the one he used for looking down patients throats perhaps, and we went deeper and deeper into the darkness. Dr Lea said quietly "Keep your voices down in case the vibration brings the roof down." I was distinctly nervous even before he said that. The thought of being instantly crushed by hundreds of tons of rock, or of being entombed with little hope of rescue, was not one I enjoyed. At last we came to the end of the tunnel and made our way out again. The daylight was most welcome.

The original purpose of this tunnel was not apparent. So far as I could see in the light of the torch it had not been mined for stone or ore. Looking at an old map of the quarry workings which my wife cleverly dredged from the Internet, the place I think we went to, in relation to the water and beach, was the site of the magazine, though it does not show whether it was in a tunnel or not.

I have one further memory of this place. I was left to go exploring by myself while Mrs Lea and the boys, including John, did something else. I don't know how this rather surprising situation arose; perhaps they were swimming and I was judged to have a cold. I climbed to the top of one of the stone hillocks and sat in the sun, eating the plentiful wild strawberries.

It was, I think, the first time that I found conscious pleasure in solitude; I savoured it for a while before rejoining the others.

Dr Lea's house was just a few minutes walk from the few shops on the main road, the Arundel Arms Hotel and bar, and the church. I was taken with John to the Arundel Arms once or twice but we had to wait in a room in the annexe, across the road, while the grown-ups had a drink. On Sundays we all walked to the morning service; it was the same every week, a few hymns, unsingable psalms and tedious sermon!

The worst reason for going to the village was to go to the hairdresser. Nanny usually took me and I hated it for two reasons: the barber was full of teasing wisecracks, and his single chair was in what must have been rather a large room, but screened into a small cubicle by hanging sheets of cloth. The unknown void behind the sheets seemed terribly sinister.

On one trip to the village with Nanny, we stopped where our side road joined the main street to watch a team of airmen manoeuvring a long transporter (we called them Queen Marys when I was in the RAF years later) with a fully assembled fighter — Spitfire or Hurricane, I couldn't see which — along the main road. The buildings stuck out on each side to make a slight dog leg in the road and the wing tips were within an inch or two of the masonry as the men on the pavement shouted instructions to the driver. They got it through!

The left hand end of the Lea's garden contained quite a big area of grass, not regularly cut as a lawn, and on this space Mrs Lea taught us to ride bicycles. They had a suitable sized bicycle, presumably Patrick's in its time, with a luggage carrier behind the saddle. Mrs Lea kept us upright by holding the carrier as we pedalled forward. It wasn't long before I was delighted, if slightly alarmed, to find I was by myself!

I put my newfound skills to the test rather too soon. The lane beside the house, Darky Lane, turns sharply downhill above the entrance to the back of the house, and having ridden round the bend I found my speed increasing alarmingly. I forget now whether the bike had no brakes or whether I hadn't got round to finding out how to use them. The solid-tyred bike was juddering badly on the rough road but I managed to steer it round into the entrance, but fearful of turning too sharply I was close to the house wall. Unfortunately a granite gate post, which was not used, was set against the wall, and when my right handlebar hit it I came a considerable cropper. My face was a bit grazed against the stonework but otherwise I, and the bike, were pretty well intact. I have been back to the house recently and what I take to be the same gate post is still there but so far in from the lane that I can't imagine how I failed to avoid it!

Near where we learnt to ride, between the tennis court and the vegetable garden, there was a bank of earth, covered by grass, a bit over 3 ft. high and of similar thickness. I guess now that it was left over from levelling the tennis court. (Old maps show a line here but I don't think it was an old hedge because there were no rocks in it.) Patrick and Roger dug a tunnel through it and started to hollow out a chamber on each side of it, driving along the length of the bank from the tunnel. A little unusually, they let John and me join in this project and between us we made two surprisingly large chambers which we lit with candles. I suppose the grass roots stopped them falling in, which they never did while I was there, although the tunnel itself partly collapsed during the winter.

The Leas employed a part-time gardener, a rather bad tempered fellow who used to threaten us with dire punishment if we put stones on the grass. He had quite a lot of it to maintain with a hand mower and I rather see his point now! We used to steal young carrots from his vegetable patch and eat them after wiping off the earth with our hands. I haven't tasted a real carrot since!

Dr Lea's great enthusiasm was fishing and occasionally he took us with him. On one trip, after a period of heavy rain, he took us to Dartmoor and I remember him running along beside the swollen river, red with Devon mud, with his rod. He explained that he was fishing with a worm and hook as trout would take a worm under these conditions. I don't think he caught anything that time.

At one stage Dr Lea invited a guest to the house for a few days, for salmon fishing, I think. This was a most irascible older man who hobbled about on a walking stick. If John or I came into the room where he was he would wave his walking stick at us and shout "I'll give you the stick!". Thinking about it now, I suppose he must have been a rich patient or ex-medical school lecturer, or some such, that Dr Lea felt obliged to placate. This was before the National Health Service, of course. John and I were careful to avoid him.

Another time Dr Lea needed some minnows for bait and showed us how to catch them. In the workshop-cum-woodshed at the end of the house he put a champagne or similar wine bottle with a deeply indented base into the vice wrapped in cloth and used a metal rod and hammer to knock out the end of the indentation, leaving most of it intact. He took us to a rather large lake with a landing stage raised on piles in the water, put some bread and a cork in the bottle and fixed it to one of the piles well below the surface, with string. We went away and did something else for an hour or so and when he pulled up the bottle it did indeed contain quite a few minnows. He said they had difficulty in turning around to swim out of the small hole he had made.

Dr Lea liked making things. Once he spotted a promising piece of split kindling in the wood basket beside the fire. He put it on the mantelpiece and from time to time worked on it with his pocket knife until he had carved a splendid paper knife. I was most impressed!

John and I used to cut the fire wood sometimes, splitting some of the smaller logs for kindling with the bill-hook. John cut the end off his finger doing this, fortunately only a slice of the fleshy bit on the end. He did tend to be accident prone. I remember his howls when he trod barefoot on a drawing pin hard enough to drive it right in, and when on one of our not infrequent visits to Exeter on the train, he slammed the carriage door on his thumb. Another mishap on the same platform at St David's occurred when we had both been given red rubber balls. I kept hold of mine on the platform but John bounced his around until, inevitably, it went on the line. There was a great fuss until a porter retrieved it for him!

I liked going on the train and I was very interested in the steam locomotives – but I hated it when they suddenly let off steam with a deafening rush. The other thing I didn't like about the railway was crossing the line on the rather scant bridge at the same time as the engine went underneath. This happened when we got back to Lifton, or rather to Tinhay where the station was, sometimes in the dark. The great rush of exhaust steam, smoke and sparks billowing round the bridge as the train started to pull away alarmed me, although there was no real danger. I always tried to hang back on the platform until the engine had passed the bridge before we crossed it.

Towards the end of the summer of 1940 we all went on a long train journey to Padstow, and thence to Polzeath, where the Leas had rented a house by the sea. On some of our trips by train we had to change, not only trains but also stations, walking between St David's and Exeter Central, but this time travelling west, we changed at Launceston. At the mainline station Mrs Lea bought John a booklet and told him that I should share it, showing the things one could see from the train on the way to North Cornwall. It was called *Ace of Spades*, ring-bound with a shiny black cover cutaway in the shape of the carriage window to show a view on the first page. I was much taken with it and slightly aggrieved that I didn't have one of my own.

I enjoyed the holiday in Polzeath enormously. We stayed in, as I now suppose, a 1930s' villa, white with a green tiled roof. The smartly tiled bathroom and lavatory were very different from the older houses I was used to and the latter, smelling pleasantly of some disinfectant, not carbolic, contained the luxury of real lavatory paper. The owner must have kept a stock from before the war, when it became unobtainable and everyone used torn up newspaper – or, as I saw later in an old propaganda film, the pamphlets dropped by the enemy seeking to persuade us to give up the hopeless struggle!

The house was separated from the foreshore by an area of grass; sea-pinks, which I hadn't seen before, grew on the seaward edge and the area was inhabited by enormous green grasshoppers which were quite exciting. A flight of steps lead down to the beach and Dr Lea showed us all sorts of things to do with the sand. Apart from sandcastles and sculptures like little cars on which we could sit, we made complicated waterways to fill as the tide came in and 'volcanoes' consisting of a mound of sand with a hole down the middle joining to a tunnel from the side. Pushing one's hand and arm into the side tunnel caused wet sand to overflow, lava like, from the top of the mound.

Dr Lea pointed out lots of interesting things in the rockpools and he showed us how to catch the rather strange black fish, I forget what he called them, using a small piece of limpet flesh tied to a length of cotton.

A short way round the headland from the bay on which Polzeath stands was a beach of small gravel, rather than sand, where the waves were often good for surfing. The Leas had a children's surfboard, nothing like today's elaborate contrivances but a simple sheet of plywood cut round at one end. Wading out within one's depth and jumping onto it as a wave came gave a satisfying ride when one timed it right! In the same bit of shoreline the sea had made a shallow cave which we called 'Cowrie Cove' because we were told that small cowrie shells could be found there. I searched diligently in the gravel and did indeed find one. It was smaller than a pea but I was very pleased with it.

There was more excitement when Patrick and Roger found an aerial gunnery target on the rocks on the other side of the bay. This consisted of a wide strip of canvas with a cable to connect it to the towing aircraft. They took it to the police station to claim the standard reward of five shillings for handing them in.

I think it was at about this time that an incident occurred which, as John's friend, I found puzzling and disturbing. I was doing something on my own one afternoon when John appeared and told me he had some money to buy something, and would I come with him. I asked where he had got the money, seven shillings and sixpence I think it was, and he said he had got it from his mother's purse. When I asked, with some anxiety, whether she knew, he said "No", and I said he should put it back at once. But he said "No it's all right" with such assurance that I almost believed that he had been given permission on some previous occasion. Not feeling very comfortable, I went with him along the back road to Tinhay to a cobbler's shop, where we bought a cobbler's hammer and some nails. I couldn't see that the wide headed hammer had any advantage over the ordinary one available to us in the workshop, but John liked it particularly.

The next day I was again doing something by myself, when Mrs Lea came up purposefully and said rather stiffly:

"John shouldn't have taken that money from my purse. The goods have been returned to the shop."

I made no comment. She didn't seem to be blaming me, or not much anyway. Nothing more was ever said about it, but the incident left me feeling uncomfortable.

I suppose it must have been towards the end of the summer of this year, 1940, that I was sent to camp for a few days with a troop of girl guides. John didn't come and I don't really know why I was sent, although I have a hazy recollection of overhearing a scrap of conversation which suggested that it would be rather convenient if I were out of the way at that time. No one really likes to hear this of themselves, but it didn't cause me any particular distress or anxiety.

The camp was held in the grounds of a fine house belonging to a Mrs Holmes-Gore, if I spell it correctly. I remember the name well enough. I had been to the house some weeks before, Mrs Lea having taken John and me there when she needed to call about something. Mrs Holmes-Gore showed us all sorts of beautiful things in her living room, which I think was of open plan style, possibly with fireplaces around a central pillar. The one I remember particularly was the Pianola, which she switched on for us. I was fascinated as the keys were depressed as if by an invisible player while the cylinder turned behind its glass panel!

The tent I slept in was pitched away from the main guides' camp, which I don't remember ever seeing, presumably so that I could go to sleep early, while the big girls were having sings songs, or whatever girl guides do, around their campfire. A big girl was in charge of the tent and I think the other girls in it were of intermediate age, but all quite a lot older than me.

I didn't have much to do with them as they went off to do girl guides things during the day and I was left to explore the woods and amuse myself as best I could. After Lifton Park this wasn't a problem.

Sanitation was provided by a rather grim earth-closet housed at the end of a conservatory on the side of the house. Our tent was pitched on a strip of grassland between some woods and a river which flowed through, or bounded, I don't know which, Mrs Holmes-Gore's property. One afternoon I came back to the tent and found that some of the big-girls were bathing naked in the river. One, standing with her back to me up to her thighs in the water, had distinct pigmentation of her buttocks beside her anus, as many people do, of course, but I hadn't come across it and was rather shocked because she looked dirty.

The highlight of this camp came a bit later the same day. The girl in charge called everyone in our tent together and asked if anyone could think of a way to store the drinking mugs so that they were not on the ground. I didn't say anything but went into the woods to find two forked sticks, which I stuck in the ground outside the tent, and with a straightish one resting between the forks, onto which the mug handles could be threaded, my rack was complete. This simple structure, using the same system as my little houses in Lifton Park, was hailed as a triumph of ingenuity and resourcefulness and I was awarded a purple-red ribbon to pin on my shirt. It seemed pretty obvious to me, but it was nice to be noticed!

About this time Mrs Lea took John and me to visit a farm and, I've no idea why, I was given a red hen. It was just for me, not for both of us. The hen lived around the outbuildings and garden at the Lea's and I don't remember anyone needing to feed it. John and I felt sure she should lay eggs and spent quite a long time looking for them. We didn't find any for a long time but eventually four turned up on a barrel full of ashes in the farthest outhouse. They were judged too old by that time!

The garden had quite a lot of apple and pear trees, including a small Cox's Orange whose apples were really delicious, and Dr Lea went to quite a lot of trouble to lay them out, not touching, on sheets of newspaper in the loft. He said they would keep for months like that.

As well as the stone-built outhouses there was an old store-room dug out under the bank behind the house, just like the air raid shelter at Moffats. This dimly lit place contained a great variety of pots of old paint, garden chemicals, animal treatments and the like. John and I entertained ourselves once by mixing as many as we could together. Nothing happened but it seemed exciting at the time. When we came back to it weeks later it had set to a whitish solid with curious raised black spots on the surface. I was to spend most of my life mixing chemicals together to see what happened, though generally in a less random way than in this experiment!

Shortly before Christmas Mrs Lea took us four boys to see the pantomime *Where the Rainbow Ends* in Exeter; I think Nanny came as well, and we travelled by train as usual. I was impressed by the big Green Dragon, and delighted by the pretty girl fairies flying high above the stage on their wires. This was the only pantomime I have ever enjoyed. I was taken to one or two in London after the war, and in due course I took my own children to a few in Newcastle. I hated them all. My children did too!

I saw very little of my parents, or of my sister, while I was with the Leas. My father came once, but I am not sure whether it was to here or to Moffats. I remember only his bristly cheek as he kissed me goodbye and an overpowering smell of cigarette smoke. My mother came at Christmas bringing a few small presents but the main impression of her visit that stays with me is that she showed me her little machine for rolling cigarettes from loose tobacco. I picked up every cigarette end I could see, took the tobacco out and kept it in a blue pencil box. When I thought it was enough I presented it to her and she dutifully rolled a cigarette and smoked it. Years later she told me it had been quite an effort!

Two or three inches of snow fell around January 1941 which was, of course, exciting for us boys. We made giant snowballs by rolling them around the grass area beside the tennis court and threw snowballs. Patrick and Roger had a sledge which went well down the fairly steep slope of the banking of the tennis court. They let John and me have a few rides but were not keen to give it up for long. I went down to the workshop-cum-woodshed to see if I could find materials to make a sledge of our own. All I could put my hands on was a single piece of timber suitable for a runner and a square of plywood, the top of a tea-chest. These I nailed together with the runner in the middle, like an aeroplane, and took it back up to the slope. It was, not surprisingly, difficult to balance well enough to stop the edges of the plywood from digging into the snow and slowing down, but on the few trips when we did manage to keep it level, it went rather well!

After I had been staying with the Leas for some time I was moved out of the bedroom I had shared with Nanny and started sharing one with John. As I have said we got on pretty well, but he could be very annoying. One morning, just after we had got up, he said something – I don't know now what it was – which, although I think I was of fairly placid disposition, roused me to instant fury. I hit him over the head with my panda pyjama case, the first thing that came to hand. This would not have done him any harm had I not forgotten in the heat of the moment ('tis the truth I am speaking, Your Honour') that as well as my pyjamas it contained my collection of mineral samples! These were a couple of chunks of quartz containing scraps of amethyst, part of a splendid hexagonal crystal of quartz and a few other stones, all of which I had collected on walks on Dartmoor. John was somewhat stunned and his scalp was slightly cut.

I felt that the Leas might not be altogether pleased to hear that I had slugged their precious child with a bag of stones, occasioning actual bodily harm, but nothing was ever said about it and John got over it soon enough.

We all played board games sometimes in the evening before bedtime. I particularly liked one called "Buccaneer" whose board was a large map of the world marked out, as usual, in squares. Each player had a little ship to move according to his throw of the dice and the ships had cargoes which could be won and lost. I liked the tiny barrels and especially the neat little brass bars representing gold.

While I was at the Leas, although I have no way of knowing just when it was [except, perhaps, a very detailed examination of Exeter war records], Nanny took me to the dentist in Exeter. The appointment was an early one in the morning and as we walked from the station to the surgery we had to step over rubble and smouldering beams strewn across the road from the previous night's air raid. This was long before the heavy raids on Exeter in 1942 and in this case the damage was isolated. I remember sitting in the dentist's chair facing a large Georgian-style window, as I would now call it, each separate pane with a diagonal cross of sticky paper strips to reduce the risk of flying glass.

Dr Lea provided John and me with a vitamin supplement in the form of a thin rectangle of white, or rather yellow, chocolate which we were given every day after lunch. I don't think John liked it but I found it delicious. I'm not sure whether the bigger boys, Roger and Patrick, got any.

Eventually John and I were deemed old enough to come into their bedroom to listen to the story Mrs Lea read to the older boys each night. I enjoyed *Emile and the Detectives* and even more Arthur Ransome's *We Didn't Mean To Go To Sea*. We had reached the stage when Jim has been knocked down and taken to hospital, and the children, left alone on the boat, realise that their anchor is starting to drag on the high tide, when I was told I was leaving to become a full-time, that is holidays as well, boarder at Ardock. I didn't find out what happened in the story until I read it to my own children forty years later.

ARDOCK

I was taken to Ardock straight after lunch, feeling rather bewildered, but I was greatly cheered to find my sister waiting for me. She had made me a flag, the Union Jack, painted on a sheet of foolscap paper and fixed to a strong stick. I was very pleased with this and ran with it up and down along the relatively narrow lawn between the front of the building and a raised flower bed. Jill's presence, and the flag, changed the tone of what would otherwise have been a pretty grim occasion.

I was, of course, separated from Nanny at this point and I never saw her again. Strangely, I remember nothing about her appearance except a seemingly clumsy built-up shoe, because she had a short leg, and a green-brown dress she often wore with buttons made by rolling up a strip of the dress material. She was quite small but I have no recollection of her face, or her hair, or her voice.

My mother told me in later years that she had employed Nanny Walsh on the recommendation of A.A. Milne's family, since she had nursed Christopher Robin [as a baby nurse; she was not the Alice of blue dressing gown fame]. I remain puzzled at this, however, as Christopher Robin was born a long time before me, in 1920. I don't know how old Nanny was, but I suppose they could have recommended her after 15 years or so.

My move to Ardock was at the beginning of March 1941, as I now know for reasons soon to be apparent, and my separation from Nanny at just five years old caused me almost no difficulty, for she had taught me to do everything for myself – except tie my shoelaces.

The routine for boarders at this time was to put on our out-door shoes straight after breakfast in a lobby near the door to the yard. We were not given much time to do it, and my efforts to copy what the other children did with their laces were not very successful and my shoes kept coming untied. After a few days I had a chance to look at a bow and devised a way of tying one. This worked quite well and I have done the same ever since. Not many years ago my sister-in-law, Roberta Greenslade, happened to see me tying my shoelaces and remarked "what a funny way you have of tying a bow!"

About a fortnight after leaving the Leas I was invited to spend the afternoon there and someone from Ardock put me on the bus. I knew perfectly well where to get off, at Tinhay and the way along the back road to their house. Mrs Lea was there but John and the elder boys were doing something else. I don't remember what we did, but it was rather dull and she did not make me feel welcome. She had, to some extent at least, taken the place of my mother, often bathing John and me together. I remember her washing what she called my 'tail', and suggesting things for us to do – like cutting a patch of lawn with scissors on one occasion, and I was fond of her. Although Nanny had looked after me from day-to-day she was, I suppose, too professional to allow any sort of maternal relationship to form. Mrs Lea's coolness on this occasion puzzled and disturbed me.

When I had been moved to Ardock, Nanny, I presume, had seen to it that my *Marvels of the Universe* and the box with my small butterfly collection, both of which she had got me, went with me but my other possessions, my Dinky aeroplanes, Shuko car, teddy bears, panda pyjama case, mineral collection and cowrie shells (the tiny one from Polzeath and a big one I had been given) and some other toys were left at the Lea's. I don't know if it was Mrs Lea's off-putting attitude or the suddenness of my departure which prevented me from asking for the things I left behind. Towards the end of the afternoon Mrs Lea suddenly jumped up and said "Oh it's time for your bus. You'd better get a move on or you'll miss it ."

It's rather over half a mile from the Lea's house to the bus stop at Tinhay [as I now see from the map] and the idea of missing the bus seemed too awful to think about. I started out running but was soon hampered by a painful stitch in my side. I kept on as fast as I could, walking then running a few yards until the stitch was too bad again. I caught the bus quite easily but throughout my life I have been troubled by the anxiety dream in which I am trying to hurry to a vital appointment but am prevented from making progress by all manner of difficulties and obstructions. I wonder whether this was initiated by the journey to Tinhay; but perhaps everyone has that dream. I wasn't invited again and I wasn't sorry.

Some 40 years later my sister found out what had gone wrong. She discovered that Dr and Mrs Lea had retired to Cornwall not far from where she was living, after giving up General Practice and becoming missionaries in Africa. Mrs Lea told her that my father had not sent them a penny to pay for my keep which should have amounted to £100. Jill gave them some money – but a fraction of what the real debt would have been by that time.

Mrs Lea also told her that John had been killed in an unlucky accident when he was sixteen. It appeared that he had been running, on a floating walk-way, with some friends, out to a boat moored at Dartmouth. Last in the line, he had evidently tripped and hit his head, finishing unconscious in the water. It was a while before his friends realised he was not there. His body was later found on the rocks at The Cobb, Lyme Regis.

Not long after I started boarding at Ardock, there were no lessons or other small children about; it must have been the Easter holiday and I was taken on various errands the school staff of had to make. Presumably they didn't want to leave me by myself at that stage and there was no one to look after me. Some of these trips were made in a pony and trap which I found a most entertaining mode of transport. On one such trip, by car this time I think, several of the staff, including Mrs Hilsden, the headmistress met at the 'Ace of Spades' a roadhouse on the road towards Launceston from Lewdown, for a drink, on the way home. I was dumped on the floor while they stood around talking. A loud tweedy woman – I'm not sure whether it was Mrs Hilsden herself – started to tell what I came to call a 'shaggy dog story' and I listened. It was the one about to the enemy agent, German of course, whose carefully laid plan to land by parachute and blow up a bridge goes awry when his 'chute fails to open. He curses that the other arrangements for him on the ground probably won't work either. I thought this was funny – I still do, but I knew instinctively that it would be a mistake to show the grown-ups that I had been listening by laughing out loud. I was learning to be defensive.

When I started boarding at Ardock I slept, with a few other children of about my age, in a dormitory [marked A on the plan] which was mainly occupied by bigger girls. At this time we were all sent to lie down for a rest after lunch and on the one such occasion one of them teased me with the spot of light from a small mirror, or some such, in the sun.

It was in this room, perhaps two or three weeks after I arrived, that I was woken in the middle of the night by one of the mistresses. She pointed to the window, which faced south, (the blackout had been taken down) and said "You had better see this. That is Plymouth burning." We looked at the orange glow on the horizon; Plymouth was thirty miles away. Her speech was perfectly matter of fact but I went back to bed knowing that things too awful to think about were happening under that glow. I had been told of the difficulties of escaping from burning buildings by the Leas.

My wife, Roslyn, has found with her computer that the raid which caused the really big fire in Plymouth was on the night of 20/21 March 1941, which shows that I must have left the Leas at the beginning of March. I thought I was there for about a year, but it was evidently rather less

Shortly after this, I think, the smaller children were moved into another dormitory ['B' on the plan] on the other side of the hall. At bedtime we collected in the dormitory and were taken in a crocodile round the gallery

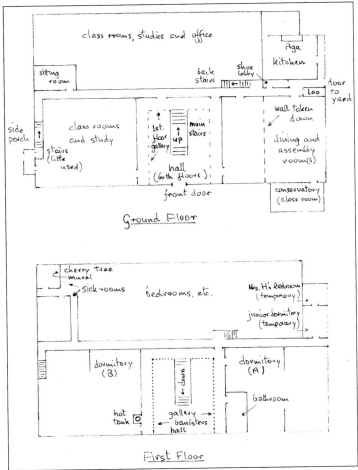

Layout of rooms at Ardock, drawn from memory and a little invention round
the back stairs. Subsequent reference to old maps shows that the building,
burnt down during renovation in 1960, was not rectangular but in the shape of
a broad T, stem towards the road, but the positions of the conservatory, side-porch
and out-buildings are essentially correct as is the missing corner. Ardock belonged
to the Baring-Gould family, noted for the eccentric Rector of Lewtrenchard, Sabine
(his paternal grandmother's maiden name), prolific author of novels, religious works
and several well-known hymns including 'Onward Christian Soldiers' and 'Now
the Day is Over'. He died in 1924; Ardock was occupied by his step-mother,
Lavinia, up to her death in 1921. In 1930 Captain W.N. Wright was living there.
(Kelly's *Directory*).

above the hall to a bathroom in the opposite corner [see plan]. This was usually done without formality and we were allowed to talk, provided we didn't make a great din. On one occasion, however, Mrs Hilsden came up the stairs as we approached and said loudly "There will be no talking. If I catch anyone they'll get this."

She held up a belt made of strips of leather plaited together in what I had heard described as Moroccan work . She walked beside us and put the rolled-up belt on a table outside the bathroom door. As she did so I turned my head to exchange glances with my neighbour in the line. I didn't speak; it would have been silly with her so close, and violent contact between that belt and one's body obviously something to be avoided. Mrs Hilsden snapped "I saw that. You're for it!"

We all carried on into the bathroom, where a few big girls were waiting to help with washing and tooth cleaning, and undressed as usual. The other children dispersed towards the helpers, but I hung about waiting uncomfortably for what would happen next. Mrs Hilsden came in holding the belt, called me over to stand on the bathmat, where she had plenty of room, and told me to bend over. Children and helpers looked on in silence while she delivered six vigorous whacks.

Happily, from my point of view, the belt did not prove as formidable as it looked. It must have hurt to some extent; she was a strong horsey woman (lucky she didn't use her riding crop!) but I have no recollection of pain. I think my relief at finding it was nothing I couldn't put up with obliterated any pain I did feel; I didn't want to be made to cry in front of all those people.

It was hard to avoid the feeling that Mrs Hilsden had brought her belt upstairs with the intention of beating someone, rather than improving behaviour in her school. I couldn't think of any reason why it should have been me especially, and I wasn't particularly upset by the strapping, which I regarded as merely another example of the oddness of grown-ups .

Looking back now I realise, however, that I must have been somewhat disturbed by the overall turn of events, because I wet my bed several times after we moved into the new dormitory, which I had not done before. I was most mortified by these accidents and very anxious that no-one should find out. It doesn't show much for the way we were looked after that no-one ever did. I quickly found an, at least partial, remedy, in the form of the hot tank in the airing-cupboard immediately next to the dormitory door, on which I could dry my sheet and pyjamas in the middle of the night.

The hall and gallery were left dimly lighted all night, and I was waiting for my things to dry on the tank when a woman came into the hall below. I didn't actually see her come through the door but in dim light, with all the outside doors covered by black-out curtains this was no surprise. She came, in any case, not from the front door, below and to my right, but towards me across the hall so that I saw her full face. She was certainly not one of the mistresses. She was dressed all in light grey, with some sort of jacket with sleeves, buttoned to the neck and a long skirt falling to the floor from a high waist in a narrow triangle. The style is called Empire-line, I believe . She was handsome rather than pretty, with high cheek bones, and her hair was tied up on the back of her head in some way I couldn't see. Her bearing was rather stiffly upright. I concluded that this woman coming in late at night (I had no idea of the time but everyone was clearly in bed) must be a guest of one of the mistresses, coming back from a dance. I'm not sure when, but I had seen women going to dances in full-length dresses.

As she came level with the stairs she turned towards them. Obviously I didn't want to be seen, but I was sharp enough not to move while she was coming towards me. As she turned, I ducked back behind the bannisters of the gallery, losing sight of her for a moment, but when I looked again she wasn't there. I supposed she must have gone beside, rather than up, the staircase and through a door in the back wall, but I was puzzled that she could have done it in the moment she was out of my sight.

If the incident was a bit puzzling the great thing was that she hadn't seen me. I looked out for the supposed guest at breakfast but she didn't come and I never saw her again. Naturally I didn't mention these nocturnal activities to anyone. I think that was the last time that particular accident befell me, and I gave the woman I had seen no further thought.

A few weeks later, unusually, I got into conversation with one of the big girls. Quite out of the blue, she said "Did you know Ardock is supposed to be haunted by a ghost of a young woman dressed all in gray who walks across the hall and up the stairs?" I made no comment. I have wondered all my life what my reaction would have been that night if I had had that conversation before I saw… whatever I saw. Subsequently I was to hear this description of the ghost many times.

Although Jill had been at Ardock to meet me when I was moved from the Leas', this was apparently by chance, though I didn't know it at the time, because she did not leave Moffats until the end of the school year, but had been invited to spend a week at Ardock to see if she would like to go there, as she did. I think the horses were a great attraction as she had been able to ride quite a lot at Moffats.

There were not many, if any, other small children boarding at Ardock through the holidays to start with, although this was to change later on, and I had to amuse myself, once again, for quite long periods. I was always keen to try to make things with the wheels with whatever materials came to hand. There was a pile of logs for the several open fires (there was no central heating, of course) in an enclosed area to the right of the main gates, as one came in, where rubbish was left for collection. I had some tacks or small nails – I've no idea now where I got them – and I tried nailing four fish-paste pot lids to a log. Not surprisingly, the tin lids buckled under my weight when I tried to ride this vehicle down the slope from the gate into the yard.

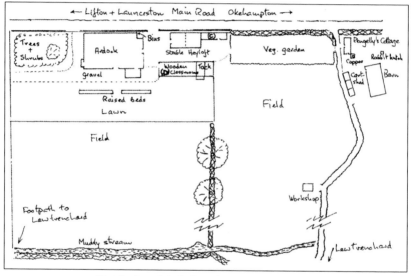

Sketch plan of Ardock and adjacent buildings at Lewdown in the 1940s, drawn from memory.

I spent a lot of time out in the fields which belonged to the school looking for wildflowers, birds, and of course butterflies, though I had no equipment to collect them. A bit later on I was given a copy of James Fisher's *British Birds*. This much prized volume disappeared from my parents' house in the 1960s. A field some way from the school building was bounded by a wire fence along the top of a fairly steep slope. One of the fence posts, made of angle-iron and set in a large long stone, much like the mast of a boat, had been dug up and removed from the fence – or perhaps left there as a replacement which had never been used. I found that by standing on the stone and rocking it from side to side with the 'mast', the whole thing would move very slowly down the slope. I did this for ages and nearly reached the bottom. A small stream flowed along the bottom of the rather large field in front of the school building and, in the corner where it came into this field, it had deposited an area of very soft mud which rather fascinated me. Somehow I managed to drop a silver coin – a florin (1/10 of a pound) I think it was – into the mud. I suppose my mother must have given it to me on one of her rare visits. I poked at the mud for days but never found it.

Occasionally grown-ups took me with them when they walked to the shop in Lewdown or to Lewtrenchard House where some of the girls boarded. This was about half a mile south of Ardock and the footpath to it led downhill through thick beech woods. One day we saw that many of the trees had been felled and a caterpillar tractor was working to drag them towards the track. One of the trees tangled with some others and I have never forgotten the sudden release of energy as the stout steel cable snapped.

I think it was at about this time that we were assembled and told that the North wing of the building, which housed the kitchen, was out of bounds for the time being and anyone found in it would be severely punished. The reason, we were told, was that work was being done on the Aga cooker and the men would be using asbestos powder, which was deadly. When the work was underway we saw the workmen coming and going to their van in the yard. They were wearing tight fitting suits with respirators; what we would call 'space-suits' these days. I find it curious that I have, quite recently, seen reports of claims for compensation by the families of men who had died of breathing asbestos dust in the 1950s and '60s rejected by their employers on the basis that the danger of asbestos was not recognized at that time.

Another piece of work I remember being done at Ardock, although I am again hazy about just when it happened, was to take down the wall between the two front rooms on the right of the front door, to make an area big enough for the whole school to assemble. A large girder (I would call it an RSJ now) had appeared beside the wall at the end of the conservatory (we used to have lunch in this when I first went there) and I wondered what it was for. I didn't see any of the work being done, which seems odd but I suppose we were kept out of the way, but when we were shown the new assembly room I inferred that the girder had been used to support the upper floor where the wall had been taken down. The rather nicely boarded floors of the two rooms had been joined by a strip of concrete where the wall had been, which I thought rather a rough job for a nice old house, though it was apparent that the two floor levels had not quite matched up!

My only recollection of the enlarged room being used, which suggests that it was not long before the juniors were moved out of Ardock, was for morning prayers. A low stage had been put up at the end of the room furthest from the hall, for the staff, and perhaps some senior girls to stand on. The hymn that day was 'Eternal Father Strong To Save'. The second time 'for those in peril on the sea' came round Mrs Hilsden gave a strangled squawk, jumped off the stage and ran out of the room. I think we had heard that a close relative (her brother?) had been killed in the Navy but my private view was that she was 'making an exhibition of herself ', to use the phrase current at the time.

In the autumn of this year, 1941, instead of lessons, one day we were taken to a local farm to help pick up the potato harvest. The rows had been ploughed so that the potatoes were on the surface, or covered by a little soil, and we went along the rows putting them into our sacks. I was working a few rows out from the hedge, not far from the corner of the field, with a farm labourer a few yards from me. I stooped to pick up a potato and suddenly found myself flying through the air to land, face first, among the brambles, nettles, thistles and similar inhospitable vegetation in the ditch beside the hedge. My attempts to move to a more comfortable position were thwarted by an irresistible force pressing down on my shoulder blades. A moment later one of the farm workers called out 'Spitfire' and, as I started to get up with the farm-hand beside me, the plane flew over thirty or forty feet above us. It is not quite true to say that I survived the war without a scratch!

Some years ago I recounted this incident to a German chemistry professor of just my age. He said he had had very much the same experience and had not been injured – until his hand was cut by flying glass when the French bombed his town after it had surrendered.

By this time a dozen or more children, all about my age, were boarding at Ardock and quite a few of them stayed through the holidays. We all spent a lot of time playing in the fields around the school. One game I can remember playing is ' pig in the middle ' where the ball is thrown back and forth between the two, or any number, of players and 'the pig' has to try to intercept it by catching it himself, then the person who threw the ball has to be 'pig'. I was always hopeless at ballgames and had disconcertingly long stints as 'pig'!

We also played 'Tom Tiddler's Ground' – a dividing line, the edge of a path or a line of sticks or stones on the ground, is chosen and someone is nominated as Tom Tiddler, usually by the formula:

Eeny, meeny, miney, mo,
Catch a nigger by his toe,
If he hollers let him go,
Eeny, meeny,miney, MO!

Each word counted off a child until the final 'Mo' fell on the chosen one. Tom Tiddler stood on one side of the line, which he was not allowed to cross, and tried to catch another player by touching them, when they had crossed onto his side, where they would sing, mockingly:

I'm on Tom Tiddler's ground,
Picking up gold and si-ilver.

The one he had caught then had to be Tom Tiddler.

The fairly small group of us, mostly girls, who stayed through the summer holiday of the following year, 1942, got on well together, though I never became particularly friendly with anyone. We used to collect black-berries, hazelnuts and wild strawberries, when we could find them, during the day and eat them for a 'midnight feast'. When we were supposed to be asleep we got out of bed, went round the gallery to the back stairs, across the yard and up the ladder to the hay-loft (see plan) where we had our feast before returning by the same route. We did this quite a few times, in daylight, but were never caught!

Lessons at Ardock were rather disjointed, taken, as far as I can remember, by a succession of young women. We made rather slow progress with reading, I suspect, and I don't remember any arithmetic, though I suppose someone must have tried to teach us some. Most of the time seemed to be taken up with 'nature study'. We grew acorns on top of medicine bottles of water and put chestnut branches with sticky buds in water to watch the leaves develop; I was interested in these experiments.

One young woman who turned up to teach us told us that we would be going out to find animal tracks and make plaster casts of them, which sounded interesting. She held out a bottle two-thirds full of water with a layer of white powder at the bottom, which she said was plaster of Paris for this purpose. I was much puzzled by this because I felt sure that plaster starts to set as soon as it gets wet, and that it wouldn't work after being kept in water for days. It didn't occur to me to say this; she seemed confident that she knew what she was doing. I looked forward to an expedition when she would try it out so that I could see whether I was right, but nothing was ever said about it again; I suppose she tried it by herself.

Another of the succession of nature study teachers gave us a lesson on the aquatic creature called 'hydra', and drew a diagram of this squid-like creature on the blackboard. For years I peered into ponds and ditches hoping to see one of these interesting things. I was about thirty when I discovered, from my wife, I think, that they are only a millimetre or so long

Not long after arriving at Ardock I was given some piano lessons. I learned to play 'Hot Cross Buns' with one finger. I can still remember the sequence of notes which started from middle C, identified as the note just to the left of the lock on the piano. Lessons stopped after the second or third!

We were expected to perform simple plays in front of the school, and perhaps a few parents, on occasions like the end of term. In one I played the cow in *The King's Breakfast*, a piece which I found rather irritating. I don't seem to have had any more aptitude for acting than for music as, according to my sister, though I don't remember it myself, during the performance the prompter said ' Speak up cow', at which I took off my cow mask, turned to the prompter and said ' I am speaking up' before replacing the mask!

On another occasion I took the part of the ' squander-bug' , dressed in a very tatty old doormat, to be vanquished by Brittania representing the Savings Stamp. In case savings stamps are unfamiliar to the reader, I should explain that one of the ways in which the Government raised money for the war was to sell these stamps at Post Offices. To the value of two shillings and sixpence or higher multiples of this half-crown, and bearing the figure of Brittania, they were stuck into a card until there were 15 shilling's worth, e.g. six half-crown stamps. The deal was that this would be redeemed for one pound ' after the war'. I had one or two of these, but I've no idea what happened to them.

In contrast, Jill was a star who could not only act but had a fine singing voice as well. I proudly saw her play a leading role, the Witch, in *Hansel and Gretel* and I remember feeling quite uncomfortable when she got pushed into the oven! I also remember her singing solos in Lewtrenchard church.

At Christmas of my first year at Ardock, 1941, my mother came and a stayed at the school for, I suppose, a couple of nights or so. She made occasional visits all through my time at Ardock, that is towards the end of 1944.

I loved to see her but her departure, all too soon, was always deeply upsetting. I think now that her own mental turmoil in having to leave us, to do what she felt was necessary as an Air Raid Warden in London, and later to serve in the ATS, (Auxiliary Territorial Service – the women's Army at that time) was communicated to me.

Name..Hugh Mac Bride........................ Term...Spring 1942......

Form..kindergarten... Age.5.years...11.months Average Age of Form.............................
 Day Pupils. Thursday. April 30th.
Days Late.......0............. Days Absent.....6.......... Next Term begins..Tuesday..April 28th.

SUBJECTS.	REMARKS.	
English	A most enthusiastic listener. Hugh thoroughly enjoys a joke and appreciates an interesting point.	J Woodroffe
Reading	Hugh is a little easily distracted but he is making good, steady progress inspite of it.	J W.
Spelling	—	
Writing	Good on the whole.	J W.
Arithmetic	He is very keen and is most capable at playing number games.	J W.
Nature	Hugh is most observant and interested. He has a genuine love of animals and plants.	J W.
Geography	Usually a quietly keen and interested member of the class, sometimes most effervescent.	J W.
History	—	
Handwork	Hugh has found knitting difficult although he has taken serious pains to learn.	J W.
Brushwork	He shows a promising trend for colour and design.	J W.
Recitation	Hugh appears to enjoy this class and is ever ready to take his part at reciting.	J W.
Singing & Rhythm / Music	Hugh has a little difficulty in reproducing correct pitch but he always works well.	E. Eaton.
Piano		
Gymnastics	Hugh's ideas are very original, he is rather heavy footed.	M.D.Chiverton
Neatness		
General Progress	Hugh is making very steady progress.	J Woodroffe.
Conduct	Hugh has settled down very well. He is a delightful little boy.	Margery Bray / Jan Ashden PRINCIPALS

My earliest surviving report from Ardock – Spring 1942.

One such occasion stands out in my mind, though I can't say when it was. After a flying visit my mother had to catch the train back from Tavistock. Somehow there was transport and I went with her to spend the few hours before the train was due. We went to the shops and she bought me a bottle of green ink, which I wanted for some reason, and then we sat on a bench in the park beside the river waiting for the time when she had to go. I have never again felt such bitter distress.

Not many years ago Jill told me that she too had loved to see mother but wished she wouldn't come because it was so upsetting.

In later years my mother told me some of her exploits as an Air Raid Warden in the Blitz. One stands out in my mind:

The Warden's Post was set up in the basement of Radnor House, a grand old building on Cross Deep overlooking the Thames and Radnor Gardens, opposite the 'Pope's Grotto' pub. (This was destroyed by a V2 towards the end of the war, killing the barman. My father was at home in Waldegrave Gardens about 100 metres away. The pub has been rebuilt now.) I don't think my mother was on duty when a bomb came through the roof and floors of the house and buried itself in the cellar floor without exploding. The wardens evacuated the building which blew up after an eight minute delay.

Not long after this my mother was out on patrol with a man who lived in the next road to Waldegrave Gardens, I have, fortunately perhaps, forgotten his name. They found the tell-tale hole made by an unexploded bomb in the middle of a main road frequently used by fire and ambulance services. Clearly one of them had to stay and keep such traffic off it while the other went back to the post (I don't know where the new one was) to alert the rescue services and get a bomb disposal squad. My mother took out a coin and said

"I'll toss you for who goes back to the post."

He just said "I can't". There seemed no point in arguing, so she stayed.

The layout of the road was such that to have any chance of stopping a vehicle coming from either direction with a torch, it was necessary to stay pretty well directly on top of the bomb. My mother told me that she was sick with fear but after a while she thought: I'll be the last person to know about it if it does go up, so why worry; which made her feel better!

Her not-so-gallant-companion, whom she pointed out to me in the street years later as he was still living in Orford Gardens, hated her from that time on and spread all sorts of fictitious gossip about her promiscuity!

Real courage, I think, is not so much a matter of not being afraid but of going on when you are.

The last serious raid on London, until such attacks were renewed, if on a smaller scale, in the early months of 1944, was on the night of 10/11 May, 1941. (L.G.S. Payne, *Air Dates*, William Heinemann Ltd. 1957.) The need for Air Raid Wardens having apparently passed, my mother applied, on November 1st 1941, for release from the ARP. She had been invited to join the ATS (Auxiliary Territorial Service, the womens' army) to do public relations work to counter a general suggestion that girls were joining the Services 'for the wrong reasons'. I suppose she was formally released by the ARP. In the ATS she had a choice of being given a commission straight away or of going to an OCTU (Officer Cadet Training Unit), the usual training for officers. She chose the latter to find out more about the Service she was to write about. During this training period the need for her PR skills evaporated because conscription was introduced for women (December 1941). Now the joker at the bar who 'knew what sort of service they wanted' was very likely to find himself elevated by his lapels and invited 'to repeat that outside' by a burly labourer whose favourite daughter had just been called up.

My mother trained instead as a Messing Officer and did this job until, I suppose, sometime towards the end of 1943. She was then appointed to a post where first class PR was a *sine qua non*: Campaigns Officer for the Army Blood Transfusion Service, Southern Command, collecting donors. I will say more about this later on.

Among the presents my mother bought me that Christmas was a rather large penknife with two blades and the inevitable tool for getting stones out of horses' hooves. Before I had had it long I was trying to cut a piece of wood in the dormitory when the knife slipped and I opened a deep cut across the middle finger of my left hand, just below the top joint. It probably needed stitching but I wrapped a hanky round it and didn't report it in case I lost the knife. None of the staff ever noticed the wound and it healed quite quickly, fortunately. Perhaps the jab mother had arranged for us both to have at the beginning of the war (TTTab, tetanus, typhoid, paratyphoid a and b), which was given to the forces, helped. I still have the scar.

Within a few months (Pearl Harbour was in December 1941) convoys of American army lorries were passing Ardock day and night. One morning we saw that the surface of the tarmac had been torn up by tank tracks. Once when I walked to Lewdown village with, I think, one of the mistresses, a GI stopped his truck and gave us a lift. He seemed a likeable fellow and he shared a bar of chocolate with us, a rare treat.

This incident, memorable if only for the chocolate, left a lasting impression on me. There was a lot of prejudice against the coloured GIs and to find that the truck driver was a cheerful agreeable fellow much like anyone else but for his dark skin was something of a revelation. Girls who associated with the coloured troops were frowned upon and the women's Services where particularly sensitive to this. Years later my mother, who finished the war as an ATS officer (with the male Army rank of Captain), told me that if any of the ATS girls were seen with a coloured man the codeword 'Burberry' was signalled to command HQ and the girl was immediately posted to another unit at the other end of the country.

In the school building at this time one was usually within earshot of a wireless set, from the kitchen perhaps. Apart from enjoying the stream of generally cheerful light music on programmes like 'Workers' Playtime' and 'Music While You Work', there was, I think, an inclination to keep in touch with any official announcements; there was always the possibility of a gas attack. As well as light music we heard the popular songs of the day, including those by Gracie Fields and Vera Lynn, recently and justly revived, like ' We'll Meet Again' and ' There'll be Bluebirds Over the White Cliffs of Dover' which matched so well the spirit of that time. There were also good songs from the shows like 'Pistol Packin' Momma' and 'She'll be Coming Round the Mountain'. There were also less worthy efforts to entertain us. The prize for the silliest, which sticks in my mind must go to the one which, with words run together, came over at first hearing as:

'Mairsy dotes and dosey dotes
And little lams-y-tivey
A kiddle-y-tivey too, wouldn't you.'

Eventually I interpreted it as, not very good, advice on animal husbandry:

'Mares eat oats and does eat oats
And little lambs eat ivy.
A kidd will eat ivy too, wouldn't you.'

It seemed to be quite popular for a while!

A seemingly tiny incident at about this time remains vivid in my mind. In the period before lunch, our class had been sent out to do some gardening, or something of the sort, in the front of the bed along the road, which had trees and shrubs further back, presumably as a screen. I was quite excited to find a chrysalis in the soil and I took it with me when we were called in to lunch. For some reason we went in through the glass side porch, next to where we had been working, which led up some stairs to, I suppose the upstairs landing, it is the only time I can remember using this entrance. On the stairs I opened my hand to show the chrysalis to the girl beside me. She slapped my hand and crushed it. I never knew whether she had maliciously destroyed what interested me, or whether she had not seen the chrysalis and thought I was inviting her to play some sort of game. I suspected the former explanation, and I now wonder if this incident contributed to the reserve I felt about some, if not all, of my classmates,

Jill has since told me that she thought that the food at Ardock was quite good, but I came to the table with some trepidation. Worst of all was rabbit stew, and only slightly better, rabbit pie, since one could eat the pastry. Irish stew, containing God alone knew what grisly animal remains, but at least lacking the cloying sweetness of rabbit, was another dish I would rather have avoided. We were not allowed to leave anything except bones on our plates but happily there was usually a dog or two knocking around to pick up the ghastliest specimens dropped surreptitiously on the floor. Other dishes included stuffed hearts, off-puttingly anatomical but actually tasting quite nice, and liver which could be quite nice but was often yellowish, powdery and full of horrible tubes. Corned beef, served with a rather basic salad, or as the meat constituent of some sort of potato pie or hash, was a prominent item in our diet which I found at least preferable to many things. Tinned luncheon meat was never far away; on a good day it was Spam, which I liked, and still do, but more often it was one of the shiny tasteless varieties. Occasionally the serving tray held slices of roast meat, greyish-brown with veins of slightly yellow fat, which was described as beef but we were all sure it was horse. It usually reappeared cold the next day, greyer and more tasteless, and shepherds' pie could be predicted for the day after that! Smoked haddock appeared from time to time but not a lot of other fish, which suited me, although I now gather that much of the country was subsisting on boiled cod.

The evening meal was served by teachers sitting at the end of long tables with eight or ten people down each side. For some time I was placed at the table in the charge of Mr Lazenby, who was the art master, the only man on the staff. I don't know whether he had medical exemption from military service – he showed no obvious disability – or whether he was a registered conscientious objector. He was an agreeable fellow and my sister has since told me that he was quite a good artist, signing his work with four letters L inside one another – his forenames were Liberty Llewellyn – but he had one habit at the meal table which caused wry amusement.

Usually the cook had put the right number of sausages, or whatever, on the serving tray but occasionally there was one left after the plates had been handed along the table. Mr Lazenby would then make a rapid circular sweeping gesture with his serving spoon which always ended by flipping the extra sausage onto his own plate; as he did this he would ask "Anyone want this last sausage? Then I'll have it." People tried saying "Yes I do," but no matter how quickly they said it they were always told they should have said so before!

Years later, from the end of 1949, I used to see Mr Lazenby on the bus, number 27A, when I was going from my parents' house in Strawberry Hill to school at St Paul's in Hammersmith. Jill told me he was the art master at Colet Court, the preparatory school for St Paul's, but he never recognized me and I never spoke to him.

At one stage, it didn't last very long, it was decreed that only French would be spoken at table. I was the only kindergarten boarder at this time and of course I hadn't done any French. After a few silent meals when I went without salt, water, mustard or whatever I would have asked someone to pass, Jill or another older girl put things right by telling me to say "Passez si vous plaît, le – comment dites-vous – mustard" or what I needed using the English word (please pass the, how do you say, mustard).

At about this time, I think, I had some minor ailment and slept in a small sick-room at the west end of the school adjacent to the main road. It was memorable for two reasons. One was the rather nice cherry tree which someone, I suspected and years later confirmed, that it was Jill, had painted on the wall opposite the single window. The other was that the black-out was not put up at night – I suppose the light bulb had been taken out – and the lights of the many passing lorries of, I presume, the US Army shone on to the wall with the cherry tree; a new experience for one who remembered only blacked-out windows at night.

Mrs. Hilsden always had a dog; I don't remember the original one when I first went to Ardock but when it died she got a pair of white Alsatians, beautiful to look at but temperamental, over-bred creatures. One disappeared fairly soon but the other, called 'Becket' was often in some sort of trouble. It had a fit and jumped out of an upstairs window, without serious ill-effect apparently, and it got into a fight with a bull-terrier we had all seen out on walks. I don't know if it was hurt but we gathered Mrs Hilsden made a fuss about it.

At Christmas of 1942 my mother gave me a carpentry set. These were not toys but real tools, a three-quarter inch chisel, mallet, tenon-saw and box-wood vice intended to be screwed to the edge of a bench, and perhaps one or two more things I've forgotten. I tried to hollow out a boat from a beech log with the chisel but drove it too far into the wood and never succeeded in freeing it. The saw enabled me to have a private war with ivy, which I had been told, not entirely correctly, would kill the tree it was attached to. I have the wood vice yet, still not fixed to a bench, now black with oil after many clamping jobs to do with car and motorcycle engines. It still makes a useful stand for an electric drill with a grinding wheel in the chuck.

From time to time we were taken out for walks 'in crocodile' along the edge of the road. I quite liked these since I could look for wildflowers in the hedges as we went by. Once, someone on the staff heard that a certain small shop had lemons in stock – a rarity indeed. We were marched for what seemed mile after mile to reach it. The mistress in charge did actually buy a bag of lemons after quite a long wait in the shop, during which I wet myself but happily nobody noticed.

Another expedition was to gather mushrooms quite early in the morning. Some were growing in the mushy rotted hay round a haystack and my shoes got saturated. They eventually dried out but the leather turned very hard and uncomfortable and they never quite lost the musty smell of rotten hay. It was a long time before anyone provided replacements – someone's cast-offs I imagine.

My mother had given me a butterfly book *Butterflies and Moths of the Wayside and Woodland*; I still have it. Many years later she wrote 'Xmas 1943' in the fly-leaf but it must in fact have been before that, 1942 probably. On one of her few flying visits, she later told me, one of the school staff told her that I was making unusually slow progress at reading. She insisted that I could read quite well and to make her point she called me over, opened the butterfly book at random and asked me to read the caption to the picture on the page. I read 'pearl-bordered fritillary' to her great satisfaction, but the test was flawed because I knew the name of the butterfly in any case, although my own memory of the incident is a bit hazy.

I did not have very much contact with the older children at Ardock but I remember watching the two older boys, Robin Howard and Reggie Selous, experimenting with making a rocket. It seemed that an elder brother or someone in the Services had sent one of them some cordite hidden in a tin of cocoa. It consisted of short orange cylinders about the diameter of macaroni. The boys rolled a single sheet of paper into a cone, put the cordite in and prepared to light the wide end. I supposed they knew what they were doing but felt intuitively that a much stronger casing with smaller exit (I would say 'venturi' now) was needed. My misgiving was confirmed when their vehicle burnt fiercely on the ground and I was rather sad to see this exciting material wasted. One of the boys had an air-rifle and shot a hole in the wing of a resting butterfly, a red admiral. It probably didn't do the insect much harm but I felt that more interesting and less wantonly destructive things could be done with the gun.

Towards the end of my time at Ardock, although I was to return for a short time, I was again ill with a cold or some such and was put in a different sick room, a rather dingy dark place. I had nothing to amuse me but there was a shelf with some books on it. I chose one pretty well at random and resolved to read it, something I had never thought of doing before. The book was *Strong Poison* by Dorothy L. Sayers. I didn't make anything of the plot, which is rather a complicated one for the circumstances, but I must have read it, or much of it, because I can remember the description of the judge's robes in the court scene. This, as I now know, is some way into the book when Harriet Vane is convicted of murder – to be saved from hanging in the nick of time by the intervention of Lord Peter Wimsey, who has of course fallen in love with her. I may not have made much of the story then, but I think it boosted my confidence in reading.

Occasionally, in the holidays, I and any juniors still around were given riding lessons on Top Hat, a gingery horse, smallest of the school's holding. I fear that, unlike my sister, I showed no great aptitude for this activity; I could never get the horse's rhythm rising on the stirrups when trotting. I have never been good at things like that: dancing lessons a dozen years on were humiliating, the girls invariably changing to another partner at the first opportunity, after an exasperated "Can't you keep the time?" Top Hat was, of course, well aware of my incompetence and had an infallible way of getting me off his back. I always fell for it, literally. After covering a short distance at a trot or lolloping canter he would stick his front legs out and stop dead, so that I sailed over his head to land in a heap on the grass in front. Remarkably, I never came to any harm.

The kindergarten class was soon to move from Ardock, although I don't think anyone told me before it happened, but I have one more vivid memory of Ardock from shortly before we left. I was alone in one of the fields not long after breakfast when I heard the drone of aircraft engines and very soon the sky was filled with wave after wave of aircraft towing gliders, an unforgettable sight.

HIGH TREES

Not long after I had seen the planes, which must surely have been D-day, 6 June 1944, with little warning as far as I was concerned, the most junior class at Ardock was moved to a 1930s, or so, villa called High Trees not far from Lewdown village. The house stood at the wide end of a fairly long tapering site with an open space in front of it giving onto a fine stand of mature beech trees and then mixed woodland down to the narrow end. The house is still there looking very much as it did then, except that the gate to the front path has been widened to make a drive round to the back of the house where the garages are. I have good reason to remember that gate. We were allowed to play in all of the area at the front of the house, but it was much more restricted than the open fields round Ardock.

The house had its own water supply collected under the floor from the roof and we had to pump the water into the cistern in the roof; it was surprisingly easy. The pump has gone from the front wall now. No modification had been made to adapt the house for use as a boarding school and it was rather cramped for the fifteen or twenty children and three or four staff.

A Mrs Morton was in charge, middle aged with grey hair, somewhat aloof but essentially agreeable. The other staff were younger women whose names I don't remember, if I ever knew them. Mrs Morton had a desk in an alcove of a room we could use and behind her chair in a corner was a tall cupboard on top of which she had a small wireless set. Notable on her desk was her fountain pen, a relatively rare possession in 1944 since they had not been obtainable since before the war. It was rather thicker than most and an unusual orange colour.

I suppose we must have had lessons at High Trees but I don't remember anything about them. We certainly spent a lot of time in the garden. One of the ways we amused ourselves when we first arrived, though we stopped doing it later on, was with organized stone fights. We divided into two roughly equal groups; I didn't think the division was completely arbitrary and there may have been some animosity. From a range of perhaps a dozen yards we each pelted the other group with stones – there were plenty about. Someone found the rusty end of a fair-sized drum and this disk of steel, jagged at the edges, was skimmed Frisbee-like between the opposing groups. Remarkably no-one was ever injured; it was not easy to see and dodge when it came your way edge-on. We called it the 'flying-jeep' after the military light aircraft of the time. This potentially lethal activity was conducted in full view of the house, but if any of the mistresses saw it from the windows they didn't do anything to stop it. I was hit square on the forehead by a stone, fortunately rather a smooth one, and I had to comb my hair a bit further forward than it naturally fell for a few days to hide the considerable bruise. After that I was, I think, instrumental in discouraging this activity and we stopped doing it. I was probably the oldest child at that time – I'm sure I was, with one other, later on.

While I was at Ardock my father had sent me a pair of Turkish leather slippers. They were yellow and had been too small for me when I got them but the leather was soft enough to turn the heel in and I used them like that; I was rather proud of them. Years later I heard that at least part of his work at the Ministry of Information was to put out propaganda aimed at discouraging Turkey from joining the Germans, as they had in the First World War. I wondered whether he had made the presumably dangerous trip to Turkey and got the slippers there, or whether he got them from a contact in this country. He never said anything about it and I never thought of asking him.

Soon after we moved to High Trees we were sleeping in the bunk beds in an upstairs dormitory. Mine was a top bunk just inside the door. One night a group of children further along the dormitory, it was four girls, went on talking quite loudly long after 'lights-out', which was forbidden, of course. I was getting rather annoyed as I wanted to go to sleep. Eventually the door, which had been ajar, burst open and one of the younger mistresses strode in. She must have been listening outside the door and clearly knew who the culprits were. As she passed my bunk she said "Can I borrow your slipper?"

I would have preferred to decline her request out of solidarity with the other children; there was always a definite feeling of 'us' against 'them', the grown-ups, but I lacked the moral courage. My muttered assent, though she had probably picked the thing up before I answered in any case, caused me a definite feeling of disloyalty. Further down the room bed-clothes were being pulled down and nighties up, a process I had seen at Ardock, and the the loud thwacks and howls which followed each muttered instruction to 'turn over' gave me he uneasy feeling that its supple Turkish leather made my slipper particularly well suited to the purpose to which it was now being put. No one seemed to hold it against me next day, however.

I'm not clear just when she arrived but a new girl joined us at High Trees. She was the same age and the same height as me, which made her a bit above average for a girl, and she was pretty with a fair complexion and red, or auburn, hair. Her name was Ursula Hurst. I don't think I took any particular notice of her when she came. I had, I now feel, rather withdrawn into the shell the of my own personality at this time and while I got on perfectly well with the other children I made no particular friends and didn't expect to.

One day we were taken out for a walk and, instead of staying on the roads, as we so often did, we crossed some open fields. I happened to be near Ursula when we both spotted a length of the black partly aluminised paper strip dropped by aircraft for the purpose of confusing the defence with false radar signals. Years later in the Air Force myself I was to learn that it is known as 'window'. We both knew that it was intended to interfere with radio signals in some way and we picked it up and formed the plan of putting it on the cupboard behind Mrs Morton's wireless. I think this was as much a scientific experiment as a jape to plague Mrs Morton, though the latter motivation was not entirely absent. We soon found a chance to put the strip on the cupboard with the wireless. Needless to say it had no effect, but the conspiracy started a friendship between us which was to bring a hitherto unknown dimension into my life – real human companionship.

Looking back now I wonder how Ursula and I knew about 'window'. I noticed recently in *The Times* obituary of one of the aircrew who took part, that it was first used by the RAF for the raid on Hamburg on the night 24/25 July 1943. I have checked this in that most informative compilation *Air Dates* by L. G. S. Payne, which stood on my father's desk at the Air Ministry where he was Chief Information Officer. I also learned that the RAF held back using it in case we came off worst if the Germans followed suit. In the Hamburg raid it was immensely successful, the defences were thrown into confusion and only 12 of seven hundred bombers failed to return. The Germans used it first in their attack on shipping at Bari, Italy, in December 1943, gaining considerable advantage, but it seems that it must have been general knowledge when we found our bit around the autumn of 1944.

Ursula and I soon started spending our time together, largely to the exclusion of the other children. We were out in the garden much of the time. I don't know what we did except that we enjoyed climbing trees, of which there were many, and being a little bigger and, perhaps, a little bolder than the other children, on whom we came to rather look down, there were some trees which only we could climb.

Not long after we became friends the children were assembled and addressed by Mrs Morton. We were told that the Germans were dropping antipersonnel bombs intended to kill civilians, or anyone who touched them. These we were told could have pretty well any shape and size and that if we saw anything at all suspicious we were to keep well away from it and tell a grown-up immediately.

Ursula and I decided that it would be rather interesting to see how people reacted to a suspicious object and we started looking round for something to make one out of. The garden hedge away from the road, which was where the 'flying jeep' came from, had been the repository for assorted rubbish over the years, and we found a quarter-pint paint tin and a more-or-less rectangular piece of shale which had clearly been cleared out of an open fire. These we attached artistically together with a bit of fence wire after punching a hole in the lid of the tin with a nail and boring through the shale with a pointed knife. With a coat of yellow poster paint the contrivance looked quite sinister.

We put our 'antipersonnel bomb' in the fork of a sycamore tree, near the pointed end of the garden, which only we could climb.

We now needed someone other than one of us to notice our device. Choosing a girl we took to be suitably gullible and obedient we attempted to point out to her a very interesting, if non-existent, bird in the branches of the tree not too far from our handiwork. This worked perfectly and she went straight to a mistress to report what she had seen.

The children were immediately banned from going near that end of the garden, as there was a suspicious object in the tree. We never heard anything about how our object was 'defused'. In these times, no doubt, everyone would be evacuated over a radius of half a mile while robots destroyed our paint-tin and clinker with a controlled explosion. I suppose the local air-raid warden, Home Guard unit, or perhaps an army bomb disposal squad took it away while we were in lessons. It is possible that one of the mistresses bravely climbed the tree to get a closer look at it, but people were pretty jittery about these things and I doubt it. Whichever it was, after a few days we were told that the end of the garden was now safe and Ursula and I saw that our thing had gone. I am sorry that my only contribution to the war might be regarded as being to the advantage of the enemy; but perhaps it provided a valuable training exercise.

Ursula and I seemed to think along very much the same lines; I don't think we ever disagreed and with her companionship the shell round my personality melted away. These were the sunniest times I had known, or was to know, for some years to come. I don't know how long they lasted;

we can't have been at High Trees for much more than four months altogether.

One day I was waiting for Ursula to come out into the garden after breakfast as usual, and indeed starting to wonder why she hadn't appeared, when I saw her being taken along the front path by two grown-ups I didn't recognize, carrying luggage, towards a black car at the gate. Although I was some way down the garden I could have called out and run forward in time to wave goodbye, but I stood in silence and watched them get into the car and drive away. She didn't look back.

I never saw her again, but it's not quite true that I never heard anything of her because I happened to see her name, assuming it to be the same person, in the Radio Times among the cast of a radio play at about the time I left school. I intended to write, care of the BBC, but I never did.

The period after Ursula was taken away was a gloomy one. When I think of it now I see the house, not from where I saw her go but from the corner looking across the front along the path to the gate, under a leaden sky.

No one got round to actually telling me, but it was by now clear that High Trees was closing down. More of the children had left, as had Mrs. Morton, leaving a dark-haired, thin-lipped, woman whose name I don't think I ever knew in charge of those who were still there. I don't remember anything else about her except that she had a dog, fortunately, for reasons which will presently emerge, one of the smaller breeds. About a week after Ursula had been taken away I got up from the breakfast table after almost everyone else, including the remaining mistresses, had left. As I did so she button-holed me and told me to follow her upstairs. She led me into the dormitory which had been vacated and the mattresses taken off the bunk frames. The black-out was partly in place so that the room was in semi-darkness. Here she launched into a tirade to the effect that my behaviour had, for some time past, been deplorable. This came as a surprise, no one had made any complaint to me and so far as I knew I hadn't done anything wrong. I was, however, aware that the grown-ups were unlikely to see the funny side of the anti-personnel bomb idea, which was weeks ago by now, particularly if there had been any difficulty or embarrassment about getting it 'defused'. While she continued rabbiting on, without making any specific accusation, I wondered if it were the APB thing that she really meant but for some reason didn't actually accuse me of. I decided that it probably wasn't. She finished by demanding:

"Are you going to improve your behaviour?"

Logical analysis of this question shows it to be of the type known as the 'forced alternative', analogous to the classic example "answer me 'yes' or 'no' have you stopped beating your wife?" While I couldn't have used this term, the logical impasse was clear enough. It was also clear that the woman intended to beat me whatever I said, and a flat 'no' didn't seem likely to make things more comfortable in the next few minutes. But 'yes', accepting her thesis, stuck in my throat. The compromise didn't really satisfy me but I settled for 'I'll try'. She held up her dog's collar.

"You'd better: next time you'll get the buckle end."

Far from being intimidated by this threat I thought 'you stupid woman; you must know that would cause actual injury and people aren't allowed to hit children with things like that.' Also the dog collar was a lot smaller than Mrs Hilsden's plaited belt. I made no comment.

'Take your trousers down'

Unbuttoning my shorts I let them fall round my ankles and stood beside the bed in my underpants, hoping but not expecting that would be enough; I had done what she said.

"And your pants. Kneel over the bed."

I complied, my arms outstretched across the diamond pattern wires of the bed frame, its steel edge cold and sharp against my middle. A moment later I was disagreeably surprised to find she could make it hurt more than Mrs Hilsden had done with her belt. I decided, however, that while I gripped the wires tightly with my fingers I could put up with her onslaught on my behind.

It happened that the evening of the same day was the time that some bigger girls came over from Ardock to help with bathing us. The girl detailed to wash me was nice, although I didn't know her, but as soon as she caught sight of the still lurid pattern of dark red tiger stripes across my rump she burst out laughing. I laughed with her; the strapping hadn't hurt enough to bother me afterwards. I feel sure now that this was the first time I had laughed since Ursula was taken away, and this entente with the older girl brought a heady moment of relief from my sadness. But she went on laughing so much while she washed me that I could not avoid the feeling that she was getting more entertainment from it than the decoration on my bottom really warranted.

A few days later we all moved to back to Ardock. It was apparent that this building was also closing down and many of the girls and staff had already left. Sooner or later, I'm not sure when, I gathered that the whole outfit was moving to a new building at Fairford, in Gloucestershire, where it was to be renamed 'Wings'. The juniors remained at Ardock for the time being.

We have a letter, or rather a letter-card, which I wrote to my mother from Ardock, saying we had 'all just come back' The postmark is clear as '1 OC 44' i.e. 1 October 1944, and this must surely have been sent during our short return to Ardock from High Trees. It is addressed to my mother (without her rank): A.B.S.D., Southmead Hospital, Bristol.

Letter-card from me to my mother, dated 1 October 1944, after we returned from High Trees and just before the Juniors moved from Ardock to Wings.

I was in an odd state of mind at this time, presumably because I was missing Ursula. If I had felt apart from the other children before, now I was entirely on my own. I was by myself a lot at this time and although I communicated with the other children from time to time it was as if there were some indefinable gap between us, across which we talked. One piece of information which reached me in this way was that the next oldest boy, I think he was called Charles, had being strapped before leaving High Trees. I was convinced by this that my punishment was not related to the APB idea, though I'm not sure now that my logic holds up.

Another bit of information (I doubt now that it was correct) was that the timber building along from the stable (C on the plan) was to be made available to us juniors as a common-room. It needed some furniture as it contained only a few old chairs, a solid fuel stove and a tall steel drum, intended presumably for fuel for the stove. This seemed quite a nice idea to me and I looked into the room, which was not locked, from time to time but nothing changed. After a few days the girl who had told me about the common room said that the idea had been scrapped because another of the girls whom I knew better than most – I think she was called Jill, like my sister – had peed in the steel drum. This seemed very odd; I thought her a sensible girl and there was a loo inside the door just along the yard. But if I was puzzled why she had done it, how she had done it was even more mysterious. To have perched on the sharp steel edge would have been agonizing and impossibly precarious. I could have done it easily enough by standing on a chair; could she have done the same? I had seen girls peeing often enough playing out in the fields around Ardock when the less inhibited ones couldn't be bothered to walk back to the building, but none of them had done it standing up. I suspected it wouldn't go the right way. I never heard any more about it and I now think that my informant had made the whole thing up. It bothered me at the time, though, and I wondered if the girl, Jill, had been falsely accused and perhaps punished.

During these temporary arrangements at Ardock the remaining small children, including me, slept in a sort of lobby which led to the room Mrs Hilsden was using. I heard she had put her foot through the ceiling while doing something in the roof and been slightly hurt. I was not unduly distressed by this news and I don't know if she was using this room because of the accident. But in any case she had to walk through our room to go to bed, probably without turning on the light. This gave me an idea. I soon found a tin of saddle-soap in the stable and, while no one else was about, spread a good layer of it on the floorboards outside her door, hoping she would slip and hurt herself. Disappointingly she didn't.

My last memory of Ardock is a short course of lessons given by a woman I did not know, in a building across from the stable (marked D on the plan). She went over the phonetic rules for English, such as that the sound of a vowel is lengthened when 'e' comes after the next consonant, as in 'at' and 'ate', etc. I had of course met all this before but her exposition was one of those learning experiences which make one feel 'why the hell didn't someone say that in the first place?'

She had brightly coloured charts with letters and numbers, she did some revision in arithmetic as well, and I have always wondered whether these were responsible for my associating letters and numbers (as well as days and months) with particular colours, although I have to admit that the rather pastel shades in my mind do not correspond with the bright colours of her teaching aids.

This gifted teacher also read us some poetry, including Southey's 'The Inchcape Rock', which I loved. I lost track of it for many years, although I remembered the name and some lines, if not the author (it's not in the *Oxford Book* – I mean the proper one selected by 'Q') and only met it again reading to my own children from an anthology. They like it too! This poem made such an impression on me that it is inseparably linked in my mind to this time in my life. I have reproduced it as an appendix.

WINGS

Two or three weeks after leaving High Trees I was taken to Wings. I do not remember the journey to Fairford, by train I presume, but I have a clear image of the building, large and rather square of red brick with Georgian-style windows. I took it to be relatively modern but the walled gardens and strangely complicated layout of the upstairs rooms, on different levels, didn't agree with that. It's last use, I was told, had been as the lunatic asylum and the local doctor had not lost the habit of keeping his hat on in the building after an inmate had bopped him on the head from behind the door.

The most memorable thing about the building was that the many upstairs rooms used as dormitories, approached by various staircases and landings, were distinguished by the names of English poets painted in remarkably neat black lettering on each door. Since I first wrote this Jill has told me that she did the lettering during the time the bigger girls were getting the building ready while I was still at Ardock. The rooms near where I slept were Herrick, Lovelace and Peacock but I have forgotten which I was in.

I didn't think there were any other children of my own age when I first arrived at Wings and once again I had to amuse myself in the large walled garden or in the open field which sloped gently away at the back of the building. I don't remember how far one could go in it. I must still have been obsessed with trying to make wheels because I remember cutting circles, or rather polygons, out of a piece of plywood I found by hammering my pen-knife through the wood to successively trim off the corners. I didn't get very far with this project.

I have no recollection of any lessons at Wings, or of where we had our meals, but I do remember very well the corridor which went past the serving hatch from the kitchen in a dog-leg shape. It was painted in institutional green (the colour I was later to learn is called light Brunswick green in the trade). At four o'clock each afternoon we all queued at the hatch for one round of white bread and margarine with some jam on it, nearly always the bright green variety which comes in large drums. (I was to meet that jam again in the Air Force!). This simple offering was always very welcome.

I don't know how long we had been at Wings when my sister, out of the blue, took me to Fairford and bought me baked beans on toast in a café. I have had many lovely meals since but none has ever equalled this one! I infer now that, for whatever reason, I wasn't getting enough to eat. Reference to her account of this time will show how, unusually, she could pay for this treat. I didn't see very much of my mother while I was at Wings except that she took me to stay with her in Salisbury for a few days. She was billeted in the Close of Salisbury Cathedral where I think she had an office. We stayed at the New Inn in the city for a few days. I remember the name because it seemed incongruous with the ancient beams and narrow passages of the hotel. While she was working during the day I was given the run of the Cathedral Close to amuse myself. I spent quite a lot of time watching the enormous trout in the Avon which runs past the beautiful lawns.

I now know that my mother had been working flat-out as Campaigns Officer for the Army Blood Transfusion Service, Southern Command, in the months leading up to D-Day. Her task was to arrange publicity for blood donors to set up a stock of blood for the coming invasion. She was given a target number of pints; she trebled it! Sadly it was after her death in 1983 that I saw a nurse, who had been on a forward medical aid unit in Normandy, interviewed on television. She said "everyone had a blood transfusion set, allied and German wounded alike." It seems they had plenty!

As well as her enormous success in collecting blood, which probably helped to save many lives, I feel that her account of some of the incidents during the campaign should be put on record. She took her team from town to town in southern England starting with a publicity campaign with posters, newspaper advertisements and sometimes lectures about blood transfusion. Some of these were given by the head of the Army Blood Transfusion Service, Brigadier Sir Lionel Whitby, but I think she tactfully discouraged him; his medically fascinating descriptions of early experiments, invariably fatal to patient and donor, had the audience reeling. A bandsman fainted through his drum!

Canvassing in the streets was done by ATS girls on the pavement while a loudspeaker car cruised along the road explaining what was happening and asking for donors. Some people made excuses when approached: the least convincing on record was "Eeh, Ah couldn't do that, me 'usband's got flat feet!" On one occasion the journalist and broadcaster Winford Vaughan-Thomas, one of my mother's team, was in the car when he saw a woman roughly push one of the girls out of her way. He told his driver to keep alongside her while he described her and said what she had done over the loudspeaker. She broke into a run and eventually disappeared down a side alley.

Part of her job was to get advertising space in the local papers, for nothing if possible, and her experience on the Derby paper and in Fleet Street must often have helped her to get on with editors, but never more so than in the Isle of Wight. Calling on the editor of the island's paper (the *Isle of Wight Mercury*, was it?) she found him distraught, hands black with ink, shouting "For God's sake don't bother me now. My compositor is ill and I have to set the type for tomorrow's paper!" Her response was "I can do that, I'll give you a hand." She was probably very good at it as she could do mirror writing as fast as ordinary. She took off her Army tunic, rolled up her sleeves and worked with him for the rest of the day and much of the night. They got the paper out on time. She was not short of advertising space in the next edition!

The blood they collected could be used in three ways: refrigerated and used as such, processed to remove the red cells and used as liquid plasma, or the water could be evaporated at low temperature to give plasma powder, which kept well and could be reconstituted with sterile water. Although their headquarters was the Army Blood Supply Depot at Southmead Hospital in Bristol (the building was standing disused in 2009 but was demolished for a replacement in 2010) the processing was done in converted farm buildings in the village of Chilton Polden (between Glastonbury and Bridgwater). The installation was camouflaged as a working farm, even to the extent of having an adjacent farmer drive the cows in and out at milking time! A row of centrifuges, built as cream separators, removed the red cells and the large vacuum pumps and refrigeration plant for the freeze drying process were housed in the old stables. The REME (Royal Electrical and Mechanical Engineers) officer in charge slept above them in the groom's room. He said that the sense which had woken the groom if his horses were in trouble alerted him when his machines needed attention!

My mother was more concerned with getting results than complying with correct army procedure and she frequently took short cuts. She was directly responsible to the Brigadier, Sir Lionel Whitby, and when staff officers rang up to complain about what she had done he told her to refer them to him. He would then say "She was acting under my direct instructions," often without waiting to hear what they were complaining about! Since he invariably out-ranked them there was no more to be said. She told me that once when she rang him up he answered with "Hello, what outrageous thing have I ordered you to do now?"

I have little doubt that it was Whitby who arranged for her to be given her 'Letters Patent', that is authorisation to use her military rank in civilian life, with the rank of Captain, when she left the ATS at the end of the war in Europe. This is interesting firstly because she had been promoted (we have an army letter addressed to her as Subaltern, the ATS rank equivalent to First Lieutenant, dated November 1944) and secondly because Captain is a male Army rank equivalent to Junior Commander in the ATS. I infer that this was because she was regarded as part of the RAMC (Royal Army Medical Corps). In my time in the RAF WAAF officers in the Medical Branch had the male RAF ranks. The Adjutant at my station, Sqn Ldr Wilberforce, used to say he was the only Squadron Leader married to a Squadron Leader (as opposed to Squadron Officer, the WAAF rank).

My mother never had the slightest intention of going round as 'Captain MacBride' but the idea amused her greatly, largely I think on account of the lines,

"She swooned and I think she'd have fallen down and died

If Captain MacBride had not been by her side."

in the *Ingoldsby Legends*, one of her favourite books. (The Captain has premature, if not actually dishonourable, designs on the rich and beautiful young widow whose elderly academic husband has just been found drowned.)

At Christmas of 1944 we were together for a couple of days or so. My mother was still collecting blood to support the allied advance across Europe. She gave me a sheet of paper and asked me to paint a picture on it. The picture was among the belongings she left when she died; it shows no great talent, I fear, but it is painted on the back of one of her campaign posters. It is reproduced here and shows how much she put into her job. (Like everything else she did. Always a good graphic artist, at the end of the 1950s she took up pottery and was soon making the 'Happy Mice of Berkeley Square', small figures of mice doing various things with apt captions of hers, or those ordered by customers. They were sold at the antique shop of Brown and Muntzer in Berkeley Square and are now collected world-wide.)

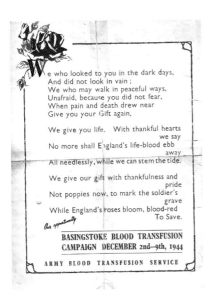

We who looked to you in the dark days,
And did not look in vain ;
We who may walk in peaceful ways,
Unafraid, because you did not fear,
When pain and death drew near
Give you your Gift again.

We give you life. With thankful hearts
we say
No more shall England's life-blood ebb
away
All needlessly, while we can stem the tide.

We give our gift with thankfulness and
pride
Not poppies now, to mark the soldier's
grave
While England's roses bloom, blood-red
To Save.

An opportunity

**BASINGSTOKE BLOOD TRANSFUSION
CAMPAIGN DECEMBER 2nd–9th, 1944**

ARMY BLOOD TRANSFUSION SERVICE

*One of my mother's campaign posters.
It was printed in green with red detail.*

I now wonder if she asked me to do the picture so that she had an excuse to keep the poster. I don't know why she should have needed one but she may have had some sort of hang-up about keeping her work. There were very few of her Express articles amongst her things (her first one that got her the job is there) and in the 1960s and '70s when we lost her on shopping expeditions she was usually in a second-hand bookshop hoping to find one of the 'pulp' novels she had written before the war to pay the gas bill, as she put it, under the pen-name of Roland Oliver. She never did and neither have we. She had no difficulty in selling these which she described as "the story of Cinderella over and over again."

My time at Wings seems to have been relatively uneventful, but one incident stays clearly in my mind. I was sitting in a downstairs room, some kind of sitting room, not a classroom, waiting, I think, to go in to lunch with one or more of the mistresses when a picture on the wall facing me unaccountably swung gently on its wire. One of the grown-ups said, "Oh! That must have been an earth-tremor."

I now feel sure that the cause was more sinister. In the Air Force I attended a training course for National Service and Short Service Armament Officers at the RAF Technical College at Henlow starting in January 1956. During a lecture on the conditions and regulations for explosives storage by one of the civilian instructors, who were all retired RAF armament NCOs, we heard about the catastrophic explosion of an underground bomb-dump at Fauld (which is in Staffordshire some 80 miles from Fairford) 'towards the end of the war '. He said that some or the bombs were showing the dangerous deterioration known as 'exudation', which occurs with ammonium nitrate-based explosives, when a crust of iridescent crystals forms round the filler-plug. These crystals are of a powerful and sensitive explosive, i.e. one which detonates very easily by shock or friction, which can initiate detonation of the bomb. The only treatment is to sponge off the crystals with warm water.

At Fauld a squad of six armourers had gone down to perform this task. They did not have long to go before their lunch break when, perhaps, someone tired of the tedious sponging process, took a shortcut, and tried scraping the dry crystals into his bucket (such compounds are much safer wet), or maybe dropped something onto the crystals. We shall never know because at this point they were evaporated at the heart of one of the biggest, perhaps the biggest, chemical explosion to happen on earth. Fauld disappeared in an enormous crater and unexploded bombs were scattered over a wide area. This much I learned at Henlow. Reference to the Internet (thank you, Julian and Kilmeny, my son and elder daughter) shows that the disaster occurred around midday on 27 November 1944. The bombs were stored in worked-out galleries of a gypsum mine supplying the raw material for a plasterboard factory, which was destroyed together with a farm. 75 people are known to have died and the crater, which appears to roughly follow the shape of the tunnels, is said to be three-quarters of a mile in its longest direction and one hundred meters deep.

The internet report suggested that there were 40,000 tons of bombs at Fauld. General Purpose bombs contain about 45% of their weight of explosive, probably the TNT and ammonium nitrate mixture known as amatol whose explosive power is greater but comparable to that of TNT itself, and other bombs in use at that time have a higher proportion (charge to weight ratio, CWR) of explosive. Had all the bombs detonated the energy release would have been equivalent to around 20,000 tons of TNT which is the estimated power of the atomic bombs dropped on Hiroshima and Nagasaki. In the event some of the bombs were left in tunnels in the ground and others, presumably from galleries at a higher level, were thrown into the air without detonating, but the explosion must have been comparable in power to those atom bombs.

A curious feature of the internet account is that an official explanation of the accident was issued in a 1973. We saw two versions: one blamed "Italian prisoners of war taking detonators out of bombs with the wrong tools," the other "an airman removing a booster pocket from a bomb with a brass chisel, causing a spark." Quite apart from the stupidity of suggesting that anyone who saw what happened could have survived, both are ludicrous. Anyone who even thought of taking a fused bomb, i.e. with a detonator in it, into such a place would have been locked up. This could not have happened accidentally because bombs are stored without their tails so that a detonator or fuse would be readily visible. The use of prisoners of war, even the docile Italians, to handle explosives seems remarkably improbable.

The booster pocket is built into the bomb and surrounds the detonator with a few pounds of an explosive more easily detonated than the main bursting charge, purified TNT or tetryl (usually known in the Service as CE, composition exploding). It is very unlikely that this dismantling work would be done by Service personnel or that there would have been any point in it at that stage of the war. But in any case all these explosives laugh at sparks; they do not, to use the technical phrase,' burn to detonation'. If you were to set fire to a pile of TNT, which would be difficult to do with a match, it would burn fiercely but there would be no detonation.

Why this rubbish should have been put out, I cannot imagine; I hope it wasn't to dodge compensation. The explanation which I heard at Henlow from armourers in the service at that time, eleven rather than twenty-nine years after the event, citing a well-known highly dangerous phenomenon, seems a lot more probable.

The reader might wonder why all of these bombs should have been put in the ground rather than dropped on the enemy. I think the reason is that a process for large scale production of the much more powerful explosive RDX (the war-time designation 'Research Department X' is still used in this country; the American name is less stuffy: 'cyclonite') had been developed and these older stores had been set aside and, if my information is correct, become dangerous.

My last recollection of Wings was that there was now a handful of children of my age mostly, perhaps all, girls. I have no memory of any contact with them. We were each allocated a small plot in an empty flowerbed along the wall of the garden. I was quite interested in this, but after some weeks we had been given no chance to dig them or plant anything. At this point, it must have been early in 1945, my mother arrived out of the blue and took me back to Lewdown. Years later she told me that she thought I wasn't getting enough to eat. I think she was right but I don't know how she knew – from Jill perhaps?

LEWDOWN

From Wings my mother took me, again I don't remember the journey, to live with Mr and Mrs Pengelly and their daughter Betty, who was three or four years older than me. They had a small farm, their house and some farm buildings occupied the corner where the side road to Lewtrenchard, which was the boundary of the Ardock land, joins the main road, so that it was the next property to Ardock towards Okehampton (see plan). Ardock was still standing empty and the vegetables in the kitchen garden, which was a strip beside the main road (see plan), had gone to seed. The onion flowers reminded me of those at the house at Angmering before the war. Betty and I would look for things to take back to Mrs Pengelly, but I don't think we found very much.

When, or perhaps before, we first met I had hoped that Betty would be a companion to replace Ursula, but the idea was short-lived. I don't remember consciously wishing that Ursula was still with me, but a sense of emptiness was ever present and persisted, to some extent at least, up to the time I made friends, with Malcolm Park in particular, in Canberra early in 1947.

Betty was fond of ball-games and spent quite a lot of time playing 'sevensies', when the ball is bounced against a wall and caught seven times before an increasingly difficult series of actions, like clapping one's hands or turning around, has to be done between throwing and catching it. To her evident disappointment and, I felt, scorn, though she was not unkind, I was hopeless so that we really had nothing in common and we didn't spend a lot of time together. In any case she attended the village school at Lewdown and I didn't go to school at all while I was there. This caused Betty increasing anxiety that I would be caught by the Schools Inspector; I don't know what she thought would happen to me if I were.

I was, however, required to go with Betty to Sunday school. I found these sessions very boring and the intensely religious atmosphere made me strangely uncomfortable.

During the first weeks I was there Mrs Pengelly took me with her when she went on the bus to Tavistock for shopping. I suppose she was nervous of leaving me to roam the fields by myself to start with, but I don't remember going more than about twice. I had a little money and the first time I bought a red dahlia in a pot. I was fascinated by the open trays of small items in Woolworths, none costing more than sixpence, including the pairs of tinplate disks with cork washers threaded onto a small nut and bolt which were intended for mending holes in saucepans and the like!

Before my last shopping trip to Tavistock, Mr Pengelly had given me a small plot in the garden to grow anything I wanted. In Woolworths I bought some seeds: sweet-corn and ocra, the latter I think because I wanted to see what would come up. Nothing much did, in the event, but the sweetcorn grew well. I also bought a reel of blue twine.

Although I was, once again, spending most of the time by myself in the fields, life with the Pengellys was agreeable enough. I certainly had enough to eat, including lots of cream. They had a small herd of cows and Mrs Pengelly used to make cream by heating a large enamel bowl of milk, filled almost to the brim, on the range to a temperature she judged with her finger, before setting it aside to clot.

The Pengellys had no bathroom, and once a week Mrs Pengelly would heat water in the 'copper' and transfer it to a small galvanized-iron bath put out in front of the range. I suppose everyone bathed in the same way. My mother came for a day or two after I had been there for a few weeks, though I don't know where she stayed; there was no room in the Pengelly's house.

At that time I had an enthusiasm for making miniature cranes from matchsticks and small bits of wood, mounted on matchboxes. With some of the blue twine wound round a piece of wire, they could lift small objects. My mother, who was totally non-mechanical (and made something of a feature of it) was amazed, and impressed by my ingenuity.

Mr Pengelly, as well as working his farm, had a workshop towards Lewtrenchard where he made gates and similar woodwork for the local farms. He took me down to the workshop one afternoon. Outside was a steel drum used as a water-butt which had rusted so that several small jets of water were coming from its sides, and when I touched it another appeared. Mr Pengelly told me to leave it alone, rather sharply, and I felt aggrieved as it seemed to me that the thing was pretty-well useless to start with. Inside the rather dingy workshop he showed me a box of nails, about 3 inch ones, and said I could amuse myself with them while he did some more work on a gate. There was a bench-vice by the nails and a hammer and I bent the nails round into loops to make a chain. It was quite a long time before Mr Pengelly saw what I had done. He didn't say much but was clearly far from pleased that I had wasted so many.

I can't now remember if there was a fall of snow that spring; perhaps there was because I found a sheet of corrugated iron lying about and attached a rope to the corners at one end to make what I called a sledge. I think I gave Betty rides on it, snow or not. Sometime later I was out watching a group of farm workers, mostly from neighbouring farms I think, working with some machine a couple of fields away from the farm. From the time of year I suppose they must have been sowing or preparing the ground in some way. After a while something went wrong with the machine and they stopped work. One said 'we need the sledge' and hearing this I volunteered to go and get it. They settled down for a break while I did so. I went back to the farm as fast as I could, pleased that my contrivance should find application in their work. The expression on their faces, when I got back, dragging the sheet of corrugated iron instead of the sledgehammer they needed, is still not a pleasant recollection.

Betty had a pet rabbit, a splendid big grey buck, and someone gave me one. It was not as impressive as Betty's but a nice enough rabbit all the same. There was a suitable box or ready-made hutch available, but it needed a run to attach to the front so that the rabbit could come out and eat grass. I found some timber, curved-sided off-cuts but adequate for the purpose, cut them to length and nailed them together, driving the nails through the side pieces into the end-grain of the end members. When Mrs Pengelly came out to see what I had done she said 'that's no good fixed like that', and produced some square section which we cut to fit the corners and re-nailed the planks to them. She was so obviously right that I felt distinctly foolish.

I don't remember having my gas-mask with me at the Pengelly's, or indeed at Wings, and if I did no-one encouraged me to practice putting it on as they had during the first years of the war. Raids had become quite sporadic by now and I suspect that many people had put their gas-masks aside out of the way. From what we know now this could have been a fatal mistake, particularly for people living in densely populated areas like London.

At the beginning of the war Churchill had announced that we would not use poison gas unless we were attacked with it, in which case we would reply in kind. At the time, I now think, he was more or less bluffing; the only war gas I know we had was mustard gas, actually a liquid, which produces nasty blisters on the skin; relatively high concentrations of the vapour can cause ultimately fatal lung damage. This was WW1 stuff, also known as Yperite after its use by the Germans in that battle. I know we were making this stuff from a letter I read in *Chemistry in Britain* (the monthly general interest publication of the Royal Institute for Chemistry) in the 1970s in which a chemist working at a plant producing it, in Liverpool I think, described a daring solution to a tricky problem by one of his colleagues. It appeared that the liquid was transferred to a road tanker by attaching an air pump to a vent at the top of its tank so that the resulting vacuum drew in the liquid. This took some time and, on one occasion, they left it too long and the mustard gas reached the level of the vent and was spraying out of the pump exhaust. He held a gas-cape (an oilskin garment issued to the forces similar to a sou'wester) over his head and shoulders as he sprinted for the pump, kicking the cut-out as he passed, and continued running for the shower discarding his clothes as he went! Remarkably he suffered no ill effect.

The Home Guard were trained to deal with it. My father was given a bottle of dark brown liquid (which sounds like pretty crude stuff) and told to put a dab of it on each of his men's wrists, which they were to remove by plucking, rather than rubbing, with absorbent material and then apply 'Ointment, Anti-gas'. My father replaced the 'gas' with Bovril; most of the men agreed that the treatment was fully effective!

I also know as the result of a curious chance, or rather a curious sequence of chances, when I was in the RAF ten years after the war, that the American Air Force, USAAF, were holding substantial stocks of mustard gas at the end of the war in Europe. At Henlow, the RAF Technical College, I happened to stay chatting with one of the instructors after his class on storage of explosives. Rather out of the blue he remarked that the Americans had been much embarrassed by their large stocks of mustard gas when the war ended. He had even heard of one case where they tried to burn it off by machine-gunning stacks of drums with tracer ammunition, but it does not burn very readily and they ended up with 'an awful mess', requiring many tons of bleaching powder to decontaminate the area.

After Henlow I was posted to RAF Bassingbourn as second deputy Armament Officer to Flt Lt Toby Wing, who had fought as air gunner until shot down and taken prisoner. Not long after I joined him he asked me to check something with the NCOs and as I came through the communicating door between our offices they were having their coffee and one, Master Tech. Cartwright I think, was saying that the wood in the road fork towards Cambridge had been used by the Americans to store mustard gas. I decided not to go there for a picnic and gave it no further thought.

Shortly after this Toby was posted to Bomber Command Headquarters at High Wycombe and replaced by Flt Lt Bert Tingle, a small Sheffield man, sharp as a razor. In due course Martin Walters, the other National Service officer, was demobbed and Bert was taken into hospital for prolonged treatment for a stomach ulcer, so that I became THE Armament Officer for six months or so.

During this time I got a call from the Station Adjutant, Sqn Ldr Wilberforce, to drop in to his office. He shoved a paper across the desk at me and said:

"Sign this."

I started to ask what it was, but immediately recognised it as a clearance certificate for land or buildings requisitioned in the war and now being returned to civilian use, stating that they were free of explosives or dangerous materials, which required the Armament Officer's signature. (I had signed a couple of these before, one for a local airfield used by the USAAF, where my squad of men picked up a large box of explosive stores, mostly rounds for the 0.5 inch Browning machine gun which, amazingly, armed all their aircraft ('Throwing squashed tomatoes at them' was my NCOs' description of this weaponry) The other was a large signals 'hut' defended by a very fierce goat which my Flight Sergeant and I just managed to outdistance to the gate after checking the building; not quite the spirit of the 'Few', I felt, as we ran for our lives.)

Glancing down the Adjutant's document I saw that it was for the wood in the road fork.

"Sign it," he repeated.

"Sorry, Sir, I need to check this one out."

"Rubbish, sign it."

"Sorry, Sir."

Muttering angrily, he grabbed the 'phone and ordered the MT Section to send a car for me. While I was waiting, I phoned the RAF Regiment Section to see if they had any gas detector powder – they hadn't.

The wood contained relatively small trees mostly with single trunks. The top cover was not very dense but there seemed to be strangely little vegetation between them, and the largely bare earth showed several rusty cans, like oil cans, some half buried. A static water tank held dark oily stagnant water, and the place was eerily quiet. I'm not sure just why but it gave me the williwaws.

I went back to the Adjutant's office and told him that I couldn't sign because I thought the place needed to be checked with proper equipment.

"Rubbish, sign the bloody thing," was his response.

I stood my ground, knowing there was nothing he could do about it, and left him growling to himself. That was the last official contact I had about the matter.

One morning six or eight weeks later I happened to arrive at the Station Armoury a little earlier than usual and met Flt Sgt Daniels on his way in, having just marched the men over from the barrack block and sent them to their places of work.

"Fraid the chaps were a bit slow off the mark this morning, Sir."

"Not to worry, Flight."

"It's difficult for them with those thirty extra men in the block."

"What are they doing?"

"They've been with us a while now, Sir. They're from 40 Group, Maintenance Command; they're digging bleaching powder into that wood up the road. Apparently it's soaked in mustard gas."

The stuff can persist for decades in the soil – it had already been there ten years – and it is far from improbable that someone digging, or children playing on the ground, would have been hurt by it: nasty for them and expensive for the RAF. Had it not been for a chance conversation at Henlow, and the sheer fluke of picking up a dog-end of someone else's chatter, I would have had no reason to refuse the Adjutant's demands, to save work I suppose, to sign the place off as safe.

Thank you, God; we got that one right.

But during the war chemists on both sides were preparing compounds which make mustard gas seem no more than a nasty nuisance. In the Chemistry labs at Cambridge University B.C. Saunders (For an account of this work see B.C. Saunders, *Phosphorus and Fluorine*, Cambridge University Press, 1957) was leading a group working on organo-phosphorus compounds (and other nasties). He was trying to make materials of the physiological type called 'cholinesterase inhibitors', generally known as 'nerve gas'. Cholinester (also called 'acetyl choline') is released at nerve endings to induce muscle contraction. This is controlled by release of the enzyme cholinesterase which breaks up cholinester (into choline and acetic acid for re-use). These inhibitors prevent this enzyme from working so that contraction continues uncontrolled (spasm) and death quickly ensues when heart and lung muscles stop pumping. The muscle that contracts the pupil of the eye is particularly susceptible, narrowing it to a pinpoint. To keep their work moving ahead as fast as possible the Cambridge chemists used this as a test for the effect they were seeking, exposing themselves to the compounds they had prepared. They used low concentrations, of course, but headaches, impaired vision and eye pain lasted up to a week; long term effects were a completely unknown quantity. I have heard it said that if you had gone to Cambridge you would not have known there was a war on. Those chemists seem to have got the message; so did my neighbour Terry Silk who was machine-gunned on the hockey pitch by a Junkers Ju 88 while a student there!

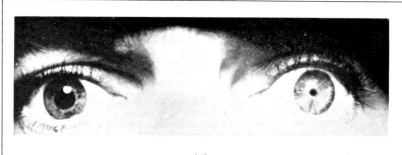

(a)

(b)

Pupil sizes. Left eye exposed to di-*iso*propyl phosphorofluoridate (0·008 mg./l.; 2 min. exposure): (*a*) 3 hr. after exposure; (*b*) 24 hr. after exposure.

The frontispiece of Some Aspects of the Chemistry and Toxic Action of Organic Compounds Containing Phosphorus and Fluorine *by Bernard Charles Saunders, Cambridge University Press, 1957.*
The Authors gratefully acknowledge the permission of CUP to reproduce this page.

In December 1941 Saunders reported to the Ministry of Supply that they had found a series of compounds which were probably viable nerve gases (actually liquids which evaporate quite readily), but it was (I guess) several months at least before their large-scale preparation of a suitable one, known as DFP, was worked out. I don't know if the process was used.

Meanwhile in Germany a group led by Schrader were working on compounds of the same type. I guess it was published work of A.R. Todd (Professor of Organic Chemistry at Cambridge at that time, later Lord Todd) on the interaction of phosphorus compounds with natural substances which gave the clue. The German group came up with three potential warfare agents, Tabun, which is destroyed fairly quickly by water, Sarin, more toxic than Tabun and similar to DFP but more toxic, and Soman, a bit more troublesome to manufacture.

At the end of the war a plant producing 100 tonnes per month of Tabun was operating and two plants for large-scale production of Sarin were under construction. What was Hitler going to do with it? Did he hope to stem the tide of the Allied advance? Probably not; war gases were to some extent effective against troop concentrations in the trenches of WW1, but are much less so in the open, fast moving fighting which he faced. Further, the soldiers had gas masks which effectively hold back these agents (at least until the absorbent, charcoal, is saturated). I strongly suspect that Hitler intended to use it for Vergeltung – revenge. He had already devoted substantial resources (to no military effect) to the V1s and V2s (V for Vergeltungswaffen: revenge weapons) which together killed rather fewer than 9000 people in England. A large scale surprise attack with nerve gas on densely populated areas like London could have made the V1s and V2s seem like a bad joke. A major strike by manned aircraft near the end of the war would surely have been shot out of the sky before it got off the ground (as you might say), but we had no defence against the V2s. With a payload of a tonne the killing power of one such weapon is frightening. I don't know the lethal concentration in the air of the German agents to humans, no doubt the Nazis did, but Saunder's figures for the less toxic DFP on rats gives us an idea of their effect. A couple of teaspoonfuls (one ninety-thousandth of the rocket's charge) evaporated into a fair sized room (36 cubic meters: 3 by 3 by 4m, say) will kill everyone in it for anything over ten minutes (well, every rat anyway). Dispersed into a hemispherical cloud at this concentration it would have a diameter of 220 meters. Air saturated with the vapour, as in the vicinity of any amount of the liquid, kills in less than a minute.

If a couple of dozen, say, of these (V3s?) loaded with Sarin had been scattered more or less simultaneously over London tens of thousands of civilians could have died gasping for breath. In the right weather conditions perhaps hundreds of thousands; an atmospheric temperature inversion with little wind, to which the Thames Valley is rather prone, keeping the warm city air near the ground, as in smog, would presumably be ideal. Even with gas-masks to hand, the first symptoms – dimness of vision and tightness of the chest – would probably not be recognised until too late unless a warning could have been given in a matter of minutes of the first strike. ARP wardens with gas-rattles?

Considering that not far short of 3000 V2s were launched between early September 1944 and the end of the following March, aimed at London or Antwerp, about 15 a day, a much larger scale attack might well have been possible. It would have to have been kept secret and our Intelligence Service, including Bletchley Park, might have been our best defence. But did Hitler envisage our victorious troops returning, with survivors unable to cope, to towns and cities populated only by the decomposing bodies of their loved ones? Revenge indeed!

Why didn't it happen? Hitler ran out of time; launching sites within range of London, 200 miles for the V2 and 150 miles for the V1, which might have been used to carry the gas although the payload was rather less and many were intercepted, were over-run by the Allies by the end of March 1945. One wonders whether some at least of the chemists and engineers needed to make it happen jibbed at the nightmare carnage to gratify a madman's whim. Or perhaps with the war clearly lost, the prospect of capture and retribution, surely hanging if the number killed even remotely approached what Hitler may have hoped for, made them drag their feet and make heavy weather of difficulties they could easily have overcome. Maybe Churchill's threat of retaliation had its effect. I guess we leaked the information that we had nerve agents to the Nazis to give that threat teeth. Hitler may not have been deterred by it but his workforce with wives and children might. The ferocity of the Allied raids on German cities can hardly have given the impression that we were concerned for the civilian population.

With Tabun and V2s in mass production it may have been a nearish thing; there seems little real difficult in putting them together. We shall probably never know, but if fear of retaliation figured in the equation, many of us alive today may owe their existence to the selfless determination of those Cambridge chemists (and I'm an Oxford man!).

Cholinesterase inhibitors have medical as well as lethal applications, which I mention because the first, treatment for paralysis of the gut after surgery and for glaucoma, were proposed by Sir Lionel Whitby, whose name keeps cropping up, in 1947. More recently they have proved effective in alleviating the effect of Alzheimer's Disease, which is associated with low levels of cholinester in the brain.

On the matter of intercepting V1s, Paynes *Air Dates* records that of the 9200 or so aimed at London, over 1000 crashed near the launch site and quite a few into the Channel. About half of the remainder were brought down, honours being almost equally divided between fighter pilots (1847 kills) and ack-ack gunners (1878). Barrage balloon wires accounted for a further 232. Many of the ack-ack batteries were 'manned' by ATS girls. My mother told me that hairdressers' quick, deft hands made them slick at setting the target's range, height, speed etc. on the dials of the gun's predictor. The girls loaded and aimed the guns but they were fired by the one man in the unit, so as to conform with the Geneva Convention's stipulation that women were not to be put in combatant positions!

It must have been about the time of VE-day (Victory over Germany was announced in the Commons by Winston Churchill on 8 May, 1945) that another 'refugee' came to stay with the Pengellys; I never knew why. He was about my age but came from a very much tougher part of London than Twickenham. He seemed agreeable enough to start with and I was looking round the farm buildings with him a few days after he came when he noticed four ropes hanging from the roof-timbers. He said he could show me an interesting trick with these and I trustingly let him tie one to each wrist and then to my ankle. Too late I realized I had been made a fool of, and ended up suspended a foot or two above the floor by each of my wrists and ankles. He left me to it, unable to release myself. Fortunately Mrs. Pengelly heard my calls for help fairly soon and untied me. This humiliating experience gave me a lifelong mistrust of seemingly well-meaning strangers, a valuable lesson no doubt.

This unpleasant boy had brought a powerful catapult with him and he was quite expert with it. My last memory of him, and indeed of my time with the Pengellys, was walking down the track to Lewtrenchard with him and Betty. He dropped back and started firing stones at us so that they ricocheted off the road surface and hit our calves painfully.

Within the next few days my mother arrived to take me back to London.

LONDON

Two things about the train journey back to London made a lasting impression on me. One was the amazing distance we travelled after seeing the first suburban houses and gardens before reaching the terminus. I had never been anywhere larger than Exeter since leaving London almost six years before. The other was the sight of the suburban electric trains proceeding without locomotives. We walked the hundred and fifty-odd yards from Strawberry Hill station (having travelled from Waterloo on one of these remarkable electric devices) to the house in Waldegrave Gardens, along Tower Road. The neglected flowerbeds beside the pavement, raised above the road level, were overgrown with rye grass scorched golden by the hot summer and dotted with brilliant red corn-poppies. I still think of Tower Road looking as it did that day.

Jill was still at Wings when we got back. The house was in a terrible mess and although my mother had made a start cleaning it, most of the walls, which were done with washable paint ('oil-bound distemper') were covered with a layer of grime; no cleaning had been done since before the war. Although I was not consciously aware of it at the time my mother was tired and run-down and the task of scrubbing the walls with sugar-soap, which made her hands sore (as during the war, rubber gloves and pretty well every-

The Bulletin

The, victim of Ted Scorfield's accompanying sketch, L. M. MacBride, was on speaking terms with Australia before coming here a month or two back to be Public Relations Adviser to the British High Commissioner at Canberra. At the beginning of the 1930's, when he was with the reorganised London "Daily Herald" as news editor, he got wind of the pending 'phone hook-up between England and these parts, and sent a cable to then Prime Minister Scullin to the effect that a confab between the Aus-

L. M. MACBRIDE.

tralian Labor P.M. and the London Labor paper as soon as the 'phone was available would be a good notion. A list of questions to be fired at the P.M. was prepared in the London office, but MacBride, who'd heard nothing meanwhile from this end, was at home in bed when the ring came. Scullin: "Good evening." MacBride: "Good morning." Then the impromptu interview, which gave MacBride the distinction of being the first London newspaperman to talk to Australia by 'phone. In 1932 MacBride changed from news editor's to foreign editor's chair, and was there till the beginning of the war, when he was asked to take charge of the British Ministry of Information's overseas feature articles department, supplying news, pictures and suchlike to the British Army, R.A.F. and Navy in all parts of the world.

JUNE 27, 1945

Above and opposite: *Two likenesses of my father, Australia 1945.*

thing else made of rubber were unobtainable), was clearly a daunting one. I was also not aware that she was considering separation from my father who was in Australia, although a few months later she asked me if I would mind if she did; at the time I didn't understand what she was asking and before I gave any answer, or could ask what she meant, she said "No, forget about it." Years later she told me that my expression when she asked me made her abandon the idea. Presumably she had inwardly made up her mind already.

One incident soon after we got back to London did, I think, give me some underlying idea that all was not entirely well with her. I was not very inclined to such games but somehow we got involved in a good-natured wrestling match on the kitchen floor by the back door. Suddenly she stiffened and sat up and said "you pinched me," which was not the case and I hotly denied it. She didn't believe me, spanked me and sent me to bed. I was not unduly upset, the spanking was nothing, but her not believing me and thinking me spiteful, a characteristic I had come to hate in other children, was painful. It was never mentioned again.

My mother had somehow acquired a cat during her last days in the Army, a dark tortoiseshell half-Siamese whom someone else had christened 'Uggly' (she was odd, but not ugly), known as 'Uggles'. She had the remarkable habit, when it was cold, of sleeping in the ash-pan of the old coke boiler, under the fire-bars so that bits of glowing coke fell on her from time to time, but she never came to any harm and didn't seem to notice! At about this time I was given a grey Persian kitten whom we called 'Spook'.

Before my sister Jill came back from Wings an ex-army friend of my mother's, Donald Robson, came to stay for a few days. He was notably fat but agreeable and took an interest in me and what I was doing. I had built a small glider from balsa wood and tissue paper. It flew quite well but the nose looked rather clumsy, made by joining the four members of the square section fuselage to a flat block. With minimum consultation with me Donald removed the block and extended the fuselage members to form a point. He did this quite neatly, but I was not totally pleased that he had taken it upon himself to change my design, though I couldn't deny that it looked better. I was never sure that it flew quite as well as before!

Also rather against my wishes he modified a model stationary steam engine which my mother had bought for me in a second-hand shop. The flywheel was carried on a shaft supported on a rather thin strip of metal, each end bent through a right-angle and drilled to form rudimentary bearings, and a thin tubular distance-piece between one of these and the flywheel controlled the end-float on the shaft. This design seemed to distress Donald considerably. The bearing area provided by the metal strip was far too small and wear was sure to result. In fact there was no sign of any wear, probably because the weight of the flywheel was quite small and the machine was only run for a few minutes from one week to the next. Nevertheless Donald, using a nail-file, widened the hole adjacent to the flywheel so that the distance-piece could be pushed through it to form a proper bearing. This clearly left nothing to take up end-float on the shaft, which didn't seem to bother him. The thing still worked but I didn't feel that he had improved it.

I am sure these tasks were done with the best intentions, including instructing me in the principles of engineering, but I suppose now that he was aiming for a longer term relationship with my mother. The day he arrived Donald brought a bottle of champagne and I was given the best part of my christening tankard full at bed-time. I don't think I realised that this was intended to ensure that I slept well, but their manner showed that there was more to it than just letting me join in the celebration!

It is appropriate at this point to note that monogamy was not part of my father's make-up, and, interpreting what my mother told me in later years, it seems to have been agreed at a fairly early stage, tacitly or otherwise, that total fidelity on either side was not an essential feature of their relationship.

Donald came two or three times during this period immediately after the war, and on one of his visits he brought a duck. It was a white Aylesbury, still in its feathers, and Donald sat in the open French window in the drawing-room with his feet on the step and plucked it, throwing the feathers to the wind. Quite a few blew back into the room. My mother was clearly unhappy about this but made no comment. At this time one was reluctant to show anything which might be construed as ingratitude for a gift of food!

One of Donald's visits coincided with the introduction of a new law that all bread must be sold wrapped. This meant, in practice, that one was handed the loaf with a wisp of paper round it. My mother reported that Donald said it was ridiculous as the crust of bread was impenetrable to bacteria. I was puzzled; wouldn't germs on the outside be just as bad? But I never said anything. Donald was a baker and knew what he was talking about.

Donald came in a fairly large car, petrol was still rationed and when he left he was anxious about having enough fuel to get back to Cumberland (as it was then). He asked me for the pint or so of methylated spirit which I had for the steam engine and poured it into his tank.

It must have been quite soon after Donald's visit that my sister came home from Wings. She was nervy, quick to take offence and frequently at logger-heads with my mother. I gathered that one bone of contention concerned a telephone call. Years later I found out what it was about. The caller had been Mrs Hilsden, headmistress of Wings, asking for Jill, who was out. Pressed by my mother to say what she wanted with Jill she said she was offering her a job helping with riding instruction at Wings. Mrs Hilsden, like, unsurprisingly, most of her staff was well known to be lesbian and my mother gave her a short answer on Jill's behalf. Quite recently Jill told me that she had no intention of going back to Wings, but she was angry that the decision had been taken over her head.

A further upset between my mother and my sister, in which I was not directly involved, arose when they went, at my mother's insistence, to see the exhibition of photographs of concentration camps taken by the liberating forces. My mother felt, as I now know, that it was important for succeeding generations to know why the war had been fought. My sister, shocked and profoundly distressed like everyone who saw those pictures, resented being brought into contact with such horrors. (A woman MP who went with a delegation from the House of Commons to see a concentration camp, Belsen I think, shortly after it was liberated, died of grief.)

Another reason why my sister was nervy at this time was that she had been entered for the 'Inter-BSC' exams in science at London University. Years later I heard that an army friend of my mother's, Brigadier Sir Lionel Whitby, head of the Army Blood Transfusion Service and her boss as Campaigns Officer (who before the war led – if from a distance – the team at May and Baker which developed 'M and B 693' the first effective anti-bacterial sulphanilamide drug; a few months later it may well have saved my life) had told her that with the teaching Jill had had, with no lab work, she had no chance of passing. She did indeed fail and her depression and loss of confidence lasted a long time.

Before long Jill had got a job as a technician in the Physics Department of the Paint Research Station at Teddington, working for Miss Tilleard who, I later discovered, was an international expert on the numerical definition of colour. Here she met a young man recently down from Cambridge, Mike Birbeck, who was employed principally to operate the electron microscope, and whom she ultimately married. The instrument is interesting; it was built by PRS staff during the war and was the second one to operate in this country (the Dunlop Tyre Company had a commercial Siemens instrument from just before the war). It was said that the magnet coils were wound by people on fire-watching duty on the roof, but I'm not sure how they could have seen what they were doing!

Curiously, I worked on the same instrument years later, when I left school before joining the RAF, in 1955. It was still working well (but the wiring, said to be Mike's work, was a nightmare, all black wires criss-crossed at all angles between the many terminals of the control panel).

Not long after Jill joined my mother and me in London we went to visit an old friend Phoebe Klitz, who lived in a beautiful house called 'Blue Shutters' at Bushy Heath. My mother's acquaintanceship with this remarkable woman has an important bearing on my family's story.

Phoebe had been the long-standing mistress of my mother's elder brother, John Hogg, who had served in the Motor Machine-gun Corps in the first world war, dashing about on a motorcycle and sidecar with a machine gun mounted on it. My mother told me that not long after he came home John had been riding a motorcycle and took a corner on the wrong side, forgetting momentarily that he was not still in France (or might he

Uncle John in the Machine-gun Corps

John's Bentley.

Right: *Uncle John at Blue Shutters in the 1920s.*

just have been going too fast?). He collided with the vicar on his bike and killed him, fracturing his own skull. Although forbidden by his doctors to get up, he insisted on attending the inquest, which accepted his explanation as a sad accident and he was not blamed. But, quite possibly by getting out of bed, he caught an incurable infection which could only be controlled by periodically scraping the bone in hospital. He lived for about 12 years like this during which time he met Phoebe whom, my mother said, he wanted to marry but she declined because she was twenty years older than him. He also set up the motor business in Great Portland Street with his younger brother, my uncle Cyril.

Phoebe had always been keen on knitting, making clothes for her friends for a little money, and when John bought a rusty old knitting-machine in a junk shop and got it going for her she never looked back. In what must have been an amazingly short time she became the owner of one of the smartest dress-shops in town, Mary Brown. Kelly's *Directory* shows that in 1924 she had premises at Mandeville Place, just off Wigmore Street, two years later at No. 98, Wigmore Street itself and by 1936 she had added Nos. 100 and 102.

Phoebe was an astute businesswoman and employed a brilliant dyer, a

Jew displaced from Germany, the origin or her own family over 100 years before. This man mixed colours which other shops didn't have, and special customers, including the Queen Mother, had their own colours which were not sold to anyone else. She also had a brilliant but irascible French fitter, Marcel, a law unto herself; no degree of social standing gave a client's bottom immunity from a jab with a pin if she didn't keep still. Phoebe made a lot of money and in the late twenties bought John a Bentley with bright yellow paintwork.

John does not seem to have been a very considerate driver, though apparently oblivious of sin. My mother recalled her, and his other passengers', amusement when a particularly discourteous bit of driving caused the other driver to shout 'Hog!' and he pulled over supposing that the man had hailed him by name!

In her seventies my mother, who married my father in 1925, told me of her annoyance, and I felt it still rankled, at John and Phoebe taking a hectoring attitude of high morality about her sleeping with my father before they were married, although they themselves had been living together for years.

Above left: *Paddy Charlton, Connie's first husband, in the Congo.*
Above right: *Connie with Topsy. When a leopard came out of the jungle and took her dog she had a rifle to hand, shot it and saved her dog.*

Connie on RMS Edinburgh Castle, *returning to the Congo after my parents Wedding in 1925. On the back she has written 'taken with Phoebe's camera'*

Phoebe was also friends with Constance, my aunt Connie, the eldest of the four Hogg children. She had married a mining engineer, Paddy Charlton, and went out with him to the Belgian Congo in 1921. She seems to have come back to this country quite often and spent time with John and Phoebe. My mother, who like Phoebe, spoke fluent French, although she never lived in France, went with them to Paris. John spoke only schoolboy French, but Connie was fluent in the Belgian-French of the Congo; in Paris her accent sounded course and ill-bred. It was as if, in London, a Cockney

Connie's and Whitney's Wedding. 1937.
(Postcard to Phoebe Klitz at
Mary Brown.)

girl had attached herself to these smart well-to-do people; taxi drivers and hotel porters would wink at her and pinch her bottom!

In 1931 Paddy committed suicide; Connie re-married to Whitney Carr, a detective in the Rhodesian police, in 1937 and remained in Southern Africa.

About two years after Paddy's death Connie was knocked off her motorcycle on a jungle road by a drunken official of the Belgian Administration, who did not stop, leaving her with a compound fracture of her arm cooking in the tropical sun. Luckily she was found before she was eaten, but her broken bone was reluctant to knit and she came back to London to recuperate. My sister had whooping-cough at that time but, brushing aside my mother's warnings, Connie came to see her, caught the disease, and coughed her arm apart again!

John made a business trip to America in about 1928 and on the ship met, and fell in love with, Elizabeth Kidd, daughter of Lady Mary Kidd, and married her in 1929 . Their honeymoon was a motoring tour in the Bentley; not a very sensitive choice perhaps. Unsurprisingly, Phoebe was very upset.

Unaccountably John and Elizabeth went out to Kenya to grow coffee. Presumably he could have come back for the periodical bone-scraping which had kept him alive for the past 12 years, but he didn't. Perhaps the hot climate aggravated his disease and he left it too late. He died in December 1930 leaving Elizabeth and their six month old daughter, Susan.

Cyril continued to run the motor business and, with my mother, kept in touch with Phoebe. He was always a keen photographer and it was thought that one of his films, left on a sunny windowsill, had caused a fire which destroyed the thatched roof at Blue Shutters. Films were made of nitrocellulose, which burns like fury, in those days; the original Molotov

Cocktail was a bottle of petrol, scored with a diamond to break easily, with a burning film attached.

Phoebe's business continued to thrive and when war came she was given an allowance of petrol to drive between Wigmore Street and Blue Shutters. On the way home one evening she picked up a hitchhiker in Canadian Army officer's uniform; it was standard practice to pick up servicemen and women in uniform, of course. He stuck a pistol in her ribs and told her to keep driving. Eventually he made her get out, drove the car at her and left her for dead. The car was found with the remains of her fur-coat stuck in the bumper, but there was never any word of anyone being arrested or questioned. It was supposed he was a spy. Phoebe survived the attack but her health was permanently impaired and she died in 1947 while we were in Australia.

On the occasion of our first visit to Blue Shutters in 1945 (we made two or three before we left for Australia in the summer of the following year) food was short and my mother was anxious to take something with us to help feed our three extra mouths, particularly as Phoebe was an invalid. She was delighted when she was lucky enough to be able to buy quite a large turbot at the fishmonger. We travelled to Bushy Heath on the Green Line bus, a service which covered greater distances with fewer stops than the London Transport buses. When the conductor came round, my mother asked for, "Two-and-a-half to Bushy Heath." As he punched the tickets, I piped up, "and one for the turbot." He punched a fourth ticket and asked for the additional fare. It took my mother and sister some time to explain that what I had said was a joke, concerning a fish. He was very angry and still wanted the money for the extra ticket he had punched. He didn't get it and eventually stomped furiously away. I felt rather foolish.

Phoebe's house was full of beautiful and expensive things. In particular I remember a pair of elegant ducks, a foot or so high, carved in rose quartz. She had been a keen gardener and could employ any help she needed; my mother said her garden had been beautiful before the war, despite the damage caused during the fire and by the following curious incident. My mother had taken my sister, then a toddler, to see Phoebe. She was playing on the floor near the open French window, which faced away from the farm land adjoining the garden, while the grown-ups were talking at the other end of the L-shaped drawing room, when Phoebe's dog came in and went up to Jill who remarked to the company in general "The dog" (she used its name, which I forget) "says there's a cow in the garden." No doubt someone answered politely, "Does he, dear. Well, fancy!" but nobody took any notice.

When they eventually went out into the garden a cow had stomped and munched her way through vast numbers of expensive plants. There seemed to be no way Jill could have seen the cow herself.

I'm not sure whether it was on our first visit after the war or the next one that Phoebe gave Jill a dress. I presume she had had it made for her; she was probably too infirm to have made it herself. It was very pretty, Lincoln green, or perhaps a shade towards lime, trimmed with red, black and white ribbon. Unfortunately Jill didn't think it suited her. I kept clear of any discussion about it, but I privately agreed with Jill; she didn't look right in it. My mother took the view that it was a lovely dress designed for her by a leading fashion expert, when dress material was in short supply, and she should be jolly grateful for it. It remained a bone of contention for a long time.

We used to go to the cinema quite often at this time, usually to the Odeon 'Luxor' in Twickenham, which stood on the corner of Cross Deep and Heath Road. The programme always contained a main film, a shorter second feature film and a newsreel. One of these, towards the end of the war with Japan, showed American soldiers clearing out Japanese resistance using flame throwers. One fired into the mouth of a cave and a Japanese soldier ran out, the back of his body a mass of flame. He covered a few yards before falling forward, his back still blazing. Perhaps someone had shot him. No one was very sympathetic towards the Japanese at that time; there had been too many stories, true or false, of atrocities – but that clip shocked me deeply.

Of the films we saw I remember *The Spiral Staircase* about a serial strangler in a large country house. We saw him putting on rubber gloves before killing the next girl, and his eye, watching her, in close-up, until it filled in the whole screen. I found it pretty scary. Another was *The Lost Weekend* about a dipsomaniac with DTs; his reaction to a mouse looking out of a crack in the wall was dramatic.

In these days of austerity not much actual food was wasted, we were too hungry, but food scraps like potato peelings were collected in a Government scheme to feed pigs, and bins were placed in every street. The 'pig-bin' in Waldegrave Gardens was fixed to the lamp-post outside the house of our neighbour on the left, Mr Raymond, a retired Navy man. We didn't see a lot of him though he was agreeable enough when we met. He was incensed at finding a corset in the pig-bin and questioned us closely about it, determined to detect the culprit, but I don't think he ever did.

Towards the end of that summer, 1945, my mother told me she thought

I should go for a holiday. She had already taken me on a day coach trip to Southend, which I don't remember enjoying particularly, but this time she said she couldn't go herself and had arranged for me to join a family who had booked a flat in Birchington. They were not friends or acquaintances; I suppose now that she answered an ad in the local paper. There were three or four children and their mother; I don't remember if their father was there. The children teased me a bit but mostly ignored me. We went to a swimming bath – I don't remember going in the sea – but as they could swim and I couldn't I didn't enjoy it much. I did like our expeditions to the Ice Cream Parlour where the 'knickerbocker glory' and similar delights were to be had, and I enjoyed walking along the foreshore and seeing the impressive silhouette of Reculver Towers in the sunset. There was a radiogram in the flat and the children played Ravel's 'Bolero' on it several times. Curiously, and to my wife's scorn, I have a nostalgic liking for the piece ever since!

I formed an attachment for another piece of music at this time. Somewhere knocking about the house I found a clockwork ('wind-up') gramophone with a record in it. It was a white children's model, my sister's presumably, and the pickup was broken. I took it to pieces and found that the sound diaphragm, attached to the needle, should have been supported between two rubber rings, but these had perished and fallen apart. I put them together by wrapping sticky tape (paper of course, this was long before Sellotape etc.) round them and reassembled the pickup. I was gratified to find that it now played quite well. The record was Saint-Saens' *Danse Macabre*.

Having seen how simple the device was I experimented with holding other things in the groove of the record; even the corner of a piece of cellophane produced recognizable music!

Someone had given me an old fishing-rod and reel and I spent quite a lot of time float-fishing, usually in the Thames at Radnor Gardens a few minutes walk from our house. I got into conversation with a fellow angler, a young man of 19 who was a stoker in the Royal Navy on some kind of extended leave. I always knew him as 'Bradley', his surname. We became friends and quite often went fishing together. He came to our house a few times and delighted my mother with some of his collection of George Formby records. I remember 'Delivering the Morning Milk', which is rather rude. I used to go with him to fish at Teddington Lock and in the gravel pits of the Ham River Grit Company in the wilderness between Teddington and Ham.

On one trip we went fishing in the lock 'cut', a deep channel for tugs and barges to approach the lock. Moored near us was a raft of five or six big square section baulks of timber lashed corner to corner with steel cable. These were used as fenders for barges to moor against while waiting to go into the lock. I was sitting between Bradley and the raft re-baiting my hook when one of a group of small boys, who had been fooling about near the raft, fell into the cut. Unable to swim, he was threshing about furiously in the water and in imminent danger of going under the raft. Bradley covered the few yards to reach him like greased lightning and pulled him out. In doing so he had run through my line and driven my hook full depth into my hand. Fish-hooks are, of course, barbed and not easy to get out, but he did it without hurting me much.

My mother remembered another incident better than I do. Neither Bradley nor I had a watch and we lost track of time and didn't appear at home at the arranged time. After waiting an hour or so my mother 'phoned the police. The man she spoke to made little effort to conceal his incredulity that she had let me go out in such circumstances with a virtual stranger. As an ex-crime reporter she took the point. She was very relieved, and Bradley was very apologetic, when we finally appeared!

Food was, of course, rationed and in short supply. Fish was often available as with the turbot, but it was usually cod which I didn't like. Most of the fish-mongers had brilliant red hunks of whale meat on their slabs but it was said to be fishy and we never tried it. Quite often we went to the restaurants in Twickenham for lunch. There was the government sponsored Civic Restaurant – they were all painted grey – where you could get a meal for a shilling but it was nearly always boiled cod, undercooked, pale blue and translucent. That left a choice between the Hygienic Bakery in York St. (just before one reached the showrooms of the Gas, Light and Coke Company), where the food was rather plain, or the Spinning Wheel (an example of which stood inside the small bull's-eye panes of its window looking over Cross Deep towards the Luxor cinema) where the food was nice but served in distinctly small portions.

Another possibility was the King's Head, in the corner of Twickenham Junction where the side road leads down to the slipway opposite Eel Pie Island; the chain-ferry would take you across for a penny. Here salads could be bought at the bar, which I was not allowed into, but we could eat and have a drink on the terrace behind the pub, quite near the river. I liked to come here because if I walked down to the slipway while my mother was finishing her drink, or smoking a cigarette, I often saw one or more of a family of cats swimming in the river, and occasionally coming ashore on the slipway. Their coats appeared to be dark brown, or perhaps mottled tortoiseshell (like Uggles), but I never saw one when it was not saturated with water, and I never got very near one. I suppose they lived on the island and caught fish in the river

Ration books were issued from a small office in Queens Road, just off Twickenham Junction, beside the Fire Station and I remember queuing for ages with my mother to get them.

Occasionally a flat wooden box would arrive by post. These contained glacé cherries, raisins, and almonds, a welcome addition which my father arranged to be sent from Australia.

In September of 1945 I started at Tower House School in East Sheen. I suppose my parents would have liked me to go to Colet Court, the preparatory school for St Paul's where my father went, and two MacBrides before him, although the previous one had been his stepfather. They didn't trouble to set an entrance test but recommended Tower House. I didn't make a very good start. In the first lesson we were told to write something, which required a dip-pen, and ink from the little inkwell let into the corner of the desk, unfamiliar equipment. I had been taught, and my last lesson in school must have been a year or so before, to write script with individual letters, and I started the task in this way. The boy sitting next to me whispered "write it, don't print it." I suppose it was kind of him, really. I looked to see what he and the other boys were doing and saw that they were keeping their pens on the paper for each word. I proceeded to do the same using the letter shapes I was familiar with. The result was horrific, and it was to be several years before I managed to make my writing reasonably neat (by partly reverting to the original script), even though I was to do extra copybook work at Tower House. It was still pretty awful when I was in the RAF, after A-levels, as I see from notebooks I still have.

The Headmaster of Tower House was a Mr Edwards, late fifties or so, rather stout and with unattractively loose lips. Soon after I started there my mother invited him to dinner at Waldegrave Gardens. I suppose she felt this would give me some advantage. What could she serve for dinner? After a rather desperate search she managed to get a lobster. It proved to be the one thing Mr. Edwards couldn't eat! I forget what happened at the meal, but she didn't repeat that invitation.

The most notable master at Tower House was a Mr Robinson, known as 'Robo', who taught English and French. In many ways he was an excellent school master but he had a regrettable inclination to beat his pupils with a gym shoe (only Mr Edwards was empowered to use the cane) but he made no secret of enjoying it. He would sometimes ask each boy round the form if he had beaten him yet. His method of teaching French vocabulary was quite effective. We were given a small book of French words divided into groups of 10 and every other day, including Saturday when we worked to 12:30, we were required to learn one block and answer a test at the beginning of the next lesson. The gym shoe was waiting for anyone who scored less than eight-and-a-half out of 10; I don't remember that anyone ever did.

Robo used to run a club for the boys one evening a week. At first I was too scared of him to go but after a few weeks I went back to the school in the evening to see what it was like. He organized all sorts of board games and the like and I enjoyed it very much and always went thereafter.

Travelling to Tower House was quite convenient: the 'Southern Electric' train from Strawberry Hill to Mortlake took just over 15 minutes and seven or eight minutes walk up Sheen Lane brought one to the school.

Robo also organized trips on school-day afternoons to see things of interest. I don't remember which of these were at this time, before we went to Australia, and which were after I returned to Tower House in 1948, but altogether we went to the films of *Henry the Fifth* and *Scot of the Antarctic* which we saw at the Odeon cinema at the junction of Sheen Lane and Upper Richmond Road, as well as looking over the sailing ship *Palmir* (at Greenwich, I think), going to the Royal Mint, the Sunday Graphic and Watney's brewery at Mortlake. I was fascinated by the production processes I saw, particularly the semi-mechanised construction of wooden beer barrels at the brewery. Before each of these trips Robo would assemble the boys and ask, "Does anyone want to go to the lavatory? Speak now or forever hold your peace." I was the only boy who ever laughed.

Robo was not a particularly big man but strong and wiry. He had been a physical training instructor in the Army and he played at scrum-half for London-Welsh. He also took us for PT, driving us for mile after mile on cross-country runs in Richmond Park, the Sheen Gate of which is quite near the school. I could run for miles for years afterwards, which was a help at the RAF OCTU (Officer Cadet Training Unit).

Tower House was also keen to increase our English vocabulary. Every night we had to take the next ten words from a list called 'The Red Spelling Book', find out their meaning and write them down on a sheet of paper to be handed-in at the first lesson, when we were given a spelling test on what we had learnt. There was a cup for the best score each week. I won it once!

We were taught Latin by the Headmaster, Mr Edwards, and our homework was mostly to memorize the declensions and conjugations from Kennedy's Latin Primer. I found this rather a chore and when another boy said "I never bother with that, I just keep the book under my desk when there's a test." The classroom we were using was small with the desks close together so that this seemed fairly easy to do and foolishly I took his advice. Unfortunately we had moved to a better room with the 12 or so desks quite widely spaced when the inevitable test came up. I knew very few of the answers which was going to be pretty embarrassing, at best. As each boy finished he took his work up to Mr Edward's desk at the front to be marked. Everyone seemed to be doing quite well, including the boy who had advised me to cheat, which wasn't a practical solution in the new room. I stayed in my seat. Eventually Mr. Edwards asked "is there anyone who hasn't been marked?" I kept silent. "Give me your mark when I call your name." When he called mine I said "14 and a half," a bit lower than most, which I judged to be uncontroversial. Was there a fleeting look of puzzlement on his face when I spoke? I'm not sure, but he went on to the next boy's name.

The school used to provide lunch, but when I told my mother that I didn't like what was served she gave me money (half-a-crown, formally equivalent to 12 and a half pence) to go to a nearby restaurant. I usually went with another boy, with whom I became good friends (he came to our house a few times) to the East Sheen branch of the Hygienic Bakeries. Occasionally we spend the money on chocolate eclairs!

Quite soon after I came back to Twickenham after the war my mother took me to the dentist; I don't think I had been to one since the trip to Exeter from the Leas. He was a friend she had met in the Army, an immensely tall Welshman whom she always called 'Tiny Williams'. He had set up a practice in the Upper Richmond Road, a short distance towards Richmond after the last shops in East Sheen. Apart from needing several fillings he found that my palate was too narrow and my teeth overcrowded. To deal with these problems I had a series of appointments after school. The surgery was the front room of an ordinary 1920s or 1930s house, and fixed to the ceiling coving where one could see it during treatment was a long strip of paper, taken I suppose from some magazine, showing the changes in clothing fashions along the ages. It's caption read 'Fashion is a Fickle Fade'. I was always puzzled by the spelling of what I took to mean 'fad', I still am; it's not in my dictionary!

At the second or third appointment, 'Tiny' extracted a tooth from each side of my top jaw to make room for the rest. These were done with injections, which I didn't enjoy then any more than I do now, but the extractions themselves hurt surprisingly little. I remember feeling only intense pressure on my jaw – and a disconcerting snap as each tooth came out. After this he made a plate to widen my palate. I was supposed to keep it in all the time, except for eating and turn the screw between the two halves one quarter turn every other day with a small spanner. I used to put it in my pocket while I had lunch, which was fine when I had a clean-ish hanky to wrap it in but otherwise I had to put it back in my mouth well coated with fluff and grit! I kept this up for quite a few weeks but somehow it got lost or broken and my mother seemed to have lost interest in it. I don't feel that my life was blighted by my failure to complete this cosmetic treatment. It is true that as a young man girls did not exactly throw themselves at my feet (or any other part) but I am not convinced that a marginally broader grin would have made all the difference.

Not long after I started at Tower House, I was walking near Twickenham Green, which was a rougher area than Strawberry Hill, when I was accosted by a group of boys and, unprovoked, one of them punched me in the face. I was not greatly hurt but much upset. When I got home my mother said I had better go to the boxing classes which the school offered one day a week after lessons. In the event I did not show particular aptitude for this sport, which I did not much enjoy, but I learned the basics of staying on my toes, keeping up my right guard to block incoming punches and looking out for a chance to score with my left. This modest achievement in pugilism was to be of great social advantage to me quite soon.

By November of 1945 there was a moderate supply of fireworks in the shops and we were invited to a fireworks party by Mr and Mrs Burge, friends of my parents, in their garden in Strawberry Hill Road. There were quite a lot of people there whom I didn't know. After the fireworks, a modest display by modern standards, we were looking forward to sausage rolls, a rare treat, which Mrs Burge had proudly cooked. Sadly she had overdone the bicarb. in the recipe and they were almost inedible.

The Burges had two sons, Charles, a couple of years or so older than me, and John a year or two younger. I got on with Charles quite well, but never really knew John. Another boy I knew was David Bartlett who lived a few houses up in Waldegrave Gardens. We didn't have much in common but used to play football with a tennis ball in the road outside my house, his being near the junction at the end of the road; there was very little traffic at that time and the game was not often interrupted to let cars go by. My mother did not approve of me playing in the road but she never noticed these games.

On one occasion Charles and John had come to my house and then we had joined up with David, in his garden. David did or said something which annoyed Charles, who was considerably bigger and easily wrestled him onto the ground, sat on his chest and sprinkled dry soil into his eyes. I was surprised and rather shocked at this bullying over-reaction by a boy I liked and thought I knew. It was a trait I was to see in him in years to come, even to the extent of being, in a mild way, on the receiving end.

The playground at Tower House was L-shaped beside and behind the school building, originally a late Victorian or Edwardian villa. It had, I think, been covered with tarmac at one time, but now it was loose gravel with lumps sticking up. Two or three weeks after the firework party I tripped over one of these and took a square inch or so of skin off my knee. I was wearing short trousers at this time, of course. My wound was washed and dressed and after a few days it was healing nicely with a good fat scab.

During the mid-morning and lunch breaks almost everyone in the school joined in a giant game of football, played with a tennis ball over the whole area of the playground. Robo quite often joined in with enthusiasm and if the ball went over the wooden fence of the next property which ran down the long side of the 'L', as it often did, he would put his hands on top of the fence and vault lightly over to get it. I was beside this fence when the ball came my way and as I went to kick it towards goal I was violently barged by a considerably bigger boy in the top form called Minis. I was flattened against the fence and the scab was scraped off my knee. My mother dressed the re-opened wound when I got home but it turned septic.

The usual dressings and hot-poultices failed to cure the infection and when I was examined by the doctor he diagnosed streptococcal infection and prescribed M and B 693, sulphanilamide, developed by Sir Lionel Whitby's group at May and Baker. Penicillin was not generally available at that time; it became a so six months later I now read (older readers may remember that Graham Green's novel and film *The Third Man* was about the black market in penicillin in Vienna in this post-war period. They might also remember that the first, rather crude, preparations of penicillin were used on a policeman suffering from streptococcal infection from the prick of a rose thorn, and that he died).

A few days before Christmas I was quite ill with a high temperature. My mother had bought a Christmas tree and Jill had blown some glass bulbs and coloured them with dye at the Paint Research Station to decorate it. They set it up in the room I was sleeping in, which was usually Jill's room. I woke up howling in terror and my mother concluded that I had had some sort of hallucination involving the Christmas tree and with Jill's help she dragged it out. Not surprisingly I don't remember the incident very well, but I think I was frightened by my usual temperature dream, which I can best, but inadequately, describe as the sensation of being over-whelmed by solid, formless noise, rather than by anything to do with the tree. My mother put it all down to the side-effects of M and B which the doctor had warned her about. From this point I got better fairly quickly and went back to school when the term began in January.

At about this time the government amazingly took sweets off the ration. There was a Maynards sweet shop between the Odeon Cinema and the upper Richmond Road and by lunchtime on the first day its shelves were totally empty. Now there were no sweets to be had. Rationing was rapidly re-imposed and we continued to buy, mostly from pharmacists' shops lemonade tablets (ostensibly to be dissolved in water to make lemonade), chloridine lozenges (flavoured as I now know with chloroform – they made one's mouth numb), 'imps' (very small and black, flavoured with very hot peppermint), liquorice root (sticks of wood which remained fibrous but tasted of liquorice when chewed) and locust beans (said to have sustained John the Baptist in the wilderness, they are dried pods, mostly crisp fibre, but with occasional deposits of sweet sticky stuff).

The wireless, in the form of the BBC's 'Home Service' and 'Light Programme', was a distinct feature in my life at this time. Most memorable was Tommy Handley's ITMA (It's That Man Again) with his quick-fire quips and team of stock characters: the bossy Miss Hotchkiss whose inevitable complaint was prefaced by a stentorian 'Mistah Handleh...'; Colonel Chinstrap, who always miss-heard what was said, and supposed he was being offered a drink, which he accepted with, 'I don't mind if I do, Sir!'; Frisby Dyke, from Liverpool, who started by asking the meaning of a long word and finished using a longer one. When asked how he knew what it meant he always said, 'I've studied its etymological derivation'; the Welshman who contradicted himself and Mrs Mopp, the char. Further comedy came from Arthur Askey, Charlie Chester, Kenneth Horne and Richard Murdoc. Tommy Handley's sudden death not long after the end of the war was a time of national mourning.

The variety program, *Monday Night at Eight,* was always worth hearing, and the daily 15- minute episode of *Dick Barton, Special Agent* was not to be missed, as he and his assistants Snowy White (Cockney) and Jock

Anderson (Scottish!) thwarted the evil schemes of adversaries, who frequently had German or Italian names and accents!

I did not quite finish the school year at Tower House because at the end of June 1946 we set out, at Government expense, to join my father in Canberra.

8th June, 1946

To-day, as we celebrate victory, I send this personal message to you and all other boys and girls at school. For you have shared in the hardships and dangers of a total war and you have shared no less in the triumph of the Allied Nations.

I know you will always feel proud to belong to a country which was capable of such supreme effort; proud, too, of parents and elder brothers and sisters who by their courage, endurance and enterprise brought victory. May these qualities be yours as you grow up and join in the common effort to establish among the nations of the world unity and peace.

George R.I.

In the years when our Country was in mortal danger

LIONEL MURRAY MacBRIDE

who served 3rd June 1940 – 31st December 1944, gave generously of his time and powers to make himself ready for her defence by force of arms and with his life if need be.

George R.I.

THE HOME GUARD

The King's message to me (left).
and to my father (above).
(There was also the matter of an
OBE for the day job!)

THEMISTOCLES

Preparations for this trip seemed to be at rather short notice. My mother bought a new cabin trunk and she and Jill packed it, and the others we already had, and stuck on the labels provided by the shipping line, Shaw, Savill and Albion: green for ' not wanted on the voyage' to go in the hold and dark-red for 'cabin'. We still have luggage (not the new one which broke years ago!) with the remains of those labels.

My mother arranged for the house to be sub-let and some money was left with the agent who promised to make sure that 'Spook', my grey Persian cat, was looked after. 'Uggles' was given into the care of Phoebe's nephew, Bill Klitz, who had been Jill's boyfriend.

SS Themistocles. (State Library of Victoria).

The luggage was taken by carrier and we set off by train for Tilbury to join SS *Themistocles*, a coal-burner built, my wife's clever keyboard finger reveals, in 1910 by Harland and Wolff alongside the *Titanic*. We heard that this was to be her last trip to Australia and back and the record shows that she was indeed laid-up in 1946, and broken up in 1947, after 79 trips to Australia.

It would be overstating the case to suggest that the move from 1946 London to life onboard ship was akin to dying and going to Heaven, but it was certainly a most agreeable change.

For one thing one could buy unlimited chocolate bars and sweets from the ship's shop. This proved a bad combination with my enthusiasm for watching the ship's headway through the rather large waves in the Bay of

Biscay, from the fo'csle, but this was the only time I was seasick. The Shaw Savill line, the government's choice for shipping the families of civil servants, was probably not the most luxurious available but the food served on board was perfectly acceptable with enough choice to avoid anything nasty. I don't remember whether rabbit stew was offered but I certainly dodged it if so!

There was a handful of children of about my age travelling with the hundred or so grown-ups on the ship. I played with one boy particularly, I think he had red hair but I had forgotten his name until Roslyn, my wife, checked the passenger list on the Internet. He was Peter Sinclair.

There were various deck-games available, deck-golf (a wooden disk was driven with a mallet round a series of 'holes', consisting of circles painted on the deck), deck-croquet (played with a similar 'puck'; one's opponent could drive yours into the 'scuppers', the drainage channels round the edge of the deck). There was also deck-tennis (more like badminton) and quoits, which I didn't like so much, lacking the necessary coordination of hand and eye for hitting and catching.

I also made friends with one of the engineer officers, a Mr Henderson, who took me round the engine-room with the three-cylinder ('triple expansion') steam engine and told me quite a lot about ships' engines which interested me greatly, even if he did have a regrettable tendency to put his hand up the leg of my shorts.

Once we got into warmer climes than Tilbury the crew rigged a canvas swimming pool on the after well-deck. One of the ship's company was detailed to help with sports and he was doing well in teaching me to swim – until water went in my ear, bringing back my old ear-ache and my mother decided I had better stay out of the water.

At one point a children's party was organized with various games. I can remember not enjoying it. One of the games was to try to take a bite out of an apple hanging on a string without using one's hands; a slightly younger boy, whom I did not really know, lost his temper after a few unsuccessful bites, tore the apple down and threw it away. I was slightly shocked by such a display in front of such a lot of people.

From time to time the 'racehorse game' was organized on the upper deck. Several wooden 'horses' moved along squares laid out on the deck according to the throw of a dice. This was really intended for grownups to bet on but we were allowed to stake small sums. It could be quite exciting but I never won!

The entertainments were interspersed by the excitement of seeing passing ships or glimpses of land, and by occasional life-boat practices. When the ship's horn gave the alarm we had to collect our life-jackets from our cabins and assemble beside our allotted life-boat. Since every metal fitting on the decks of the ship appeared to be composed of solid rust, and the continuous creaking and groaning of the hull, even in light seas, did not reassure me that it too was not seriously corroded, I paid careful attention to the instructions for abandoning ship should the need arise.

After what must have been two or three weeks the African coast appeared on the horizon and we docked at Cape Town.

Themistocles carried cargo as well as passengers and I was interested to watch the sailors unloading it. The cargo hatches were on the fore and after well-decks covered by canvas sheets secured to rails round their edges, which were a couple of feet above deck level, by wooden wedges; stout planks closed the hatches under the canvas. The cargo was lifted out on derricks, held up against the mast while at sea, using the (very rusty) steam winches on the deck. These ran at one speed and raising and lowering the load was controlled by a sailor putting more or less tension on the free end of the lifting rope, with a few turns round the winch, so that it gripped or slipped as needed. Coal was loaded by cranes on the dock.

These operations took some time so that we had a few days at each port when we could go ashore. Cape Town is, of course, overshadowed by Table Mountain, an impressive view from the harbour, but I was acutely uncomfortable in the streets and shops of the town. Apartheid was enforced at that time and all public facilities were segregated into 'White' and 'Africaans'. The resentment of the native population for the whites was unmistakable and to me, as a white child, the atmosphere was rigid with hatred; I was always relieved to get back to the ship.

From Cape Town we sailed around the Cape to Durban where we were met by my Aunt Connie, my mother's elder sister, who lived in Salisbury and was married to a detective, Witney Carr, in the Rhodesian police.

The same atmosphere or racial hatred pervaded Durban and my discomfort was aggravated by Connie's clearly displayed attitude that the native population was a lower form of life, unworthy of consideration. Apart from the racial situation, this was a different world; I was interested to watch a customer chose and buy an automatic pistol over the counter of a department store.

I remember that we went to the beach, although going in the water was out of the question because of sharks. I found a small jellyfish on the sand, a perfectly featureless sphere of clear jelly, I tried to pick it up on a layer of sand but it rolled off. Jill said "Oh, it's fallen on its face!"

One afternoon we visited the Snake Park. As well as seeing many varieties of snake confined behind glass, the keepers held what we were lead to believe were very poisonous species in their hands. I don't think my mother liked snakes very much, despite her general enthusiasm for wildlife, and seemed to find the experience disturbing, not least when the keeper let a python (which is not poisonous) loose in the crowd. He put his foot on its tail when it seemed to be taking a more than the healthy interest in one bystander.

We had several days in Durban therefore setting off across the Indian Ocean for Freemantle, the longest leg of our voyage without sight of land. I was delighted by the flying-fish gliding from the ship's bow wave, porpoises swimming along beside us and occasionally a whale spouting in the distance. The velvety tropical sky, frequently lit-up by flashes of 'summer lightning' which produced no sound, now showed the Southern Cross instead of the Plough.

There was always a sweepstake on the distance we had travelled in the last 24 hours. The ship, as I now know, was supposed to be capable of 15 knots (i.e. 360 nautical miles in 24 hours, neglecting ocean currents) but my recollection is that the winning figure was often less than 300; I never got it right.

As well as the deck-games with the other children, or with grown-ups who wanted to play, I amused myself by carving miniature ships from matchsticks with a razor blade. When I needed a new blade I bought a packet of 'Valet' blades, stiffer than the 'Gillette' type and with one blunt edge. I had got to know a man in a cabin next to ours and I offered him the packet of blades to shave with before I used them but he said they wouldn't fit his razor and could I change them. We were both a bit embarrassed when I had to admit that these were the type I needed!

In Cape Town I had bought a small battery operated electric motor, neater than any I had seen in England, and I put it in its box on the dressing table in our cabin. After some days I found it was missing. No one knew anything about it and I had to conclude that the rolling of the ship had slid it off the edge into the waste-paper basket, which the steward had emptied.

If I ran out of things to do during the day my mother was usually to be found on the upper deck with a long ' Tom Collins' (gin with lemonade and Angostura bitters) in conversation with other passengers and she would usually wave to the steward to bring me an iced ginger ale.

After three weeks or so we reached Australia and docked at Freemantle. This proved to be a fairly short stop and we didn't have a chance to go to Perth. The only expedition ashore was with my mother to some wasteland with railway sidings to look for Australian wildflowers. I pressed the samples we found in a cheap exercise book; I think I still have it somewhere.

Our next port of call was Adelaide, again for a short stop and I don't remember going ashore. From there we went to Melbourne where we stopped for a couple of days or so. I was impressed by the uniform geometrical layout of the streets, unlike anywhere else I had seen. My mother bought me a cheap fishing-rod and I caught a small puffer-fish in the harbour. I was told later that they could be quite dangerous to touch but I suffered no ill-effect.

The last leg of our journey on *Themistocles* was to Sydney where we were due to disembark on arrival. In the event we could not leave the ship for a day or two because it was raining and the stevedores declined to off-load our luggage in the wet! One passenger, anxious to be on his way, said he had offered to hold an umbrella over them!

Finally, we left by train for Canberra, or rather for Queenbean, a few miles outside Canberra, which is where the station was. Once again I don't remember the railway journey.

CANBERRA

We were to rent a house in Canberra, No 13 Mugga Way, but the owner, a professor of botany I was told, was not yet ready to leave and we spent several weeks staying at the Canberra Hotel, not far from Parliament House where my father worked in the Office of the High Commissioner.

In 1946 Canberra was more of an idea then a city. An artistic, but very confusing, network of roads had been laid out with sweeping curves, concentric circles and many small roads joining them together. There were houses along some of the roads but most of the areas enclosed in the pattern were covered by rough grass. There were two 'shopping centres', the only shops, a parade of half a dozen or so shops opposite the cinema at Manuka – I remember only a greengrocer and an ice-cream parlour – and a short-ish street with shops on both sides at Civic. The lake, so prominent on the today's map of Canberra, did not exist; only the meanders of the small turgid Murrumbidgee River.

The Canberra Hotel (I think it was *The* Canberra hotel) had a central building with the reception desk, a foyer with tables where drinks were served and a dining room. The bedrooms were in several relatively long wings radiating from the main building, in front of which were well-kept lawns and shrubberies with a drive up to the entrance.

Although we reached Canberra at the end of August I did not go to school for some time. My mother hired a bicycle for me, a lethal contraption with no brakes and a fixed wheel (i.e. no free-wheel so that the pedals went round all the time the wheel was turning); the pedals were the only way to slow down. Fortunately there was not much motor traffic. I still had that bike when we moved to Mugga Way and, on one trip down the fairly steep hill to Manuka, my feet came off the pedals, which were of course still flying round. I managed to stop by holding my foot against the front wheel, just short of the more or less blind junction with the main road at the bottom of the hill.

Another problem with that bike, while we were still at the hotel, was that the back tyre was worn into a hole exposing the inner tube. When I rode over a hose on the hotel drive the tube burst. I was able to buy a repair kit and surreptitiously borrowed some spoons from the dining room to use as tyre levers, a technique learned at the Leas, and so got mobile again.

Two other guests at the hotel, with whom we had got into conversation, kindly provided some entertainment for me. One was Professor Brunovsksy, well known on the radio in programs like the Brains Trust and adviser to the wartime government on fuel and power. He arranged for me to be shown round the Canberra Power Station which interested me greatly, although I was a bit nervous on the ladders and cat-walks of single, rather thin, widely-spaced steel rods quite high above the turbines and generators.

The other was a rather loud American woman called Madeleine Zapp. She had a big American car and invited me to join a party she was driving to Brindabella, quite high in the mountain range to the West of Canberra. It was an interesting trip and there was a dusting of snow amongst the gum trees at our highest point. I was, however, rather anxious in the car, particularly on the narrow mountain roads, because she kept turning her head to speak to the back-seat passengers while she was driving. I had seldom, if ever, been in a car since I left the Leas.

The house in Mugga Way was quite small, on one storey, as were the majority in Canberra then and indeed they still are. I won't call it a bungalow because this term is derogatory in Australian usage, more like 'shack'. It stood in the acute angle where Dampier Crescent joins Mugga

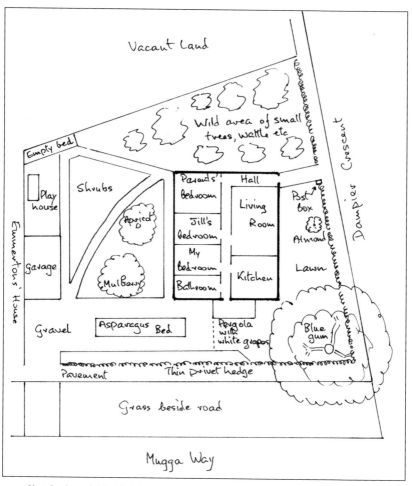

Sketch plan of No 13, Mugga Way, Canberra in 1947, drawn from memory.
A larger single storey house now covers much of the site.

Way surrounded by quite a nice garden with a fair-sized blue gum, on the rather bare lawn, nearest to the road junction. Behind the house a mulberry and an apricot tree, the latter particularly, gave amazing crops of wonderful fruit. A large bed of asparagus, not very beautiful under a covering of ashes, from the open fires at each end of the living room presumably, was also highly productive. Growing things in this garden was remarkably rewarding; later on I planted some rock-melon seeds and we were eating the melons in about six weeks!

There was a wooden play-house in the garden and a garage, which we didn't use, where the owner had left an unlabelled glass flask, containing a colourless liquid which smelled sickly-sweet. I now realize that it was benzene, currently regarded as dangerously toxic; I don't remember what I did with it.

Hitherto I had not made friends with any other children. There was a girl next door, Beverly Emmerton, whose father was Black Rod in the Australian Parliament, but she was a couple of years older than me end we never seemed to have anything in common so that I never got to know her. During this time before I started at school my mother, I suppose, got into conversation with a retired couple, called McFarlane, who lived in the next house across the side road. Their son had long ago left home and made a very successful career in finance – he was Secretary to the Treasury and his signature was on the Australian banknotes! They had kept some of his toys including an enormous Meccano set and they lent it to me. I made a crane along the lines of the one we had all worked on at the Leas, but I don't think I was inventive enough to realize the full potential of the set.

Looking back, I think I must have started at Canberra Grammar School in the middle of the term which had, I presume, started in September because I don't remember waiting as long as the next one in January. The school was less than a mile away, set in open ground beside Flinders Way which at that time joined the end of Mugga Way (the modern map shows Mugga Way continuing into a large built-up area). I went on my bike, replaced at about this time by the hirer, with a better one which had a free-wheel and back-pedal brake (i.e. one could stop pedalling and backward pressure on the pedals applied a brake to the back wheel).

My start at the school was not a pleasant one. I was in the lowest form in the charge of a Mr Moore who wore gold-rimmed glasses and was known to the boys as 'Greazy' because he smarmed his hair down with Brylcreem or something of the sort. He taught us all day, unlike Tower House where subjects were taken by different masters, and he was desperately boring. But worse than this was the continuous teasing I got from the other boys. I heard later that I had replaced another English boy whose life must have been made a misery. The onslaught was purely verbal; I was not shown or threatened with any violence; that was to come from me. I put up with it for a few days – Tower House had not been a bed of roses – but in the form room after lunch, before the afternoon class, I was alone with a rather nondescript boy who said something that touched a raw nerve, I don't remember what it was, and I socked him. I expected him to come back at me with his fists but to my amazement he turned his back and ran away! I chased him round between the desks literally boxing his ears until he escaped into the playground.

Quite soon this boy returned with some others in our form who were apparently considered leaders. The boy indicated me and said

'He can fight'.

This produced a unanimous decision that I should fight Doug Jenkins who was acknowledged to be the best fighter in the form. Doug was American, the son of a US Trade Attaché. The bout was immediately arranged in the playground and Doug and I squared up to one another with bare knuckles inside the traditional circle of boys.

Doug was an enthusiastic fighter and came at me with fists flying, but he lacked any training in boxing and I had no difficulty in blocking his punches with my guard while scoring with my left. Before long I landed a rather more solid straight left to his eye and the circle of adjudicators awarded me the bout. Doug appeared next day with what was usually called 'a real shiner'.

My prowess established I was now required to meet the best fighter in the next form up, who was quickly produced and turned out to be called Alexander. He was, in all fairness, pretty much my own size but older and wiry. He was a distinctly better boxer than me but I managed to defend myself well enough to avoid any more damage than a slightly split lip. The circle of adjudicators soon decided that Alexander was the winner but were clearly impressed by my performance.

Doug's father, Doug Jenkins Senior, worked in Parliament House like my father and they knew one another quite well. After our fight he accosted my father with "Say, your son has blacked Doug's eye!" I imagine my father was pleased, and probably surprised, that I had shown so much gumption; we didn't know one another very well at this stage (I don't think we ever did, actually). He started, however, some sort of apology but Doug Senior roared with laughter. Evidently fisticuffs between boys at school was not contrary to his conception of the clean-living all-American way of life. I doubt if my father missed the opportunity to exchange a few rounds of drinks, perhaps quite a few, though he didn't mention it when he recounted the incident.

From this point on everyone was very friendly and I became good friends with Doug Jenkins and a boy called Malcolm Park. He was Malcolm Mungo Steel Park, a direct descendant of the African explorer Mungo Park (1771-1806).The three of us went round together quite a lot.

Not long after this Greazy Moore had a good idea. It was possibly the only one and as things turned out perhaps not such a good one. He asked everyone in the form to collect any interesting insects and similar wildlife and bring them to school preserved in meths or something similar. Some of the boys lived in rather wild places outside Canberra and there was soon quite an impressive, at   least to me accustomed to English insects, collection in the form room. Some-one brought a distinctly dangerous looking snake coiled round in a large glass jar and there was a quite enormous centipede, each section of its back the size of a man's thumbnail. Malcolm, Doug and I had not found any specimen to contribute until, exploring on Red Hill, a ridge behind Mugga Way which had Canberra's reservoir on the top, we opened a cover over a valve and found an exceptionally large and colourful red-back spider. Not an unusual thing to find in such a place, the red-back is dangerously poisonous. Although not as deadly as the trap-door (funnel-web) spider its bite is occasionally lethal. We were well aware of this unpleasant characteristic of our specimen but managed to put a match-box over it and shut it without mishap. Doug put the box in his pocket. In the evening he asked his father to help him kill it with meths, but Doug Senior immediately threw the matchbox on the fire. We never did add anything to Greazy's collection.

At the school I also made friends with Mario Santos, younger son of the Brazilian ambassador. The embassy was on Flinders Way on the opposite side from the school, near the junction with Mugga Way and I was invited there quite often. I think Mario was expected to stay in the embassy grounds, which extend for some way behind the house, because I didn't go round on my bike with Mario as I did with Doug and Malcolm.

On one visit Mario produced a round of .303 ammunition, which his brother had pinched from the school Corps. There was a deep dry gully at the end of the Embassy land and we lit a fire of twigs in the bottom of it, put the cartridge in the fire and took cover outside the gully. When nothing had happened for a few minutes we crept forward to look over the edge, at which point there was a loud bang and bits of brass cartridge case whistled past our heads. Luckily neither of us was hit. At the time I was interested to see that the bullet itself had gone less than a foot or so. Later I was to learn that, compared with other explosive stores, small-arms ammunition does not pose a major hazard in fires.

Mario had a (not terribly satisfactory) air-gun which he swapped for the rather good collection of marbles which I had brought from England. I was pleased with this and spent quite a lot of time shooting at paper targets in the garden at Mugga Way. This proved to be about the only one of my boyhood interests in which my father ever participated. Despite his poor eyesight he had apparently become quite a good shot in the Home Guard, and he showed me the correct 'prone' position for firing and the basics of holding and aiming. I'm not sure whether this early instruction contributed to my representing my school, university and the RAF at rifle shooting in years to come.

Shortly after we settled in Mugga Way we were given a pair of kittens, one all-black and one all white which we called 'Mulberry' and 'Mistletoe' (respectively!). I don't know where they came from but there was some tie-up with the Army Officer Cadet Training Unit, stationed a little way outside the city, because when Mulberry went missing the entire contingent of cadets was mobilised on an exercise to find her, which they did. I'm not sure how this happened but I think my sister had a hand in it!

Another boy I played with occasionally, again always in his own house, was Marnix van Aersen whose father represented the Netherlands; their

Mulberry and Mistletoe in the gum tree at Mugga Way.

Legation was just across the road from our house in Mugga Way. Marnix had two elder sisters and lots of expensive toys. I remember particularly a splendid electric train set; the engine had a light at the front and the light bulb had a depression on top in which a tablet could be put to make white smoke come out of the funnel!

Across the rough field behind the Jenkins' house was the home of a rather older boy called Moss Allen. He was passionately keen on cricket and recruited a group of boys to play on a rough wicket in that field. Doug became very enthusiastic about these games and Malcolm and I played a few times but cricket was not my game and Malcolm and I drifted away and saw less of Doug out of school.

Towards the end of my first term at Canberra Grammar School a boy called Hickman, who was a boarder at the school whom I hardly knew, invited me to come and stay for a fortnight at his parents' homestead. My parents having no objection, I went with him when his father picked him up on the last day of term in his ' utility'; what would be called a pick-up in this country with a closed cab and a small open truck body. I think the drive to his homestead took about a couple of hours. I don't think I ever knew where it was. On the way I noticed a large tree beside the road ahead completely covered in pink blossom – but as we approached the 'blossom' took off in the form of a large flock of pink cockatoos leaving the dead 'ring-barked' tree a grey skeleton. (The majority of trees on agricultural, i.e. grazing, land had been killed years before by cutting a groove round the trunk with an axe, in the belief that they were an unnecessary drain on groundwater. The dead branches always seemed to be reaching out in contorted shapes as if they had writhed in the death-throes of the tree.)

As soon as we reached the homestead Mr Hickman asked me, with some apparent anxiety, if I could ride a horse. My riding lessons at Ardock (I don't think I went near a horse at Wings) had not been a major success, my main recollection being my aerial trips over 'Top Hat's' head, but I didn't want to miss anything so, with some inner misgiving, I said I could. Horses were immediately produced and we set off to ride round the perimeter of the Hickman's land. Fortunately my equestrian skills were not tested beyond keeping the docile horse going the same way as the others at walking pace. Perhaps it would have done this without any guidance from me!

The most interesting thing about the Hickman's house was the electricity generating set, with shelves of car batteries to provide power when the engine was not running. I was initially surprised to see batteries used to produce mains voltage, but knew enough to realize that this could be done by connecting enough of them in series.

We spent most of the time exploring the fields round the homestead, on one occasion having to run like mad for the fence to escape a furious cow with large horns! I also remember standing on an elderly tractor whose steel front wheels had lost the original central guiding rim so that as we went across a slope the driver had to keep to the wheels turned hard up the slope to make the machine go straight.

My companion and I were both keen on playing marbles which we did in the dust of the yard, but the high-light of my visit happened when we wandered into the stock-yard, while the men were taking a break. One was holding a stock-whip, which is long enough to redirect an errant cow by cracking it from a considerable distance. This man said something to one of the others, who picked up a dried stalk of dock and held it out between his teeth. The stockman stepped back, raised his whip and cracked it in front of his friend's face: the stalk fell, cut off under his nose! He then invited me to hold the stalk in my mouth. The thought of what might happen if he got it wrong was daunting, but reason told me that he was very unlikely to try the trick with a visiting child unless he was perfectly confident of not hurting me so, not wishing to appear cowardly, I agreed. I made rather a point of keeping still till the whip cracked close to my face and the stalk fell. He had left it slightly longer in my case, just beyond the end of my nose, I noticed.

After the holiday I went back to Greazy Moore's class. The routine was the same; when we arrived each morning he would have written a sentence on the blackboard and we were required to 'parse and analyse' it, i.e. to identify the verb, subject etc. I could do this easily enough, having done English grammar, French and Latin at Tower House. These last two were not started until one was 14 or so in Australian schools. Greazy never followed up this exercise with any further points of grammar but always went on to another subject.

Greazy was the only teacher we had, with one exception, and we had to stay in his classroom listening to his boring lessons all day, every day. The exception was music. For this a rather un-masculine, as it seemed to me, young man took us to another room where there was a piano. Here he attempted to teach us to sing Handel's 'Where E're You Walk', a lovely piece to be sure but perhaps not an obvious choice for a class of eleven year olds consisting predominantly of out-back farmers' sons with a sprinkling of diplomatic and white collar boys. It was not a great success and the music master left at the end of the term, leaving Greazy to teach us to sing 'Waltzing Matilda' without the piano.

One of Greazy's subjects was history: this meant Australian history, being accounts of the journeys made by the various explorers who opened up Australia. The school text was about the size of a Penguin book, which I found encouraging compared with the interminable saga of English, let alone European, history. It was more interesting than Greazy's other material and not too difficult to remember; he did not seem to be aware of any other history. We had worked almost to the end of this book when Greazy disappeared and was replaced by a Mr Pollock, out from England. Years later my mother told me that Greazy had been sent packing after she and my father had repeated my accounts of his classes to the Headmaster, Canon Edwards, at a social function.

Mr Pollock went about on an ancient bicycle which he referred to as 'Half-a-leg'. (I perceived the origin of this as Tennyson's *Charge of the Light Brigade* – 'Half a league, half a league, half a league onward...'). I presume he brought it from England because the handle-bars were of the straight English style, unlike Australian bikes which used handlebars of the 'dropped' shape but turned up, so that one's hands were above the steering-head, with the ends pointing forward. I liked this upright riding position, which I was later to refer to as 'sit up and beg' in motor-cycling circles. My parents gave me such a bike, a 'Malvern Star', much heavier than contemporary British makes, for my eleventh birthday to replace the hired one.

Mr Pollock taught English history, though I don't remember that he made it particularly interesting to me, let alone the Australian boys. He taught grammar more systematically than Greazy had, however. I suppose both masters taught arithmetic (I don't think algebra or geometry were on the syllabus) but I don't remember anything about it. I expect I had done it before at Tower House. Overall Mr Pollock's classes were less dull.

Greazy Moore had occasionally punished boys by hitting their calves with a small cane, but Mr Pollock had brought a different weapon. Known, I believe, as a 'tawse' in Scottish schools, it was a heavy plaited leather thong six or seven inches long beyond the handle, which was applied to the palm of a culprit's hand. He used it on me once; it hurt enough to make one feel that a repetition was to be avoided if possible, which is, I suppose, what a school punishment should do.

One afternoon we were taken from school to the Civic Cinema to see a performance (I think it was the last rehearsal) of scenes from *Les Sylphides* by the Canberra Ballet, a distinctly amateur group. I knew nothing about ballet, but had the idea that it was intended to be graceful. These large rather gawky women clumping about the stage amid clouds of dust, groping frantically for one another's hands, struck me as hilarious even at that tender age. I'm not sure where I picked it up, but there was a general feeling in Canberra that this was 'Culture' with a capital 'C'.

Another cultural feature of Canberra Grammar School was its orchestra. At one end of term function they were required to play the National Anthem. A bar or so after the final chord the bass drummer realized that he should have contributed to it and gave his drum a mighty thump!

Canberra had its own radio station '2CA Canberra' which seemed to be manned largely by students; their time checks were frequently wrong! There was a children's programme in the afternoon and if I got home quickly I could hear the next episode of an adventure serial set in the South American rain forest; the arch-villain was constantly threatening to bury his adversaries up to their waists in an ant-hill, snarling "I'll make you squirm!" One afternoon I got home to hear the announcer say 'I'm afraid we've just dropped the record of the next episode, but we'll play you what's left of it! 'This didn't turn out to be very much, so I never did find out how the hero extricated himself from the dire predicament in which he had, as usual, been left at the end of the previous episode.

Later in the evening 2CA broadcast a series of fifteen minute serials starting at 6.15 with 'Justice Rides the Range', a Western, followed by 'Martin's Corner', which was about a shop and I found it rather dull, but the best one was 'Danger Unlimited' at 6.45 (brought to you by the makers of 'Bex', an aspirin formulation) where the hero/heroine pair were confronted by master-criminals, shut in gas chambers, threatened by vampires, etc., etc. At 7.00 there was a news program followed by more serials including 'Nick Carter' (the American private eye) but I was losing interest by this time and went to bed soon afterwards.

More than once Malcolm and I cycled to the Australian War Memorial and museum which was near Civic, on the slopes of Mount Ainsley, a small steep mountain on the edge of the city. It contained various weapons used by the Australian forces in the two World Wars and a Japanese miniature submarine caught in Sydney Harbour, after cutting through the defensive netting, fortunately before its two-man crew could do any damage.

The Governor General (i.e. the senior representative of the Crown) when we went to Canberra was the Duke of Gloucester and when he finished in this position he gave a farewell party for his children, two boys,

My parents at a Diplomatic Function in Canberra.

The A.D.C. in Waiting is desired by
Their Royal Highnesses
The Governor-General & The Duchess of Gloucester
to invite
Mrs. L. M. MacBride and Hugh
to Government House, Canberra on *Tuesday*
3rd December 4 to 6 o'clock
Children's Party
An answer is requested.

To give the Diplomatic Corps and the High Commissioners
and their staffs the honor of bidding farewell to His Royal Highness
the Duke of Gloucester, Governor-General of Australia,
and Her Royal Highness the Duchess of Gloucester
The American Ambassador and Mrs. Butler
request the honor of the company of
Mr. and Mrs. L. M. MacBride
at a Reception
on Friday, twentieth December
at five o'clock to seven o'clock
The guests are requested to
arrive promptly at 5 o'clock.
R.S.V.P.

To Celebrate the Inauguration of
Indian Independence
The High Commissioner for India in Australia
requests the pleasure of the company of
Mr. L. M. MacBride
Mugga Way, Canberra, at the Ceremony of
Flag Hoisting,
[Frid]ay, August 15, 1947, at 12 noon.
R.S.V.P.
Private Secretary

Some notable invitations.

William and Richard, both younger than me. The elder, William, was born in 1941 and died in an air crash in 1972. My mother kept the invitation and I still have it – but I didn't enjoy the party very much.

My parents were evidently still worried about my ears, although I don't remember (and I'm sure I would) any ear-ache after the swimming incident on board ship. Years later my mother told me that the Duke's children had a similar problem and he had recommended a specialist in Sydney.

My mother and I flew to Sydney for an examination by the specialist. I gather that he recommended that I should drink plenty of milk, which I particularly disliked; I don't know how much he charged. We flew from a small airfield outside Canberra in a Dakota (Douglas DC2). I was disappointed that our seats were above the wing so that we couldn't see very much. I watched the rivets on the engine cowling turning slowly with the vibration and a streak of black oil steadily creeping back in the slip-stream. The trip, my first, as it was for my mother, in an aeroplane was pretty bumpy and became much more so as we circled between land and sea waiting to land at Sydney. The plane seemed to drop like a stone for several seconds, presumably as we flew out of thermals (up-currents) from the warmer land. My mother was clearly not liking it at all, and she dabbed a drop of blood out of her ear before we landed.

We reached Sydney before the mosquito season was supposed to have started so that our hotel had not put out mosquito nets, but they came early that year and with a tree outside our window I was soon covered in itching bites. After I think it was three, more or less sleepless nights I was near to delirium. I have no memory of the visit to the specialist, or the flight home, and my only recollections of Sydney are taking the Manley Ferry across the harbour, with the fins of innumerable sharks swimming round the boat, and my anxiety that I would get caught between two of the trams going in opposite directions, where there seemed to be barely enough room to stand.

According to my mother she sent for the doctor as soon as we got back to Mugga Way; he put me out for 24 hours and treated the bites with picric acid ointment. I woke up covered in bright yellow patches but feeling a lot better!

My sister Jill had got into Sydney University to study Medicine starting in September 1947, so I didn't see so much of her after that, but she was still in Canberra for my eleventh birthday and asked me what I wanted for a present. I had seen a hand-drill in the tool shop in Civic costing 37/6d (that is one pound seventeen shillings and six pence; Australia was still using English money but an Australian pound was worth only three-quarters of an English one). I was hesitant about asking for something that cost so much, but she got it for me. I still have it and use it in preference to an electric one when I need to drill close to a wall or something. During my life I have, apart from drilling innumerable holes, used it to wind kite strings, and an induction coil, as a stirrer for chemical experiments, to wind up rubber-powered model aeroplanes and goodness knows what else!

In the closing months of 1947 my father's contract with the Commonwealth Relations Office finished and he was flown back to England. We followed at a more leisurely pace on the Shaw, Savill and Albion line as before.

Just before we left a boy from school called Scott, whom I didn't really know at all well brought me a leaving present - an interesting bird he had shot and a copy of *Australian Bird Life*. Malcolm gave me another copy of the same book!

Our ship the *Akaroa* (*Themistocles* having been broken up!) sailed from Melbourne, whence we travelled by train starting from the nearest station to Canberra at Queenbean. In New South Wales the railway gauge was four feet eight and a half inches, as in Britain, but in Victoria the gauge was 3'6" and we had to change trains in the middle of the night at the State boundary, at Albury. The second part of the journey was in a very modern train, the 'Spirit of Progress', which ran on rails with tongued-and-grooved joints giving a distinctly smoother and quieter ride than the traditional 'clickety-clack' track in NSW.

RMS *Akaroa* was, like *Themistocles*, built in Belfast but three years younger and had been converted to burn oil. We called at Adelaide to pick up more passengers then crossed the Indian Ocean to Cape Town. I don't think we stopped there for very long – perhaps because fuelling was quicker with oil – but our next stop, at Las Palmas in the Canaries, lasted a few days and we did some sightseeing. I was intrigued by the homes of the cave-dwellers, each cave-front being filled in and fitted with a door and windows, perched in a cliff-face high above the road. We were shown round a historic building, a cathedral or something, part of which was very high and one got vertiginous glimpses of the ground through gaps in the dilapidated masonry we were standing on. I sensed that my mother was extremely uncomfortable at that point! We also visited an orangery with rather curious yellow oranges on the trees. A woman-worker broke off a small branch with several oranges on it and gave it to me. I said 'Gracias' which pleased my mother very much indeed!

Commemorative Dinner on the Akaroa.

My mother was fond of chess and played regularly for her clubs in Canberra and Richmond, though not on the top boards. Captain Williams, Master of the *Akaroa*, was also a keen chess-player and my mother played him several times during the voyage. On one occasion, she told me, there was a knock on his cabin door and the First Officer put his head in to say:

"Looks like dirty weather ahead, Sir." Without looking up from the chess-board the Captain said:

"Cat below hatches."

The officer departed with a smart "Aye, aye, Sir."

A few minutes later he returned to report: "Cat below hatches, Sir."

The Captain then reeled off a series of nautical checks and precautions to be put in hand.

There was another boy of my age on the boat, Ian Shales, whose father was travelling as the Company's Representative. Ian had, I think, made several such trips and got rather good at deck games, particularly deck golf. I was not bad at it and we entered the ship's tournament together. We won round after round and everyone was quite excited when we had to play a couple in their thirties in the final. I think many of the passengers felt that they should make sure that Ian and I won, but my mother had got to know the couple and told me that they said they didn't want to throw the match, but were rather relieved when we beat them fair and square. I was pleased with the result; for some time to come it was to be my best, not to say only sporting achievement!

LONDON AGAIN

We docked at Southampton on, as I now know thanks to my wife's skill at the keyboard again, 21 November and we went back to Waldegrave Gardens by train via Waterloo.

My father had flown back to this country, to take up the post of Chief Information Officer at the Air Ministry, in September but he had had little opportunity, or perhaps inclination, for housework before we arrived and the house had been left in a terrible mess. Various pieces of furniture had been thrown higgledy-piggledy into the small bedroom above the hall, in which we had left all sorts of things of our own, and which was supposed to have been left locked. The garden was overgrown with weeds – we heard later that the neighbours had complained to the Ministry of Agriculture about them. Apparently our tenant, a Commander Watkins, RN, had sacked the gardener, whom we called 'Ring', who had come for one afternoon each week. My mother used to give him a cup of tea which he always drank from the saucer, the only person I have seen actually doing this! The Commander was burgled twice during his stay and we wondered whether these facts were related; a 'careless' word overheard in the pub perhaps?

There was no sign of Spook. Enquiry revealed that the person entrusted to feed her had just pocketed the money. We never knew whether she had died or run away. Bill Klitz, who was looking after Uggles, had disappeared and, as Phoebe had died we had no way of finding him.

I don't remember where she came from but we soon acquired a cat called 'Buttercup', a tabby and white female. At that time cats were given a bath from time to time to discourage fleas, and Buttercup, unlike most cats, really enjoyed it. She was fascinated by water and would often come in when someone was having a bath and sit on the edge putting her paw down to touch the water. She fell in more than once and swam happily around until fished out! Perhaps she was related to the Eel Pie cats, of whom there was no sign by this time – and a footbridge had been built to replace the chain-ferry.

My parents and I (Jill had stayed on at Sydney University) were invited to spend the Christmas of 1947 at Wadebridge in Cornwall with Uncle

Cyril, his wife, Zoe and her daughter, Betty, by whose own account Zoe had given a grim childhood; I don't know what happened to her father. She had found happiness married to a man called Franklin, but he died of cancer before they had been married long and she was back with her mother. For me, the few days we spent there were strangely memorable. I was aware that the atmosphere in the house was tense but I spent almost no time in it during the day, having been hustled out to fish in the estuary. I had brought my rod but had only coarse fishing tackle unsuitable for the shallow sand banks and sea water. I tried for a while without success and spent most of the time exploring by myself. The weather was overcast and windy with occasional light rain on the wind, conditions which I found invigorating. I don't remember the Christmas dinner. When I was older my mother told me that the visit had been a total disaster. Zoe had been impossible and refused to cook anything or help in any way (she was a trained caterer) leaving my mother and Betty, I suppose, to do all the food. I've no idea why we were invited in the first place.

Before re-starting at Tower House for the Spring Term I had some time to start clearing up the garden. Adjacent to the path from the back door was a brick-built coal-house in which we kept coke for the, now pretty ancient, boiler and coal for the open fire in the drawing room. This shed was supposed to be screened from the garden by a trellis on which the unruly climber polygonum had been planted. Untrimmed, its weight had pulled the whole thing down and I set about rebuilding it. My Malvern Star bike had been shipped back to this country in a crate of fairly thin redgum planks which I found could quite easily be split into strips, and with some stouter posts at the corners I made them into a new trellis and set the polyganum to climb on it again. It was still standing when my mother left the house after my father's death in 1968.

My bike had only the back-pedal brake for the back wheel which I suspected was not legal in this country, and didn't seem very safe in London traffic in any case, so I bought and fitted a calliper brake to act on the front wheel. I also set the handlebars to the 'dropped' position, a bit reluctantly, fearing that the Australian up in the air style would look ridiculous. A disadvantage of the dropped position was that one tended to look at the road immediately in front rather than watching further ahead. This led to an embarrassing incident in East Twickenham, approaching Richmond Bridge, when I failed to notice that my side of the road was closed and that the control man was waving a red flag at me. I turned onto the other side of the road but, misjudging the distance to the end, was soon confronted by a bus coming towards me in the only lane. I rode between the flags (this was long before plastic cones) onto the new tarmac which was being laid, where my wheels left deep grooves to the fury of the shouting, shovel-waving workmen!

Another hazard, less easy to avoid than those associated with not looking where one was going, which confronted cyclists in London at that time was due to the trolleybuses. These operated on certain routes alongside motor buses and ran on tyres with normal steering but were powered by electricity from a pair of overhead wires. The pickup arms were long enough to allow normal traffic manoeuvres without coming off the wires. When one came to pass a bus standing at a stop the drivers were not inclined to wait for the convenience of the odd cyclist and would often pull away before one had got past. One could usually beat the modest acceleration of the motor buses and get in front, but the trolleybuses were quicker off the mark and one had no chance. The only option was to brake frantically and pull over behind it, hoping that the following traffic had not closed the gap.

A legacy of the trolleybuses' predecessor, in the form of tram-lines, made another trap for the unwary cyclist. No longer used, these were still laid in the road at Twickenham Junction, Station Road and other places. One had to take care to cross them at a broad angle; if the front wheel went into the groove against the slippery steel one was almost sure to come a cropper.

Back at Tower House I soon made friends with a boy called Dennis Geeson who lived quite near the school in Palewell Park, a turning or two from Sheen Lane along the Upper Richmond Road, with his father who had an electrical business in Wimbledon. His mother had walked out and I don't think she made much effort to keep in touch with him. His father joined in everything he wanted to do and gave him everything he wanted, including a splendid 00-gauge model railway which he built on a shelf round Dennis' playroom. We went on various trips together: one was to Ashdown Forest. There was a pre-war Brownie Popular box camera knocking about at Waldegrave Gardens and I bought a 620 film for it and took pictures of the scenery, experimenting with time exposure. I was rather pleased with the results, but I never used the camera again.

We had no particular hobby or interest, although Dennis liked birds' nesting, which I didn't approve of and I think that was what we eventually fell out about. Wondering what to do one day Dennis said "Lets get some chemicals to mix up." (His father had some knowledge of chemistry and may have started the idea). Having no alternative suggestion I agreed and asked how we should start. Dennis said "Let's get some calcium carbine." (He meant carbide, of course.) This substance liberates the flammable gas acetylene (properly called ethyne in today's nomenclature) on contact with water. It powered car headlamps before electric ones came in and some cycle lamps still used it so that it was available over the counter in bike-shops. It is considered too dangerous (rightly, for various reasons) for open sale these days. I'm not sure just what we did with it, though no doubt it involved putting water on it and setting fire to the gas. These experiments satisfied Dennis' interest in chemicals and we did something else, but I started collecting what chemicals I could persuade chemist's shops to sell me. I knew the names of some, like copper sulphate, from my time at the Leas. I tried mixing them together to see what would happen, usually without any very exciting result, and I think there was an element of simply collecting compounds, but I was hooked.

When Dennis' father heard that he had taken an interest in chemistry, he built him a bench in an alcove of his playroom with shelves for chemicals and a gas supply for a Bunsen burner. A firm called Beck, who basically made chemistry sets, also sold small bottles of chemicals and some (not very satisfactory) glassware and Mr Geeson equipped Dennis' lab with what I imagine was their entire catalogue. Beck's stock was intended for children so that most of the more interesting (i.e. dangerous) chemicals were not included.

At about this time I did something sensible (about time, the reader might well feel) which may well have shaped the rest of my life. I bought a chemistry book from a shop in the Upper Richmond Road a few shops to the left of Sheen Lane. It was not an 'interesting experiments for boys' type of book but a School Certificate text *Fundamental Chemistry* by Henry Wilkins. I was fascinated by what I read and quite soon understood chemical formulae and how to write, and balance, chemical equations.

Aside from the book my interest was turning inevitably towards fireworks and explosives and I found out, I don't know how, that the latter could be made with, among other things concentrated nitric acid. I was still friends with Charles Burge who took an interest in my chemical enthusiasm and he built me a neat shelf for chemicals by reconstructing a wooden apple crate. The book had shown me how to make nitric acid by heating potassium nitrate with concentrated sulphuric acid and Charles helped me to try it. The former substance, a constituent of gunpowder, could be bought from some chemists but others refused. I have forgotten where I

Me with Charles' chemical shelf.

got the acid; maybe Charles brought it. Our apparatus consisted of a small flask (one of Beck's) connected by a cork to a glass tube, which led via another cork to a bottle cooled in a bucket of water (to condense the product). Unfortunately we had not provided any way for pressure to escape (a common mistake of students I was to find later in life) and soon after we started heating the flask, the first acid vapour having rotted the cork, the joint blew apart ejecting the hot acid onto the floor. Fortunately neither of us was hit by it but the linoleum bore the marks ever after, as did the cover of Henry Wilkins' book which I still have.

A supply of nitric acid came rather unexpectedly from Dennis. It certainly didn't come from Becks and I assume that his father got it from someone who worked in a lab. It didn't have a supplier's label and was in a 250ml reagent bottle with a glass stopper, nearly full. What I didn't know, but was soon to discover, was that the stopper didn't fit properly.

I set out carrying the bottle to walk to Mortlake station but by the time I got there the acid slopping about in the bottle had seeped past the stopper and a film of it was running down the outside on to my hands. The train came fairly soon and I got into a compartment by myself, but by then my hands had started to itch seriously. I tried rubbing them on the upholstery of the train seat, but it didn't help. The train seemed to take its time reaching Strawberry Hill but at last I got out, ran home and got my hands under the tap. This stopped the itching and although my hands were bright yellow for some days they were not blistered.

Not very long after this generous, if troublesome, gift from Dennis we had a violent argument while walking in Richmond Park. As I've said, I think it was about bird-nesting. We made it up on the 'phone after a few days and I went to his house. A short while before we fell out, I had carved a small – about 4 in. long – yacht hull out of balsa wood. It may have been too small to sail but I was pleased with the shape and Dennis had asked if he could borrow it to show his father. I noticed it now split in two in the waste-bin of his playroom/lab. I wasn't particularly bothered by this and made no comment but I felt it gave me some insight into the boy's mind and we soon drifted apart.

I had formed two new friendships at school, with Peter Charlesworth, who lived a few minutes' walk from my home, in Walpole Road near Twickenham Green, and Dermot O'Flaherty. Peter, known as Chas, and Dermot, known as Dibs, were interested in my chemical experiments and one day we made a mixture which we, or perhaps I, expected would burn with an interesting pyrotechnic effect. It disappeared in an instantaneous flash when ignited. This seemed likely to make a satisfying explosion if confined and we filled a small thin-walled glass bottle with it and stuck a roll of newspaper in the neck. We lit the paper at the bottom of the garden and quickly got well clear. Nothing happened. After a not very long time, and contrary to my advice, Dibs walked over and kicked it. There was a loud bang and bright flash. Luckily he wasn't hit by any of the glass. I wasn't very happy about the unprofessional way this experiment had gone but we were pleased with the result and christened our composition DMC 1, the letters standing for the casual names of its inventors Dibs, Mac and Chas.

Although we soon became a lot more expert in making fuses for such experiments DMC 1 proved a bit unreliable and sometimes didn't go off.

Uncle Cyril with Bill after the war.   *Uncle Cyril and my mother in 1955.*

With increasing chemical know-how we changed one of the constituents to get a better mixture DMC 2, before long.

My uncle Cyril had stayed in the RAF with the rank of Flight Lieutenant after the war, and at this time he was stationed at Pembroke Dock, in Wales, where he was an Air Traffic Controller for the Sunderland flying boats which operated from there. While in Australia, we had seen him on a newsreel, looking through binoculars from the control tower, as Sunderlands were being used in the Berlin Airlift. He came to see us occasionally with his Cocker Spaniel 'Bill'and on one visit he brought me a splendid model yacht. He said it had been made by a pair of ancient Irishmen who sailed about the Irish Sea in a similarly ancient boat, kept afloat on their last trip only by pumping all night!

According to my mother Cyril's service to his country began at the age of 16 when he enrolled for the Army in 1916. He gave his age as 17 but the enrolling officer said "You're a big chap you look 18." Cyril took the hint: "Yes 18, I'm sorry, Sir, I made a mistake." He was signed on. The enrolling officer was his Godfather!

Unlike his brother John, whose service in the Motor Machine-gun section of the Machine-gun Corps, and promotion in the field from the ranks to Honorary Second Lieutenant is reasonably well documented, the Army records available now give no indication of Cyril's service; an entry for an A.C. Hogg may refer to him but gives no detail. His mother related in later years that for some time after the war he suffered terrible nightmares, swearing horribly as he tore his pillow to shreds. He was the gentlest, and the most courteous, person I ever met.

I have no doubt that my uncle Cyril joined up in one of the armed forces at, or very likely before, the outbreak of war in 1939 but I don't know what he was doing for the first year or so, and what he did next is recorded only by word of mouth. I cannot, however, say that it has never been written down until now, as the curious circumstance noted below reveals. He never mentioned any of this to me but once told my mother, late at night after quite a few drinks.

In the 1930s Cyril had been a keen sailor and had his own yacht, the *Eiderduck*. Towards the end of 1940 he joined a sailing friend and his wife on their boat (I once knew the names of both) on a trip to the Mediterranean on behalf of some department of military intelligence. Their mission was to survey possible landing places on the North African coast. I guess he was taken out of uniform to make this trip.

Uncle Cyril at the helm of the Eiderduck *before the war.*

Some way into the Med their rudder was damaged and put out of action. The girl repaired it, working under water. Near Greece his friend told Cyril that his wife was pregnant and had to be put ashore in Greece; this was some six months before the German invasion and the allies had a considerable military presence there, so she could probably have got home. (Or was she being placed as a spy?)

Cyril and his friend went on and sailed along the North African coast, but they were spotted and a Stuka dive-bombed the boat. I guess Cyril jumped overboard in the nick of time because he knew that his friend was killed. He was in the water for many hours before being picked up by a freighter bound for New York. Here he was interned as an alien on Ellis Island, obviously having no way to establish his identity or explain how he had ended up floating in the Med.

My uncle was a very well-coordinated man; my mother always said he could have made a fine career as a dancer, and a boxing champion at his school, Rossall. When a fellow internee expressed loud pro-Nazi opinions Cyril knocked him flying. This evidently pleased the guards, who would have liked to do the same, so much that they let him out!

On the waterfront, Cyril found a Norwegian freighter, the MS *Heina*, waiting to sail for England but unable to do so because the navigating officer, last seen dead drunk, had not appeared. Cyril was signed on as a replacement, nominally as mess-boy, presumably because he had no official qualifications, and the next day, 6 Jan 1941 (thanks again to Roslyn for the details of this voyage) they put to sea. At this point it appeared that his predecessor had funded his drinking bout by selling all the ship's charts! A school atlas was the best that could be found.

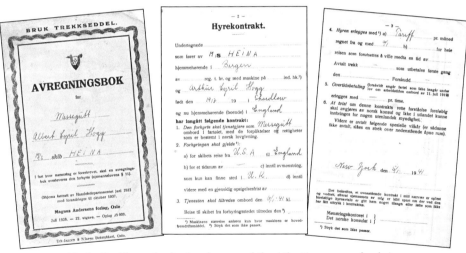

Uncle Cyril's pay book when he crossed the Atlantic as crew after being picked up in the Mediterranean by a US freighter.

We know the name of the ship because, remarkably, his pay-book was among my mother's papers (see photo). He signed-on on 5 Jan. 1941, and, as internet records for this ship show, she sailed from New York on 6 Jan. for Halifax and arrived there to join convoy HX 102 on 8 Jan. and they set out to cross the Atlantic three days later. Being in convoy must have helped the navigational problem; the trip was not without incident since the convoy was dispersed by hurricane force winds not far out of Halifax, but managed to re-form, although the escort ship turned back to look for them and went back to Halifax. *Heina* docked at Liverpool on 29 Jan. and Cyril joined, or re-joined, the RAF.

To my uncle's total surprise the first instalment of an account of this trip into the Med. appeared in a yachting magazine, *Yachting World*, I think, around 1950 with the title 'Cruise of the [name of the boat]'. The Authorities banned any further instalments on the grounds of National Security, and Cyril said he was completely puzzled as to who could have written it. But I think I can guess. More than once he mentioned a close friend in the RAF, Flt Lt Pepper and I'm sure they must have spent a lot of time drinking together in the mess. This chap was a writer (rather a good one, I think) because Cyril told me that he was the author of the series 'Rockfist Rogan' in the boy's weekly *Champion* of which I was an avid reader. I suppose he didn't ask Cyril's permission to publish because he knew it wouldn't be given. Apart from the Official Secrets Act I don't think he would have wanted it, particularly so soon after it happened. Integrity ran in my uncle's veins in place of blood.

During my time at Tower House after coming back from Australia, I'm not sure just when it was, Uncle Cyril invited me to stay with him in the Officers' Mess at RAF Pembroke Dock for a few days. I went on the train, the first long trip I had made by myself.

My uncle had to work most of the day but he found time to take me sailing, more than once I think, in an airborne lifeboat converted to conventional sailing rig, which I enjoyed a lot, even if the rather high vertical ladder from the dock to get into the boat had been a bit daunting at first!

While he was working I explored the dock. There were several German E-boats (the equivalent of the Allies' motor torpedo boats) pulled up on a slipway; most removable souvenirs had already been taken but I got a rather nice navigation lantern from one. I gave it to Peter Charlesworth, who greatly admired it, in the end.

One afternoon I was on the dock when the driver of a steam crane, which ran on railway tracks along the dock, climbed down and put chocks under the wheels having finished work for the day. He saw my interest in his machine and invited me into the driving cab. He explained the various controls and then asked me if I would like to drive it along the track. Obviously I said yes. He showed me how to open the steam valve slowly but as I did so the whole thing reared alarmingly up in the air! The driver hastily closed the valve; he, and I, had forgotten he had chocked the wheels!

At Tower House we were taught maths by Mr Ellinger, a nice enough chap but new to the job presumably, since the only thing I can remember him teaching me was the equation of the parabola – work at least three years beyond the Common Entrance syllabus. I don't think any of us made much of it but I suppose he got some of the basic stuff into us.

Tower House Rugger Team, 1949.

The school sports were soccer, rugger (it was never called 'rugby' at that time) and cricket and we had occasional matches against other prep schools. I don't think I ever represented Tower House at soccer or cricket but I was in the rugger team when I finished, probably because I was among the fifteen biggest boys in the school rather than for any particular aptitude for the game, which I strongly disliked. I played prop forward. One match stands out in my mind. It was against Colet Court, a formidable opponent, and it was played on Saturday morning on the Richmond Athletic Ground, which made us feel quite important! We lost about forty-five nil. After the match we went to Mathias' Café at the end of the Kew Road for buns and lemonade, but it was a dismal occasion.

Early in the summer term of 1948, as I infer it must have been the first cricket term after I came back from Australia, I went as a spectator with the cricket team to play, again against Colet Court, on their splendid ground at Brook Green. I was not passionately interested but as I watched a Colet Court boy was lying on the ground near me keeping the score in a large book with pages formally printed for this purpose. Suddenly he jumped up and thrust his pencil into my hand and said "Take over would you, I have to go for a minute." I had no real idea how to keep the score, but looking at what he had done I thought I could see what was needed. He had put a dot for each ball that was bowled and I went on doing the same, but was thrown into total confusion when the bowling changed ends after only six balls! I had played the game quite a lot in Australia and was perfectly well aware that there were eight balls to an over. I left rather quickly when the scorer returned before he could see what I had done to his score-sheet!

At this time (the Incoming Passenger Lists show it was May 1948) my sister came back from Australia to live with us at Waldegrave Gardens, having decided not to go on with her medical course at Sydney University, although she qualified to do so. She took a job at a firm called HOSA which did clinical analysis, like blood counts and pregnancy tests, the latter depending on the response of a South American toad to a hormonal (urine, I suppose) sample. It was hard work for a bullying boss but enabled her to get a much better job at Hammersmith Hospital.

At Tower House I continued, as before the Australia trip, to buy lunch at a local restaurant, usually still the Hygienic Bakeries. I usually went with

Me with Jill in1949.

Dermot as by this time Peter had left to attend a technical school in Twickenham. As before, we used to visit various pharmacists' shops to get substitutes for sweets, which were still rationed, and were to remain so for another four years or so. In one of these shops we bought, I've no idea why, a small bottle of eucalyptus oil. Back in the playground we offered to put a few drops of this on the handkerchiefs of anyone who wanted to smell it. Rather unfortunately a few recipients found it amusing to grab smaller boys and hold it to their faces, and things were getting a bit out of hand when the bell went for afternoon classes.

A bit before four o'clock we were in the room at the top of the tower (which gave the school its name), the form room for the top class, A1, being taught by Robo. The Headmaster came in and told him that the mother of one of the junior boys, who finished at 3.30, had 'phoned to say that her son had been made dizzy with eucalyptus oil. He left again and Robo asked who had the oil. Dermot and I put up our hands and Robo said eagerly "I'm going to beat you both," relishing, no doubt, this windfall opportunity to whack a pair of bottoms.

The dormitory where the punishment was to take place was the first door on the right in the corridor leading from the class-room. He went in with Dermot, told me to wait outside and pushed the door partly shut. Through the remaining gap I could see him swinging his hips as he wielded the gym-shoe, each thwack eliciting an involuntary yelp from Dermot. A moment later in the dormitory I was told to touch my toes (something I have never actually been able to do), my blazer was folded up my back and I heard myself giving the same yelps that Dermot had made.

But the six whacks were not the end of the punishment; we were told to hand-in an essay of five hundred words on eucalyptus next morning. We returned, not altogether comfortably, to our wooden seats and Robo went on with his lesson.

At home my mother was quietly sympathetic about the beating, though she need not have been. I rang Peter and we both laughed about it. Peter was quite familiar with Robo's use, or perhaps abuse, of the gym-shoe. He had been a boarder at the school while I was in Australia and Robo had caught them larking about after lights-out and beaten them in their pyjamas. From the way he spoke about it I gathered that the experience had left its mark on him after the bruises had healed.

The five-hundred word essay was a fish but my mother was very helpful with suggestions for things to put down so it didn't take too long. In the morning Robo glanced at the length and threw it in the bin with Dermot's.

While I took the beating in good part there was another incident before I left the school which I did resent. I was sitting in the back row in the same form-room and Robo had required us to translate a passage, which he had written on the black-board containing the word 'sugar', into French. I really knew the French, 'sucre', for sugar but couldn't think of it at once and knowing it was similar to the English word I wrote 'le sugar', hoping to put it right when I remembered the word. Robo was somewhere behind me as I worked but I didn't know he was reading what I had written over my shoulder – until I was almost knocked off my seat by an open-handed slap across my right ear which left my head ringing. Robo muttered furiously 'Le sugar indeed'.

Some six years later I attended a medical exam for pre-selection for a commission in the RAF and during a (rather painful) inspection of my inner ear the doctor remarked that there was a scar on my ear-drum. I hadn't noticed any actual injury after the class-room assault but I always wondered whether or not the scar was due to my infant ear-ache problems. A few years ago I had a hearing test and ear examination and I asked the audiologist if that blow might have affected my hearing, but she said that the responses of my two ears were the same so presumably it didn't. She couldn't see the scar that the RAF man had noted.

During this period we made one or two visits to my father's mother, Granny Phyllis, at the flat she shared with her friend Miss Prendergast, 'Prendy', near Guildford. The flat was full of valuable, and it seemed to me precarious, antique ornaments and furniture which made me nervous. My grandmother seemed rather a fussy old stick and I didn't enjoy these visits, but Jill said she had been good fun on her regular visits to Strawberry Hill before the war, and what I have heard about her since seems to bear this out.

Granny Phyllis had led rather a sad life. One of six daughters and a son of a noted army doctor, Lt Col Francis Arthur Davy who had campaigned, successfully in the end, for reduction of the severity of the soldiers' physical training, she had run away and married an actor, Roberts Carter. Travelling round in repertory they had paid out an unpleasant landlady by tacking a kipper to the bottom of the table before they left! At the end of March 1901 the census shows that they were living in Finborough Road, Kensington, but before my father was born in January 1902 the prospect of life with a baby seems to have been too much for him and he deserted her.

Her family's response was to send her to Ceylon (Sri Lanka now) to find a new husband, leaving my father in the care of Col and Mrs Davy and his aunts in Richmond.

In 1908 Phyllis married Robert Johnstone Knox (Tom) MacBride, in Government Service in charge of woods and forests. We have a letter from the Crown Prince of Germany thanking him for organising a hunting trip! His father, Robert Knox MacBride, CMG, had been Director of Public Works and in charge of the Naval dockyard at Trincomali. My father changed his name at this time.

Above: *Mrs Davy, my
Great Grandmother.*
Right: *Col. Davy.*

Phyllis and Tom MacBride in Ceylon.

*Phyllis' and Tom's bungalow
in Ceylon.*

Colombo, 12th December 1910.

Sir,

      I am directed by His Imperial Highness the Crown Prince of Germany to convey to you His best thanks for all the trouble you had in connection with His shooting trip.

      His Imperial Highness expressed particular regret at not being able to thank you personally and commanded me to forward to you registered a Cigarette Case as a memento.

           I have the honour to be,

                Sir,

                Your obedient servant,

                Freudenberg

                Imperial German Vice-Consul.

R. J. K. Mac Bride Esq,
    P. W. D., Trincomalie.

Thank you letter from the Crown Prince of Germany to my father's stepfather.

Phyllis told my parents some funny stories of these times; one became a family joke ever after. It seems that the native girls advertised what they had to offer the sailors as they came ashore with the phrase "All pink inside, like Queen Victoria!" I doubt if that monarch would have been amused. It's surprising how many everyday situations it can be applied to. Another that she told, on the theme that an elephant never forgets, is so improbable that one feels it can only be true. Way back, the wife of a young diplomat, annoyed by an elephant waving its trunk near her, spitefully

Above left: *My father aged 3.* Above right: *'Lionel MacBride, aged 5yrs & 10months. November 1907' taken shortly before Phyllis returned to Ceylon to marry Robert Johnstone Knox MacBride (Tom).*

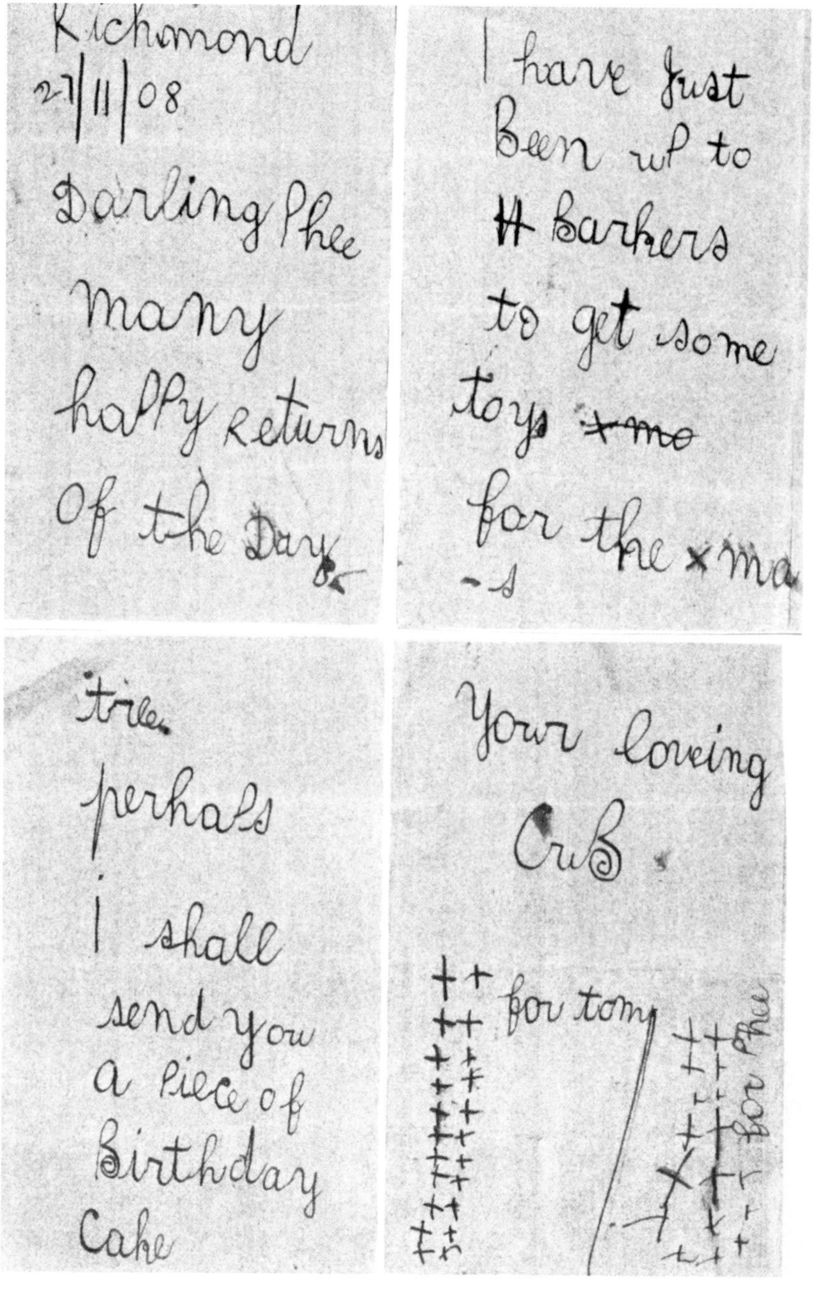

Richmond
27/11/08.

Darling Phee
many
happy returns
Of the Day

I have just
Been up to
H Barkers
to get some
toys xmo
for the xma
~s

tree.
perhaps
i shall
send you
a piece of
Birthday
Cake

Your loveing
Cub.

++ + for tom

for Phee

Left: *My father – ready for rain!*

Below: *Enlargement from Phyllis'
personal notebook.*

Opposite: *Letter from my father (Cub)
sent to his mother for her birthday
in 1908.*

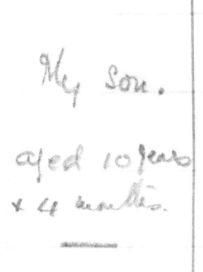

My Son.

aged 10 years

+ 4 months.

jabbed it with a hat-pin. Years later, the diplomat having risen to a senior position, she sat next to him in the front row to watch a traditional procession. The elephant was in it and when it came level with her it swung out its trunk, wrapped it round her ankles, and lifted her up in the air. This would have been embarrassing enough had it not been the custom among European women, in that hot climate, to wear ankle-length skirts with nothing underneath! The diplomat had to be posted to another country.

Granny Phyllis became expert on gemstones and we still have a splendid smokey star sapphire, now set in a ring, which she spotted uncut in the gravel path of the tennis club at Trincomali.

Tom MacBride, although he was not many years older than Phyllis, died in 1918 shortly before the end of the First World War and she returned to this country. Her ship was torpedoed off Southern Ireland and she struggled ashore with no papers. When she gave her name as MacBride she was arrested in case she was the revolutionary Maud Gonne MacBride, a strange idea as Phyllis was quite petite while Maud Gonne was a giant of a woman, well over six feet tall! I don't think she was held for very long.

My father can have seen very little of his mother up to the age of sixteen, when she came back from Ceylon, although we know from the shipping records that she visited this country from time to time, and was here at the time of the 1911 Census. He lived in an all-female establishment with his grandmother and four aunts, since Col. Davy stayed at 13 Ellerker Gardens when the others moved a few streets away to 2 Spring Terrace in 1913.

Mrs Davy was very musical and rather eccentric. We have a letter in which her son-in-law describes her as 'a very difficult lady' and says Phyllis' youngest sister, Gwen, his wife, used to run errands between the two establishments. The story goes that Mrs Davy got off the train at Richmond and started an intensely musical conversation with a friend she met at the ticket barrier. At first she didn't notice the ticket-collector holding out his hand for her ticket, but when he politely attracted her attention she shook it warmly and went on talking. When he withdrew his hand and held it out once more she stopped what she was saying and asked, with some irritation:

"My good man, what *do* you want?"

In the house in Spring Terrace my father's favourite aunt, Margot, died in tragic and mysterious circumstances. Her body was found in the tiled hall-way after she had fallen, for no apparent reason, over the bannisters. A dozen or so years later my parents lived in this house, with Phyllis, for a while after they were married and, returning late from the paper after my mother had gone to bed, my father encountered what he described as a horrific, terrifying 'presence', on the stairs; but there was nothing to be seen. He was not given to flights of fancy and inevitably associated this strange experience with Margot's death.

The mother of my friend Peter Charlesworth, Chas, told me of a rather similar experience in their house in Walpole Road, when she sensed someone's weight passing her on the stairs. This happened at about the same time each evening and she got in quite a state about it, bravely sitting on the bottom step waiting for it to happen. I assume Mr Charlesworth was away. It transpired, on his return perhaps, that the Victorian semi-detached villa was built with the stair treads extending through the wall into the next house, and the mysterious phenomenon was her neighbour going up to bed!

I suggested some such mundane explanation to my parents but they could not see how this could apply to the grander house in Spring Terrace. It was odd that the cats, usually ubiquitous creatures, never went up the stairs.

My father's only uncle, Murray Davy, had left home to make a career as a famous opera singer, resisting family pressure to join the army. He was christened Arthur Macdonald (his paternal great-grandfather was Hugh Macdonald, descended from the Lords of the Isles) but chose instead to be known as Murray (his maternal great-grandmother was Maria Murray of the Murrays of Philiphaugh, another ancient Scottish family) to dissociate himself from the military lineage. We have a Covent Garden poster for 1909 with Murray Davey (he added the 'e') taking leading rolls in *Samson and Delilah* and *Faust* as Mephistophiles, his favourite part. He also took engagements entertaining the guests at social functions in grand houses. On one such occasion he took offence because a professional dancer had also been engaged and when asked to perform he refused with: 'No, no; tonight we dance,' and proceeded to cavort about the room jumping over the furniture.

I can't remember just when I sat the Common Entrance exams for St Paul's but it must have been near the end of the Spring Term of 1949. By that time, from a virtually scratch start, though I could read fairly well, I had been at Tower House for three terms (1945-6), cut slightly short when we left for Australia, a two year gap when I learnt nothing useful except perhaps some adventitious geography, three terms in 1948 and at least most of the Spring Term in 1949, amounting to a scant, interrupted, seven terms' teaching. My parents can hardly have been optimistic that I would get into

Murray Davey's debut in Paris. He has written on the programme:
'To my well-beloved Mother in remembrance of my first debut at the Opera.
Paris Oct 1905'.

St Paul's. I did, however, have the advantage of being what appeared to be the fourth generation to attend that school. My father went there but the previous boys were his step-father (and his brother) and their father (there is some doubt about this one), though I don't suppose my father elaborated this point!

When the results came I had not done too badly but I had to re-take the Latin paper. In the hope of improving my performance, my parents arranged extra tuition for me with Mr Goodman, a young man with a sallow complexion and black curly hair, who taught History at the school. For these sessions I had to go to Waterloo and take the Edgware branch of the Northern Line to Belsize Park where he had a flat. I don't remember that he set me any work to take away and I was a bit surprised when, working through an unseen, he asked me what a 'defile' was, which I knew, if a bit hazily.

In due course my father rang Dr James, the High Master, to ask how I had done in the re-sit. "Worse, if possible, than the first time," was his answer. But the family connection won the day it seems – I was in!

When I started at St Paul's I was in the lowest form, 4C, (the 3rd form was for boys some-how admitted a year early) and the lowest set for Maths, 4.3. But my French set was the highest, 4.1. Robo's teaching methods may not have accorded with modern practice but I can't say they weren't effective!

My ultimate progress through that famous old school was to prove distinctly unconventional. I came top of 4C by a big margin – and my tutor threatened to cane me for it! But that is another part of the story.

APPENDIX

The Inchcape Rock

No stir in the air, no stir in the sea,
The ship was as still as she could be,
Her sails from heaven received no motion,
Her keel was steady in the ocean.

Without either sign or sound of their shock
The waves flow'd o'er the Inchcape Rock;
So little they rose, so little they fell,
They did not move the Inchcape Bell.

The good old Abbot of Aberbrothok
Had placed that bell on the Inchcape Rock;
On a buoy in the storm it floated and swung,
And over the waves its warning rung.

When the rock was hid by the surges' swell,
The mariners heard the warning bell;
And then they knew the perilous Rock,
And blessed the Abbot of Aberbrothok.

The sun in heaven was shining gay,
All things were joyful on that day;
The sea-birds screamed as they wheeled round,
And there was joyance in their sound.

The buoy of the Inchcape Bell was seen
A darker speck on the ocean green;
Sir Ralph the Rover walked his deck,
And he fixed his eye on the darker speck.

He felt the cheering power of spring,
It made him whistle, it made him sing;
His heart was mirthful to excess,
But the Rover's mirth was wickedness.

His eye was on the Inchcape float;
Quoth he, 'My men, put out the boat,
And row me to the Inchcape Rock,
And I'll plague the priest of Aberbrothok.'

The boat is lowered, the boatmen row,
And to the Inchcape Rock they go;
Sir Ralph bent over from the boat
And he cut the bell of the Inchcape float.

Down sank the bell, with a gurgling sound,
The bubbles rose and burst around;
Quoth Sir Ralph, 'The next who comes to the Rock
Won't bless the Abbot of Aberbrothok.'

Sir Ralph the Rover sailed away,
He scoured the seas for many a day;
And now grown rich with plundered store,
He steers his course for Scotland's shore.

So thick a haze o'erspreads the sky
They cannot see the sun on high;
The wind hath blown a gale all day,
At evening it hath died away.

On the deck the Rover takes his stand,
So dark it is they see no land.
Quoth Sir Ralph, 'It will be lighter soon,
For there is the dawn of the rising moon.'

'Canst hear,' said one, 'the breakers roar?
For methinks we should be near the shore;
Now where we are I cannot tell,
But I wish I could hear the Inchcape Bell.'

They hear no sound, the swell is strong;
Though the wind hath fallen, they drift along,
Till the vessel strikes with a shivering shock;
Cried they, 'It is the Inchcape Rock!'

Sir Ralph the Rover tore his hair,
He cursed himself in his despair;
The waves rush in on every side,
The ship is sinking beneath the tide,

But even in his dying fear
One dreadful sound could the Rover hear,
A sound as if with the Inchcape Bell,
The fiends below were ringing his knell.

ROBERT SOUTHEY

224